C-553    CAREER EXAMINATION SERIES

*This is your*
*PASSBOOK for...*

# Oiler

*Test Preparation Study Guide*
*Questions & Answers*

# COPYRIGHT NOTICE

This book is SOLELY intended for, is sold ONLY to, and its use is RESTRICTED to individual, bona fide applicants or candidates who qualify by virtue of having seriously filed applications for appropriate license, certificate, professional and/or promotional advancement, higher school matriculation, scholarship, or other legitimate requirements of education and/or governmental authorities.

This book is NOT intended for use, class instruction, tutoring, training, duplication, copying, reprinting, excerption, or adaptation, etc., by:

1) Other publishers
2) Proprietors and/or Instructors of "Coaching" and/or Preparatory Courses
3) Personnel and/or Training Divisions of commercial, industrial, and governmental organizations
4) Schools, colleges, or universities and/or their departments and staffs, including teachers and other personnel
5) Testing Agencies or Bureaus
6) Study groups which seek by the purchase of a single volume to copy and/or duplicate and/or adapt this material for use by the group as a whole without having purchased individual volumes for each of the members of the group
7) Et al.

Such persons would be in violation of appropriate Federal and State statutes.

PROVISION OF LICENSING AGREEMENTS – Recognized educational, commercial, industrial, and governmental institutions and organizations, and others legitimately engaged in educational pursuits, including training, testing, and measurement activities, may address request for a licensing agreement to the copyright owners, who will determine whether, and under what conditions, including fees and charges, the materials in this book may be used them.  In other words, a licensing facility exists for the legitimate use of the material in this book on other than an individual basis.  However, it is asseverated and affirmed here that the material in this book CANNOT be used without the receipt of the express permission of such a licensing agreement from the Publishers. Inquiries re licensing should be addressed to the company, attention rights and permissions department.

All rights reserved, including the right of reproduction in whole or in part, in any form or by any means, electronic or mechanical, including photocopying, recording, or by any information storage and retrieval system, without permission in writing from the Publisher.

Copyright © 2024 by
## National Learning Corporation

212 Michael Drive, Syosset, NY 11791
(516) 921-8888 • www.passbooks.com
E-mail: info@passbooks.com

PUBLISHED IN THE UNITED STATES OF AMERICA

# PASSBOOK® SERIES

THE *PASSBOOK® SERIES* has been created to prepare applicants and candidates for the ultimate academic battlefield – the examination room.

At some time in our lives, each and every one of us may be required to take an examination – for validation, matriculation, admission, qualification, registration, certification, or licensure.

Based on the assumption that every applicant or candidate has met the basic formal educational standards, has taken the required number of courses, and read the necessary texts, the *PASSBOOK® SERIES* furnishes the one special preparation which may assure passing with confidence, instead of failing with insecurity. Examination questions – together with answers – are furnished as the basic vehicle for study so that the mysteries of the examination and its compounding difficulties may be eliminated or diminished by a sure method.

This book is meant to help you pass your examination provided that you qualify and are serious in your objective.

The entire field is reviewed through the huge store of content information which is succinctly presented through a provocative and challenging approach – the question-and-answer method.

A climate of success is established by furnishing the correct answers at the end of each test.

You soon learn to recognize types of questions, forms of questions, and patterns of questioning. You may even begin to anticipate expected outcomes.

You perceive that many questions are repeated or adapted so that you can gain acute insights, which may enable you to score many sure points.

You learn how to confront new questions, or types of questions, and to attack them confidently and work out the correct answers.

You note objectives and emphases, and recognize pitfalls and dangers, so that you may make positive educational adjustments.

Moreover, you are kept fully informed in relation to new concepts, methods, practices, and directions in the field.

You discover that you are actually taking the examination all the time: you are preparing for the examination by "taking" an examination, not by reading extraneous and/or supererogatory textbooks.

In short, this PASSBOOK®, used directedly, should be an important factor in helping you to pass your test.

# OILER

## JOB DESCRIPTION
Under direct supervision, is responsible for the lubrication of power plant, pumping and/or construction equipment. Performs related work.

## EXAMPLES OF TYPICAL TASKS
Lubricates and cleans pumps, engines, blowers, compressors, motors, gears, ejectors and other operating equipment. Reads meters, gauges and other operating equipment. Assists in the operation, maintenance, and repair of this equipment. Keeps logs.

## SCOPE OF THE EXAMINATION
The multiple-choice test may include questions on lubrication and maintenance of electro-mechanical power plant, pumping and construction equipment; proper application of lubricating greases and oils; proper use of tools and lubricating devices; safety, reports, basic mathematics, standards of proper employee ethical conduct; and other related areas.

# HOW TO TAKE A TEST

I. YOU MUST PASS AN EXAMINATION

A. *WHAT EVERY CANDIDATE SHOULD KNOW*

Examination applicants often ask us for help in preparing for the written test. What can I study in advance? What kinds of questions will be asked? How will the test be given? How will the papers be graded?

As an applicant for a civil service examination, you may be wondering about some of these things. Our purpose here is to suggest effective methods of advance study and to describe civil service examinations.

Your chances for success on this examination can be increased if you know how to prepare. Those "pre-examination jitters" can be reduced if you know what to expect. You can even experience an adventure in good citizenship if you know why civil service exams are given.

B. *WHY ARE CIVIL SERVICE EXAMINATIONS GIVEN?*

Civil service examinations are important to you in two ways. As a citizen, you want public jobs filled by employees who know how to do their work. As a job seeker, you want a fair chance to compete for that job on an equal footing with other candidates. The best-known means of accomplishing this two-fold goal is the competitive examination.

Exams are widely publicized throughout the nation. They may be administered for jobs in federal, state, city, municipal, town or village governments or agencies.

Any citizen may apply, with some limitations, such as the age or residence of applicants. Your experience and education may be reviewed to see whether you meet the requirements for the particular examination. When these requirements exist, they are reasonable and applied consistently to all applicants. Thus, a competitive examination may cause you some uneasiness now, but it is your privilege and safeguard.

C. *HOW ARE CIVIL SERVICE EXAMS DEVELOPED?*

Examinations are carefully written by trained technicians who are specialists in the field known as "psychological measurement," in consultation with recognized authorities in the field of work that the test will cover. These experts recommend the subject matter areas or skills to be tested; only those knowledges or skills important to your success on the job are included. The most reliable books and source materials available are used as references. Together, the experts and technicians judge the difficulty level of the questions.

Test technicians know how to phrase questions so that the problem is clearly stated. Their ethics do not permit "trick" or "catch" questions. Questions may have been tried out on sample groups, or subjected to statistical analysis, to determine their usefulness.

Written tests are often used in combination with performance tests, ratings of training and experience, and oral interviews. All of these measures combine to form the best-known means of finding the right person for the right job.

## II. HOW TO PASS THE WRITTEN TEST

### A. NATURE OF THE EXAMINATION

To prepare intelligently for civil service examinations, you should know how they differ from school examinations you have taken. In school you were assigned certain definite pages to read or subjects to cover. The examination questions were quite detailed and usually emphasized memory. Civil service exams, on the other hand, try to discover your present ability to perform the duties of a position, plus your potentiality to learn these duties. In other words, a civil service exam attempts to predict how successful you will be. Questions cover such a broad area that they cannot be as minute and detailed as school exam questions.

In the public service similar kinds of work, or positions, are grouped together in one "class." This process is known as *position-classification*. All the positions in a class are paid according to the salary range for that class. One class title covers all of these positions, and they are all tested by the same examination.

### B. FOUR BASIC STEPS

#### 1) Study the announcement

How, then, can you know what subjects to study? Our best answer is: "Learn as much as possible about the class of positions for which you've applied." The exam will test the knowledge, skills and abilities needed to do the work.

Your most valuable source of information about the position you want is the official exam announcement. This announcement lists the training and experience qualifications. Check these standards and apply only if you come reasonably close to meeting them.

The brief description of the position in the examination announcement offers some clues to the subjects which will be tested. Think about the job itself. Review the duties in your mind. Can you perform them, or are there some in which you are rusty? Fill in the blank spots in your preparation.

Many jurisdictions preview the written test in the exam announcement by including a section called "Knowledge and Abilities Required," "Scope of the Examination," or some similar heading. Here you will find out specifically what fields will be tested.

#### 2) Review your own background

Once you learn in general what the position is all about, and what you need to know to do the work, ask yourself which subjects you already know fairly well and which need improvement. You may wonder whether to concentrate on improving your strong areas or on building some background in your fields of weakness. When the announcement has specified "some knowledge" or "considerable knowledge," or has used adjectives like "beginning principles of…" or "advanced … methods," you can get a clue as to the number and difficulty of questions to be asked in any given field. More questions, and hence broader coverage, would be included for those subjects which are more important in the work. Now weigh your strengths and weaknesses against the job requirements and prepare accordingly.

#### 3) Determine the level of the position

Another way to tell how intensively you should prepare is to understand the level of the job for which you are applying. Is it the entering level? In other words, is this the position in which beginners in a field of work are hired? Or is it an intermediate or advanced level? Sometimes this is indicated by such words as "Junior" or "Senior" in the class title. Other jurisdictions use Roman numerals to designate the level – Clerk I, Clerk II, for example. The word "Supervisor" sometimes appears in the title. If the level is not indicated by the title, check the description of duties. Will you be working under very close supervision, or will you have responsibility for independent decisions in this work?

**4) Choose appropriate study materials**

Now that you know the subjects to be examined and the relative amount of each subject to be covered, you can choose suitable study materials. For beginning level jobs, or even advanced ones, if you have a pronounced weakness in some aspect of your training, read a modern, standard textbook in that field. Be sure it is up to date and has general coverage. Such books are normally available at your library, and the librarian will be glad to help you locate one. For entry-level positions, questions of appropriate difficulty are chosen – neither highly advanced questions, nor those too simple. Such questions require careful thought but not advanced training.

If the position for which you are applying is technical or advanced, you will read more advanced, specialized material. If you are already familiar with the basic principles of your field, elementary textbooks would waste your time. Concentrate on advanced textbooks and technical periodicals. Think through the concepts and review difficult problems in your field.

These are all general sources. You can get more ideas on your own initiative, following these leads. For example, training manuals and publications of the government agency which employs workers in your field can be useful, particularly for technical and professional positions. A letter or visit to the government department involved may result in more specific study suggestions, and certainly will provide you with a more definite idea of the exact nature of the position you are seeking.

## III. KINDS OF TESTS

Tests are used for purposes other than measuring knowledge and ability to perform specified duties. For some positions, it is equally important to test ability to make adjustments to new situations or to profit from training. In others, basic mental abilities not dependent on information are essential. Questions which test these things may not appear as pertinent to the duties of the position as those which test for knowledge and information. Yet they are often highly important parts of a fair examination. For very general questions, it is almost impossible to help you direct your study efforts. What we can do is to point out some of the more common of these general abilities needed in public service positions and describe some typical questions.

1) General information

Broad, general information has been found useful for predicting job success in some kinds of work. This is tested in a variety of ways, from vocabulary lists to questions about current events. Basic background in some field of work, such as sociology or economics, may be sampled in a group of questions. Often these are principles which have become familiar to most persons through exposure rather than through formal training. It is difficult to advise you how to study for these questions; being alert to the world around you is our best suggestion.

2) Verbal ability

An example of an ability needed in many positions is verbal or language ability. Verbal ability is, in brief, the ability to use and understand words. Vocabulary and grammar tests are typical measures of this ability. Reading comprehension or paragraph interpretation questions are common in many kinds of civil service tests. You are given a paragraph of written material and asked to find its central meaning.

3) **Numerical ability**

Number skills can be tested by the familiar arithmetic problem, by checking paired lists of numbers to see which are alike and which are different, or by interpreting charts and graphs. In the latter test, a graph may be printed in the test booklet which you are asked to use as the basis for answering questions.

4) **Observation**

A popular test for law-enforcement positions is the observation test. A picture is shown to you for several minutes, then taken away. Questions about the picture test your ability to observe both details and larger elements.

5) **Following directions**

In many positions in the public service, the employee must be able to carry out written instructions dependably and accurately. You may be given a chart with several columns, each column listing a variety of information. The questions require you to carry out directions involving the information given in the chart.

6) **Skills and aptitudes**

Performance tests effectively measure some manual skills and aptitudes. When the skill is one in which you are trained, such as typing or shorthand, you can practice. These tests are often very much like those given in business school or high school courses. For many of the other skills and aptitudes, however, no short-time preparation can be made. Skills and abilities natural to you or that you have developed throughout your lifetime are being tested.

Many of the general questions just described provide all the data needed to answer the questions and ask you to use your reasoning ability to find the answers. Your best preparation for these tests, as well as for tests of facts and ideas, is to be at your physical and mental best. You, no doubt, have your own methods of getting into an exam-taking mood and keeping "in shape." The next section lists some ideas on this subject.

## IV. KINDS OF QUESTIONS

Only rarely is the "essay" question, which you answer in narrative form, used in civil service tests. Civil service tests are usually of the short-answer type. Full instructions for answering these questions will be given to you at the examination. But in case this is your first experience with short-answer questions and separate answer sheets, here is what you need to know:

### 1) Multiple-choice Questions

Most popular of the short-answer questions is the "multiple choice" or "best answer" question. It can be used, for example, to test for factual knowledge, ability to solve problems or judgment in meeting situations found at work.

A multiple-choice question is normally one of three types—
- It can begin with an incomplete statement followed by several possible endings. You are to find the one ending which *best* completes the statement, although some of the others may not be entirely wrong.
- It can also be a complete statement in the form of a question which is answered by choosing one of the statements listed.

- It can be in the form of a problem – again you select the best answer.

Here is an example of a multiple-choice question with a discussion which should give you some clues as to the method for choosing the right answer:

When an employee has a complaint about his assignment, the action which will *best* help him overcome his difficulty is to
    A. discuss his difficulty with his coworkers
    B. take the problem to the head of the organization
    C. take the problem to the person who gave him the assignment
    D. say nothing to anyone about his complaint

In answering this question, you should study each of the choices to find which is best. Consider choice "A" – Certainly an employee may discuss his complaint with fellow employees, but no change or improvement can result, and the complaint remains unresolved. Choice "B" is a poor choice since the head of the organization probably does not know what assignment you have been given, and taking your problem to him is known as "going over the head" of the supervisor. The supervisor, or person who made the assignment, is the person who can clarify it or correct any injustice. Choice "C" is, therefore, correct. To say nothing, as in choice "D," is unwise. Supervisors have and interest in knowing the problems employees are facing, and the employee is seeking a solution to his problem.

## 2) True/False Questions

The "true/false" or "right/wrong" form of question is sometimes used. Here a complete statement is given. Your job is to decide whether the statement is right or wrong.

SAMPLE: A roaming cell-phone call to a nearby city costs less than a non-roaming call to a distant city.

This statement is wrong, or false, since roaming calls are more expensive.

This is not a complete list of all possible question forms, although most of the others are variations of these common types. You will always get complete directions for answering questions. Be sure you understand *how* to mark your answers – ask questions until you do.

## V. RECORDING YOUR ANSWERS

Computer terminals are used more and more today for many different kinds of exams.
For an examination with very few applicants, you may be told to record your answers in the test booklet itself. Separate answer sheets are much more common. If this separate answer sheet is to be scored by machine – and this is often the case – it is highly important that you mark your answers correctly in order to get credit.
An electronic scoring machine is often used in civil service offices because of the speed with which papers can be scored. Machine-scored answer sheets must be marked with a pencil, which will be given to you. This pencil has a high graphite content which responds to the electronic scoring machine. As a matter of fact, stray dots may register as answers, so do not let your pencil rest on the answer sheet while you are pondering the correct answer. Also, if your pencil lead breaks or is otherwise defective, ask for another.

Since the answer sheet will be dropped in a slot in the scoring machine, be careful not to bend the corners or get the paper crumpled.

The answer sheet normally has five vertical columns of numbers, with 30 numbers to a column. These numbers correspond to the question numbers in your test booklet. After each number, going across the page are four or five pairs of dotted lines. These short dotted lines have small letters or numbers above them. The first two pairs may also have a "T" or "F" above the letters. This indicates that the first two pairs only are to be used if the questions are of the true-false type. If the questions are multiple choice, disregard the "T" and "F" and pay attention only to the small letters or numbers.

Answer your questions in the manner of the sample that follows:

32. The largest city in the United States is
   A. Washington, D.C.
   B. New York City
   C. Chicago
   D. Detroit
   E. San Francisco

1) Choose the answer you think is best. (New York City is the largest, so "B" is correct.)
2) Find the row of dotted lines numbered the same as the question you are answering. (Find row number 32)
3) Find the pair of dotted lines corresponding to the answer. (Find the pair of lines under the mark "B.")
4) Make a solid black mark between the dotted lines.

## VI. BEFORE THE TEST

Common sense will help you find procedures to follow to get ready for an examination. Too many of us, however, overlook these sensible measures. Indeed, nervousness and fatigue have been found to be the most serious reasons why applicants fail to do their best on civil service tests. Here is a list of reminders:

- Begin your preparation early – Don't wait until the last minute to go scurrying around for books and materials or to find out what the position is all about.
- Prepare continuously – An hour a night for a week is better than an all-night cram session. This has been definitely established. What is more, a night a week for a month will return better dividends than crowding your study into a shorter period of time.
- Locate the place of the exam – You have been sent a notice telling you when and where to report for the examination. If the location is in a different town or otherwise unfamiliar to you, it would be well to inquire the best route and learn something about the building.
- Relax the night before the test – Allow your mind to rest. Do not study at all that night. Plan some mild recreation or diversion; then go to bed early and get a good night's sleep.
- Get up early enough to make a leisurely trip to the place for the test – This way unforeseen events, traffic snarls, unfamiliar buildings, etc. will not upset you.
- Dress comfortably – A written test is not a fashion show. You will be known by number and not by name, so wear something comfortable.

- Leave excess paraphernalia at home – Shopping bags and odd bundles will get in your way. You need bring only the items mentioned in the official notice you received; usually everything you need is provided. Do not bring reference books to the exam. They will only confuse those last minutes and be taken away from you when in the test room.
- Arrive somewhat ahead of time – If because of transportation schedules you must get there very early, bring a newspaper or magazine to take your mind off yourself while waiting.
- Locate the examination room – When you have found the proper room, you will be directed to the seat or part of the room where you will sit. Sometimes you are given a sheet of instructions to read while you are waiting. Do not fill out any forms until you are told to do so; just read them and be prepared.
- Relax and prepare to listen to the instructions
- If you have any physical problem that may keep you from doing your best, be sure to tell the test administrator. If you are sick or in poor health, you really cannot do your best on the exam. You can come back and take the test some other time.

## VII. AT THE TEST

The day of the test is here and you have the test booklet in your hand. The temptation to get going is very strong. Caution! There is more to success than knowing the right answers. You must know how to identify your papers and understand variations in the type of short-answer question used in this particular examination. Follow these suggestions for maximum results from your efforts:

### 1) Cooperate with the monitor

The test administrator has a duty to create a situation in which you can be as much at ease as possible. He will give instructions, tell you when to begin, check to see that you are marking your answer sheet correctly, and so on. He is not there to guard you, although he will see that your competitors do not take unfair advantage. He wants to help you do your best.

### 2) Listen to all instructions

Don't jump the gun! Wait until you understand all directions. In most civil service tests you get more time than you need to answer the questions. So don't be in a hurry. Read each word of instructions until you clearly understand the meaning. Study the examples, listen to all announcements and follow directions. Ask questions if you do not understand what to do.

### 3) Identify your papers

Civil service exams are usually identified by number only. You will be assigned a number; you must not put your name on your test papers. Be sure to copy your number correctly. Since more than one exam may be given, copy your exact examination title.

### 4) Plan your time

Unless you are told that a test is a "speed" or "rate of work" test, speed itself is usually not important. Time enough to answer all the questions will be provided, but this does not mean that you have all day. An overall time limit has been set. Divide the total time (in minutes) by the number of questions to determine the approximate time you have for each question.

**5) Do not linger over difficult questions**

If you come across a difficult question, mark it with a paper clip (useful to have along) and come back to it when you have been through the booklet. One caution if you do this – be sure to skip a number on your answer sheet as well. Check often to be sure that you have not lost your place and that you are marking in the row numbered the same as the question you are answering.

**6) Read the questions**

Be sure you know what the question asks! Many capable people are unsuccessful because they failed to *read* the questions correctly.

**7) Answer all questions**

Unless you have been instructed that a penalty will be deducted for incorrect answers, it is better to guess than to omit a question.

**8) Speed tests**

It is often better NOT to guess on speed tests. It has been found that on timed tests people are tempted to spend the last few seconds before time is called in marking answers at random – without even reading them – in the hope of picking up a few extra points. To discourage this practice, the instructions may warn you that your score will be "corrected" for guessing. That is, a penalty will be applied. The incorrect answers will be deducted from the correct ones, or some other penalty formula will be used.

**9) Review your answers**

If you finish before time is called, go back to the questions you guessed or omitted to give them further thought. Review other answers if you have time.

**10) Return your test materials**

If you are ready to leave before others have finished or time is called, take ALL your materials to the monitor and leave quietly. Never take any test material with you. The monitor can discover whose papers are not complete, and taking a test booklet may be grounds for disqualification.

## VIII. EXAMINATION TECHNIQUES

1) Read the general instructions carefully. These are usually printed on the first page of the exam booklet. As a rule, these instructions refer to the timing of the examination; the fact that you should not start work until the signal and must stop work at a signal, etc. If there are any *special* instructions, such as a choice of questions to be answered, make sure that you note this instruction carefully.

2) When you are ready to start work on the examination, that is as soon as the signal has been given, read the instructions to each question booklet, underline any key words or phrases, such as *least, best, outline, describe* and the like. In this way you will tend to answer as requested rather than discover on reviewing your paper that you *listed without describing*, that you selected the *worst* choice rather than the *best* choice, etc.

3) If the examination is of the objective or multiple-choice type – that is, each question will also give a series of possible answers: A, B, C or D, and you are called upon to select the best answer and write the letter next to that answer on your answer paper – it is advisable to start answering each question in turn. There may be anywhere from 50 to 100 such questions in the three or four hours allotted and you can see how much time would be taken if you read through all the questions before beginning to answer any. Furthermore, if you come across a question or group of questions which you know would be difficult to answer, it would undoubtedly affect your handling of all the other questions.

4) If the examination is of the essay type and contains but a few questions, it is a moot point as to whether you should read all the questions before starting to answer any one. Of course, if you are given a choice – say five out of seven and the like – then it is essential to read all the questions so you can eliminate the two that are most difficult. If, however, you are asked to answer all the questions, there may be danger in trying to answer the easiest one first because you may find that you will spend too much time on it. The best technique is to answer the first question, then proceed to the second, etc.

5) Time your answers. Before the exam begins, write down the time it started, then add the time allowed for the examination and write down the time it must be completed, then divide the time available somewhat as follows:
    - If 3-1/2 hours are allowed, that would be 210 minutes. If you have 80 objective-type questions, that would be an average of 2-1/2 minutes per question. Allow yourself no more than 2 minutes per question, or a total of 160 minutes, which will permit about 50 minutes to review.
    - If for the time allotment of 210 minutes there are 7 essay questions to answer, that would average about 30 minutes a question. Give yourself only 25 minutes per question so that you have about 35 minutes to review.

6) The most important instruction is to *read each question* and make sure you know what is wanted. The second most important instruction is to *time yourself properly* so that you answer every question. The third most important instruction is to *answer every question*. Guess if you have to but include something for each question. Remember that you will receive no credit for a blank and will probably receive some credit if you write something in answer to an essay question. If you guess a letter – say "B" for a multiple-choice question – you may have guessed right. If you leave a blank as an answer to a multiple-choice question, the examiners may respect your feelings but it will not add a point to your score. Some exams may penalize you for wrong answers, so in such cases *only*, you may not want to guess unless you have some basis for your answer.

7) Suggestions
    a. Objective-type questions
        1. Examine the question booklet for proper sequence of pages and questions
        2. Read all instructions carefully
        3. Skip any question which seems too difficult; return to it after all other questions have been answered
        4. Apportion your time properly; do not spend too much time on any single question or group of questions

5. Note and underline key words – *all, most, fewest, least, best, worst, same, opposite,* etc.
6. Pay particular attention to negatives
7. Note unusual option, e.g., unduly long, short, complex, different or similar in content to the body of the question
8. Observe the use of "hedging" words – *probably, may, most likely,* etc.
9. Make sure that your answer is put next to the same number as the question
10. Do not second-guess unless you have good reason to believe the second answer is definitely more correct
11. Cross out original answer if you decide another answer is more accurate; do not erase until you are ready to hand your paper in
12. Answer all questions; guess unless instructed otherwise
13. Leave time for review

b. Essay questions
1. Read each question carefully
2. Determine exactly what is wanted. Underline key words or phrases.
3. Decide on outline or paragraph answer
4. Include many different points and elements unless asked to develop any one or two points or elements
5. Show impartiality by giving pros and cons unless directed to select one side only
6. Make and write down any assumptions you find necessary to answer the questions
7. Watch your English, grammar, punctuation and choice of words
8. Time your answers; don't crowd material

8) Answering the essay question

Most essay questions can be answered by framing the specific response around several key words or ideas. Here are a few such key words or ideas:

M's: manpower, materials, methods, money, management
P's: purpose, program, policy, plan, procedure, practice, problems, pitfalls, personnel, public relations

   a. Six basic steps in handling problems:
      1. Preliminary plan and background development
      2. Collect information, data and facts
      3. Analyze and interpret information, data and facts
      4. Analyze and develop solutions as well as make recommendations
      5. Prepare report and sell recommendations
      6. Install recommendations and follow up effectiveness

   b. Pitfalls to avoid
      1. *Taking things for granted* – A statement of the situation does not necessarily imply that each of the elements is necessarily true; for example, a complaint may be invalid and biased so that all that can be taken for granted is that a complaint has been registered

2. *Considering only one side of a situation* – Wherever possible, indicate several alternatives and then point out the reasons you selected the best one
3. *Failing to indicate follow up* – Whenever your answer indicates action on your part, make certain that you will take proper follow-up action to see how successful your recommendations, procedures or actions turn out to be
4. *Taking too long in answering any single question* – Remember to time your answers properly

## IX. AFTER THE TEST

Scoring procedures differ in detail among civil service jurisdictions although the general principles are the same. Whether the papers are hand-scored or graded by machine we have described, they are nearly always graded by number. That is, the person who marks the paper knows only the number – never the name – of the applicant. Not until all the papers have been graded will they be matched with names. If other tests, such as training and experience or oral interview ratings have been given, scores will be combined. Different parts of the examination usually have different weights. For example, the written test might count 60 percent of the final grade, and a rating of training and experience 40 percent. In many jurisdictions, veterans will have a certain number of points added to their grades.

After the final grade has been determined, the names are placed in grade order and an eligible list is established. There are various methods for resolving ties between those who get the same final grade – probably the most common is to place first the name of the person whose application was received first. Job offers are made from the eligible list in the order the names appear on it. You will be notified of your grade and your rank as soon as all these computations have been made. This will be done as rapidly as possible.

People who are found to meet the requirements in the announcement are called "eligibles." Their names are put on a list of eligible candidates. An eligible's chances of getting a job depend on how high he stands on this list and how fast agencies are filling jobs from the list.

When a job is to be filled from a list of eligibles, the agency asks for the names of people on the list of eligibles for that job. When the civil service commission receives this request, it sends to the agency the names of the three people highest on this list. Or, if the job to be filled has specialized requirements, the office sends the agency the names of the top three persons who meet these requirements from the general list.

The appointing officer makes a choice from among the three people whose names were sent to him. If the selected person accepts the appointment, the names of the others are put back on the list to be considered for future openings.

That is the rule in hiring from all kinds of eligible lists, whether they are for typist, carpenter, chemist, or something else. For every vacancy, the appointing officer has his choice of any one of the top three eligibles on the list. This explains why the person whose name is on top of the list sometimes does not get an appointment when some of the persons lower on the list do. If the appointing officer chooses the second or third eligible, the No. 1 eligible does not get a job at once, but stays on the list until he is appointed or the list is terminated.

## X. HOW TO PASS THE INTERVIEW TEST

The examination for which you applied requires an oral interview test. You have already taken the written test and you are now being called for the interview test – the final part of the formal examination.

You may think that it is not possible to prepare for an interview test and that there are no procedures to follow during an interview. Our purpose is to point out some things you can do in advance that will help you and some good rules to follow and pitfalls to avoid while you are being interviewed.

*What is an interview supposed to test?*

The written examination is designed to test the technical knowledge and competence of the candidate; the oral is designed to evaluate intangible qualities, not readily measured otherwise, and to establish a list showing the relative fitness of each candidate – as measured against his competitors – for the position sought. Scoring is not on the basis of "right" and "wrong," but on a sliding scale of values ranging from "not passable" to "outstanding." As a matter of fact, it is possible to achieve a relatively low score without a single "incorrect" answer because of evident weakness in the qualities being measured.

Occasionally, an examination may consist entirely of an oral test – either an individual or a group oral. In such cases, information is sought concerning the technical knowledges and abilities of the candidate, since there has been no written examination for this purpose. More commonly, however, an oral test is used to supplement a written examination.

*Who conducts interviews?*

The composition of oral boards varies among different jurisdictions. In nearly all, a representative of the personnel department serves as chairman. One of the members of the board may be a representative of the department in which the candidate would work. In some cases, "outside experts" are used, and, frequently, a businessman or some other representative of the general public is asked to serve. Labor and management or other special groups may be represented. The aim is to secure the services of experts in the appropriate field.

However the board is composed, it is a good idea (and not at all improper or unethical) to ascertain in advance of the interview who the members are and what groups they represent. When you are introduced to them, you will have some idea of their backgrounds and interests, and at least you will not stutter and stammer over their names.

*What should be done before the interview?*

While knowledge about the board members is useful and takes some of the surprise element out of the interview, there is other preparation which is more substantive. It *is* possible to prepare for an oral interview – in several ways:

**1) Keep a copy of your application and review it carefully before the interview**

This may be the only document before the oral board, and the starting point of the interview. Know what education and experience you have listed there, and the sequence and dates of all of it. Sometimes the board will ask you to review the highlights of your experience for them; you should not have to hem and haw doing it.

**2) Study the class specification and the examination announcement**

Usually, the oral board has one or both of these to guide them. The qualities, characteristics or knowledges required by the position sought are stated in these documents. They offer valuable clues as to the nature of the oral interview. For example, if the job involves supervisory responsibilities, the announcement will usually indicate that knowledge of modern supervisory methods and the qualifications of the candidate as a supervisor will be tested. If so, you can expect such questions, frequently in the form of a hypothetical situation which you are expected to solve. NEVER go into an oral without knowledge of the duties and responsibilities of the job you seek.

### 3) Think through each qualification required

Try to visualize the kind of questions you would ask if you were a board member. How well could you answer them? Try especially to appraise your own knowledge and background in each area, *measured against the job sought*, and identify any areas in which you are weak. Be critical and realistic – do not flatter yourself.

### 4) Do some general reading in areas in which you feel you may be weak

For example, if the job involves supervision and your past experience has NOT, some general reading in supervisory methods and practices, particularly in the field of human relations, might be useful. Do NOT study agency procedures or detailed manuals. The oral board will be testing your understanding and capacity, not your memory.

### 5) Get a good night's sleep and watch your general health and mental attitude

You will want a clear head at the interview. Take care of a cold or any other minor ailment, and of course, no hangovers.

*What should be done on the day of the interview?*

Now comes the day of the interview itself. Give yourself plenty of time to get there. Plan to arrive somewhat ahead of the scheduled time, particularly if your appointment is in the fore part of the day. If a previous candidate fails to appear, the board might be ready for you a bit early. By early afternoon an oral board is almost invariably behind schedule if there are many candidates, and you may have to wait. Take along a book or magazine to read, or your application to review, but leave any extraneous material in the waiting room when you go in for your interview. In any event, relax and compose yourself.

The matter of dress is important. The board is forming impressions about you – from your experience, your manners, your attitude, and your appearance. Give your personal appearance careful attention. Dress your best, but not your flashiest. Choose conservative, appropriate clothing, and be sure it is immaculate. This is a business interview, and your appearance should indicate that you regard it as such. Besides, being well groomed and properly dressed will help boost your confidence.

Sooner or later, someone will call your name and escort you into the interview room. *This is it.* From here on you are on your own. It is too late for any more preparation. But remember, you asked for this opportunity to prove your fitness, and you are here because your request was granted.

*What happens when you go in?*

The usual sequence of events will be as follows: The clerk (who is often the board stenographer) will introduce you to the chairman of the oral board, who will introduce you to the other members of the board. Acknowledge the introductions before you sit down. Do not be surprised if you find a microphone facing you or a stenotypist sitting by. Oral interviews are usually recorded in the event of an appeal or other review.

Usually the chairman of the board will open the interview by reviewing the highlights of your education and work experience from your application – primarily for the benefit of the other members of the board, as well as to get the material into the record. Do not interrupt or comment unless there is an error or significant misinterpretation; if that is the case, do not hesitate. But do not quibble about insignificant matters. Also, he will usually ask you some question about your education, experience or your present job – partly to get you to start talking and to establish the interviewing "rapport." He may start the actual questioning, or turn it over to one of the other members. Frequently, each member undertakes the questioning on a particular area, one in which he is perhaps most competent, so you can expect each member to participate in the examination. Because time is limited, you may also expect some rather abrupt switches in the direction the questioning takes, so do not be upset by it. Normally, a board member will not pursue a single line of questioning unless he discovers a particular strength or weakness.

After each member has participated, the chairman will usually ask whether any member has any further questions, then will ask you if you have anything you wish to add. Unless you are expecting this question, it may floor you. Worse, it may start you off on an extended, extemporaneous speech. The board is not usually seeking more information. The question is principally to offer you a last opportunity to present further qualifications or to indicate that you have nothing to add. So, if you feel that a significant qualification or characteristic has been overlooked, it is proper to point it out in a sentence or so. Do not compliment the board on the thoroughness of their examination – they have been sketchy, and you know it. If you wish, merely say, "No thank you, I have nothing further to add." This is a point where you can "talk yourself out" of a good impression or fail to present an important bit of information. Remember, *you close the interview yourself*.

The chairman will then say, "That is all, Mr. _____, thank you." Do not be startled; the interview is over, and quicker than you think. Thank him, gather your belongings and take your leave. Save your sigh of relief for the other side of the door.

*How to put your best foot forward*

Throughout this entire process, you may feel that the board individually and collectively is trying to pierce your defenses, seek out your hidden weaknesses and embarrass and confuse you. Actually, this is not true. They are obliged to make an appraisal of your qualifications for the job you are seeking, and they want to see you in your best light. Remember, they must interview all candidates and a non-cooperative candidate may become a failure in spite of their best efforts to bring out his qualifications. Here are 15 suggestions that will help you:

1) **Be natural – Keep your attitude confident, not cocky**

If you are not confident that you can do the job, do not expect the board to be. Do not apologize for your weaknesses, try to bring out your strong points. The board is interested in a positive, not negative, presentation. Cockiness will antagonize any board member and make him wonder if you are covering up a weakness by a false show of strength.

2) **Get comfortable, but don't lounge or sprawl**

Sit erectly but not stiffly. A careless posture may lead the board to conclude that you are careless in other things, or at least that you are not impressed by the importance of the occasion. Either conclusion is natural, even if incorrect. Do not fuss with your clothing, a pencil or an ashtray. Your hands may occasionally be useful to emphasize a point; do not let them become a point of distraction.

3) **Do not wisecrack or make small talk**

This is a serious situation, and your attitude should show that you consider it as such. Further, the time of the board is limited – they do not want to waste it, and neither should you.

### 4) Do not exaggerate your experience or abilities

In the first place, from information in the application or other interviews and sources, the board may know more about you than you think. Secondly, you probably will not get away with it. An experienced board is rather adept at spotting such a situation, so do not take the chance.

### 5) If you know a board member, do not make a point of it, yet do not hide it

Certainly you are not fooling him, and probably not the other members of the board. Do not try to take advantage of your acquaintanceship – it will probably do you little good.

### 6) Do not dominate the interview

Let the board do that. They will give you the clues – do not assume that you have to do all the talking. Realize that the board has a number of questions to ask you, and do not try to take up all the interview time by showing off your extensive knowledge of the answer to the first one.

### 7) Be attentive

You only have 20 minutes or so, and you should keep your attention at its sharpest throughout. When a member is addressing a problem or question to you, give him your undivided attention. Address your reply principally to him, but do not exclude the other board members.

### 8) Do not interrupt

A board member may be stating a problem for you to analyze. He will ask you a question when the time comes. Let him state the problem, and wait for the question.

### 9) Make sure you understand the question

Do not try to answer until you are sure what the question is. If it is not clear, restate it in your own words or ask the board member to clarify it for you. However, do not haggle about minor elements.

### 10) Reply promptly but not hastily

A common entry on oral board rating sheets is "candidate responded readily," or "candidate hesitated in replies." Respond as promptly and quickly as you can, but do not jump to a hasty, ill-considered answer.

### 11) Do not be peremptory in your answers

A brief answer is proper – but do not fire your answer back. That is a losing game from your point of view. The board member can probably ask questions much faster than you can answer them.

### 12) Do not try to create the answer you think the board member wants

He is interested in what kind of mind you have and how it works – not in playing games. Furthermore, he can usually spot this practice and will actually grade you down on it.

### 13) Do not switch sides in your reply merely to agree with a board member

Frequently, a member will take a contrary position merely to draw you out and to see if you are willing and able to defend your point of view. Do not start a debate, yet do not surrender a good position. If a position is worth taking, it is worth defending.

### 14) Do not be afraid to admit an error in judgment if you are shown to be wrong

The board knows that you are forced to reply without any opportunity for careful consideration. Your answer may be demonstrably wrong. If so, admit it and get on with the interview.

### 15) Do not dwell at length on your present job

The opening question may relate to your present assignment. Answer the question but do not go into an extended discussion. You are being examined for a *new* job, not your present one. As a matter of fact, try to phrase ALL your answers in terms of the job for which you are being examined.

*Basis of Rating*

Probably you will forget most of these "do's" and "don'ts" when you walk into the oral interview room. Even remembering them all will not ensure you a passing grade. Perhaps you did not have the qualifications in the first place. But remembering them will help you to put your best foot forward, without treading on the toes of the board members.

Rumor and popular opinion to the contrary notwithstanding, an oral board wants you to make the best appearance possible. They know you are under pressure – but they also want to see how you respond to it as a guide to what your reaction would be under the pressures of the job you seek. They will be influenced by the degree of poise you display, the personal traits you show and the manner in which you respond.


ABOUT THIS BOOK

This book contains tests divided into Examination Sections. Go through each test, answering every question in the margin. We have also attached a sample answer sheet at the back of the book that can be removed and used. At the end of each test look at the answer key and check your answers. On the ones you got wrong, look at the right answer choice and learn. Do not fill in the answers first. Do not memorize the questions and answers, but understand the answer and principles involved. On your test, the questions will likely be different from the samples. Questions are changed and new ones added. If you understand these past questions you should have success with any changes that arise. Tests may consist of several types of questions. We have additional books on each subject should more study be advisable or necessary for you. Finally, the more you study, the better prepared you will be. This book is intended to be the last thing you study before you walk into the examination room. Prior study of relevant texts is also recommended. NLC publishes some of these in our Fundamental Series. Knowledge and good sense are important factors in passing your exam. Good luck also helps. So now study this Passbook, absorb the material contained within and take that knowledge into the examination. Then do your best to pass that exam.

# EXAMINATION SECTION

# EXAMINATION SECTION
# TEST 1

DIRECTIONS: Each question or incomplete statement is followed by several suggested answers or completions. Select the one that BEST answers the question or completes the statement. *PRINT THE LETTER OF THE CORRECT ANSWER IN THE SPACE AT THE RIGHT.*

1. The texture of an aluminum-soap lubricating grease is  1.____

    A. smooth  B. fibrous  C. spongy  D. stringy

2. The property of a lubricant that allows it to adhere to metallic surfaces is known as  2.____

    A. antifoam  B. cloud point
    C. viscosity  D. oiliness

3. The physical appearance of a grease with a consistency number of four is MOST NEARLY  3.____

    A. hard  B. medium hard
    C. semifluid  D. soft

4. The one of the following measures that is COMMONLY used to represent a rate of oil feed is drops per  4.____

    A. minute  B. pound
    C. foot  D. square inch

5. The MOST important single property of a lubricating oil is its  5.____

    A. fire point  B. pour point
    C. floc point  D. viscosity

6. The rate of change of the viscosity of a petroleum oil with its temperature is indicated by its  6.____

    A. SUS number  B. kinematic index
    C. centistokes number  D. viscosity index

7. The neutralization number of an oil is an indication of its  7.____

    A. inorganic or demineral acidity
    B. emulsifying and demulsifying capacity
    C. organic or mineral acidity
    D. precipitate carbon residue

8. Graphite is a form of  8.____

    A. lard oil  B. animal oil
    C. wool wicking  D. anthracite coal

9. The BASIC ingredient in the manufacture of lubricating greases is  9.____

    A. gum  B. an inhibitor
    C. soap  D. fatty acid

10. A test of grease that identifies greases and indicates uniformity in their manufacture is known as the _____ test.

    A. penetration  
    B. consistency  
    C. temperature-pour  
    D. dropping-point

11. The bearing materials usually called *white metals* or Babbitt metal consist MAINLY of

    A. tin and copper  
    B. tin and lead  
    C. copper and antimony  
    D. copper and lead

12. It is GOOD practice in the installation of three new packing rings in a stuffing box to require that the joints of the packing be spaced _____ degrees apart.

    A. 90  B. 120  C. 140  D. 230

13. The objective in the use of applicators for wire-rope lubrication is to apply a smooth even film at a temperature conducive to the

    A. penetration of the wire strands  
    B. safety of the operator  
    C. prevention of dust accumulation  
    D. even brushing-on of lubricant

14. The one of the following metals that is non-ferrous is

    A. galvanized iron  
    B. cast iron  
    C. chrome-nickel steel  
    D. copper

15. The common terms *heavy* and *light,* applied to an oil, refer ONLY to the oil's

    A. weight  
    B. color  
    C. viscosity  
    D. emulsification

16. The ring in ring-oiled bearings has a diameter that is USUALLY _____ the journal diameter.

    A. twice  
    B. the same as  
    C. one and one-half times  
    D. one and one-quarter times

17. A boiler feedwater regulator automatically controls the _____ the boiler.

    A. feedwater treatment to  
    B. water temperature in  
    C. water pressure to  
    D. water supply to

18. The dirty oil to be purified in an operating DeLaval Purifier enters the purifier bowl from the

    A. top of the machine  
    B. bottom of the machine  
    C. side of the machine  
    D. priming tank

19. The APPROXIMATE rpm of a Sharpies oil purifier is

    A. 7,000  B. 10,000  C. 16,000  D. 25,000

20. In order to have effective separation or purification in a DeLaval Purifier, it is recommended that the oil to be cleaned be heated to an APPROXIMATE temperature of

    A. 80° F      B. 100° F      C. 120° F      D. 160° F

21. The one of the following that is NOT a method for removing contaminants from oil is

    A. settling      B. filtering
    C. centrifuging      D. centripeting

22. An engine indicator is an instrument that is used on a reciprocating engine to determine the _____ the engine.

    A. oil pressure in      B. temperature in
    C. operating speed of      D. performance of

23. The MAXIMUM bearing oil discharge temperature at which a turbine beating may satisfactorily operate is

    A. 220° F      B. 200° F      C. 180° F      D. 160° F

24. Generally, at what point should a turbine-driven generator, with an integral lubricating oil system, put the lube oil cooler in operation?

    A. As soon as the turbine is started
    B. When the sump oil temperature is at 150° F
    C. Before the turbine is started
    D. When the temperature of the hottest bearing reaches 100° F

25. In modern practice, the method by which turbine-generator reduction gear surfaces NORMALLY receive lubrication oil is

    A. pressure circulation lubrication
    B. oil wick systems
    C. gears dipping in sump oil
    D. oil rings

26. Lubrication for modern reciprocating air compressors is GENERALLY supplied by

    A. a gravity feed
    B. grease cups
    C. a wick feed
    D. a mechanical force-feed oiler

27. Aftercoolers are put on MOST air compressor installations to

    A. cool air compressor lube oil
    B. function as unloaders
    C. cool air compressor jacket water
    D. condense moisture from compressed air

28. A pipe fitting having a male thread at one end, a female thread at the other end, and shaped to a ninety-degree bend is called a(n)

    A. street elbow      B. 90-degree elbow
    C. elbow      D. 90-degree nipple

29. The one of the following actions that MUST be taken during normal operation to clean a knife edge (cuneo) strainer is    29.____

    A. washing it in kerosene
    B. disposing of the element
    C. changing the basket
    D. rotating the cleaner blades

30. Detergents are used in lubricating oils to    30.____

    A. prevent oxidation of the oil
    B. control the oil color
    C. prevent corrosion
    D. keep insoluble matter in suspension

31. The purpose of adding an inhibitor to lubricating oil is to _____ the engine.    31.____

    A. lower the pour point of the oil to
    B. prevent sludge and varnish formation on parts of
    C. improve the adhesiveness of the lubricant to
    D. reduce the tension of small bubbles that may form in the oil for

32. The relationship between lubricating oil viscosities and temperature is that the viscosities    32.____

    A. decrease with a temperature decrease
    B. decrease with a temperature increase
    C. increase with a temperature increase
    D. are not affected by temperature changes

33. The one of the following fluids that should be used when cleaning filter bags of pressure-type lube oil filters is    33.____

    A. carbon tetrachloride          B. gasoline
    C. kerosene                      D. hot soapy water

34. The precaution, or precautions, that an oiler must take when he is using absorbent type lubricating oil filters is to    34.____

    A. make sure that straight mineral oils are not used
    B. make sure that the particular oil additives are not removed by the filter
    C. make sure that all water is removed from the oil before it passes through the absorbent type filter
    D. do both A and C above

35. The specific gravity of lubricating oil is USUALLY measured by means of a    35.____

    A. venturi meter                 B. hydrometer
    C. calorimeter                   D. purifier

36. Of the following, the MOST important requirement of a refrigerator lubricant is that it have    36.____

    A. a good dielectric strength
    B. freedom from water
    C. a good pour-point temperature
    D. a good wax separation capability

37. The one of the following faults that would MOST generally cause a sudden increase in oil pressure in a lubricating line to a bearing is

   A. a clogged strainer
   B. too low an oil temperature
   C. too high an oil temperature
   D. water in the system

37.____

38. The wick used in a gravity oil-feed system is USUALLY made of

   A. asbestos
   B. nylon
   C. saran fiber
   D. wool

38.____

39. A thrust bearing is LEAST likely to be found on a(n)

   A. auxiliary turbine driving a pump
   B. impulse turbine
   C. reciprocating pump
   D. reaction turbine

39.____

40. A valve that allows oil to flow in one direction only is GENERALLY called a _____ valve.

   A. globe      B. stop      C. check      D. gate

40.____

# KEY (CORRECT ANSWERS)

| | | | |
|---|---|---|---|
| 1. D | 11. A | 21. D | 31. B |
| 2. D | 12. B | 22. D | 32. B |
| 3. A | 13. A | 23. B | 33. C |
| 4. A | 14. D | 24. D | 34. B |
| 5. D | 15. C | 25. A | 35. B |
| 6. D | 16. A | 26. D | 36. B |
| 7. C | 17. D | 27. D | 37. A |
| 8. D | 18. A | 28. A | 38. D |
| 9. C | 19. C | 29. D | 39. C |
| 10. D | 20. D | 30. D | 40. C |

# TEST 2

DIRECTIONS: Each question or incomplete statement is followed by several suggested answers or completions. Select the one that BEST answers the question or completes the statement. *PRINT THE LETTER OF THE CORRECT ANSWER IN THE SPACE AT THE RIGHT.*

1. The one of the following types of oils MOST preferred for the hydraulic governor of a reciprocating steam engine is _____ oil.   1.___

    A. compounded
    B. foaming additive
    C. non-additive turbine type
    D. wetting additive

2. The one of the following pumps that does NOT have moving parts to be lubricated is a _____ pump.   2.___

    A. jet
    C. centrifugal
    B. propeller
    D. rotary

3. The LARGEST class of lubricants in common use is   3.___

    A. water
    C. vegetable oil
    B. mineral oil
    D. animal oil

4. The sealing fluid in lubricating oil centrifuges is   4.___

    A. the dirty oil
    C. the clean oil
    B. water
    D. kerosene

5. In a well-operated lubricating oil and grease storage facility, lubricating oil is NOT normally removed from large drums by   5.___

    A. a hand pump
    B. siphoning out of the top of the drum
    C. an air-operated pump
    D. gravity

6. The one of the following that is NOT the identification of a type of gear is a _____ gear.   6.___

    A. needle
    C. herringbone
    B. worm
    D. rack and pinion

7. The one of the following that is NOT an anti-friction bearing is the _____ bearing.   7.___

    A. tapered roller
    C. ball thrust
    B. helical
    D. roller

8. There are five belts in the drive of a certain fan unit. One of the belts is very loose. The PROPER action to take to correct this condition is to   8.___

    A. take up the slack
    B. replace the loose belt
    C. replace all belts with new belts
    D. remove the loose belt and do not replace it

9. The one of the following activities that need NOT be performed before starting a forced-draft fan unit that has been shut down for some time is to

   A. check around the fan for loose tools and rags, and that it is closed up and ready to operate
   B. check to see that the motor drive is free of tools and rags
   C. check the electric distribution panel to make sure that the motor switch is not *worker tagged*
   D. open up the suction air valve

10. The oil at the bearing surface of a steam turbine is USUALLY hotter than the bearing oil discharge temperature by _____ degrees F.

    A. 5 to 10    B. 10 to 20    C. 50 to 80    D. 100 to 120

11. General experience indicates that the lubricating oil temperature for the bearings of steam turbines should NOT be permitted to go above _____ degrees F.

    A. 70 to 80    B. 80 to 90    C. 90 to 100    D. 110 to 120

12. The FIRST step in determining the reason why the bearings of a ventilating fan are *running hot* is to

    A. put graphite in the oil
    B. shut down the unit
    C. check the oil flowing to the bearings
    D. check the electrical circuit

13. AGMA Grade 1 lubricant is MOST NEARLY equivalent to SAE number

    A. 75    B. 90    C. 120    D. 140

14. The letters *AGMA*, used when referring to a gear lubricant, are an abbreviation for the

    A. Association of Gear Manufacturers Alliance
    B. Alliance of Gear Manufacturers of America
    C. American Gear Manufacturers Association
    D. Association of Gear Manufacturers of America

15. When the ignition characteristics of a fuel are represented by a cetane number, the fuel is NORMALLY used in a

    A. gasoline engine
    B. diesel engine
    C. reciprocating steam engine
    D. steam turbine power unit

16. The resistance to flow of a liquid is measured by a(n)

    A. manometer         B. anemometer
    C. petrometer        D. viscosimeter

17. The MOST economical and effective method to get lubricating oil into a horizontal super-heated-steam reciprocating engine is to

    A. swab the piston and valve rods with the oil
    B. atomize the oil into the steam at the steam inlet
    C. direct the feed of the oil to the cylinder and valves
    D. oil through the indicator ports

18. The parts of the valve in a poppet valve engine that require lubrication are the _____ guide.

    A. poppet mechanism and the
    B. cam and tappet mechanism and the valve steam
    C. slide-valve mechanism and the
    D. sealing-valve ring and the

19. The purpose of the seals that close the small openings between shafts in machinery, and the housings through which they extend, is to

    A. prevent leakage of steam
    B. prevent the escape of air
    C. exclude dirt and prevent the escape of lubricant
    D. prevent the leakage of air into the machine

20. Lubricants in a diesel engine perform all of the following functions EXCEPT

    A. acting as a cooling agent
    B. acting as a vibration absorber
    C. assisting in sealing the piston-cylinder wall clearance
    D. cleaning and carry away dirt and other foreign matter from bearings

21. The one of the following signs that would indicate that the oil supply passage to a hydraulic lifter on a diesel engine is plugged up is

    A. a high exhaust temperature from the affected cylinder
    B. noise from the affected valve
    C. overheating of the piston
    D. a piston slap noise

22. A pyrometer on a diesel engine is used for measuring

    A. vacuum                B. pressure
    C. temperature           D. viscosity of fuel oil

23. Water GENERALLY enters a diesel engine lubricating oil system because of

    A. a leaky crankcase cover
    B. rain dripping down its vents
    C. condensation of combustion products
    D. all of the above

24. Two gears are meshed together and have a gear ratio of to 1. If the small gear rotates 120 revolutions per minute, the large gear rotates at _____ rpm.

    A. 20            B. 40            C. 60            D. 720

25. The vacuum side of a compound gage reads 14 inches of vacuum. The barometer reading is 29.76 inches of mercury. The equivalent absolute pressure of the compound gage reading, in inches of mercury, is MOST likely

   A. 15.06   B. 15.76   C. 43.06   D. 43.76

26. The fraction 5/8, expressed as a decimal, is

   A. 0.125   B. 0.412   C. 0.625   D. 0.875

27. If 300 feet of a certain size pipe weighs 450 pounds, the number of pounds that 100 feet will weigh is

   A. 1,350   B. 150   C. 300   D. 250

28. As an oiler, you work for a facility that has automobiles that use, on the average, 600 quarts of one grade of lubricating oil every month. The number of one-gallon cans of the above oil that SHOULD be ordered each month to meet this requirement is

   A. 100   B. 125   C. 140   D. 150

29. The purpose of a fuse in an electric circuit operating at a set voltage is to protect against

   A. high frequency  B. capacitance
   C. reactance       D. too much current

30. A fuse in an electric circuit has the SAME function as a

   A. receptacle       B. condenser
   C. circuit breaker  D. commutator

31. Electric current is measured in

   A. volts   B. amperes   C. ohms   D. farads

32. Of the following, the one that is a good surface color for the commutators and slip rings of electrical generators is

   A. light straw       B. jet black
   C. chocolate brown   D. bright copper

33. The type of fire extinguisher that SHOULD be used in fighting an electrical fire is

   A. soda acid       B. foam
   C. carbon dioxide  D. carbon tetrachloride

34. The MOST important precaution to take in giving first aid to a severely injured man when there is a possibility of broken bones is to

   A. raise him to a sitting position and console him until the doctor arrives
   B. move him no more than is absolutely necessary and call a doctor
   C. lower his arms and legs to make him comfortable and call a doctor
   D. bundle him into an automobile and get him to a hospital immediately

35. An oiler who is working on a repair job which has to be EXPEDITED is working on a job that must be done

   A. slowly                   B. carefully
   C. as quickly as possible   D. safely

36. An oiler who is ADEPT at his job is one who is

   A. skilled
   B. developed
   C. honest
   D. cooperative

Questions 37-40.

DIRECTIONS: Questions 37 through 40, inclusive, are to be answered in accordance with the following paragraph.

    Synthetic detergents are materials produced from petroleum products or from animal or vegetable oils and fats. One of their advantages is the fact that they can be made to meet a particular cleaning problem by altering the foaming, wetting, and emulsifying properties of a cleaner. They are added to commonly used cleaning materials such as solvents, water, and alkalies to improve their cleaning performance. The adequate wetting of the surface to be cleaned is paramount in good cleaning performance. Because of the relatively high surface tension of water, it has poor wetting ability, unless its surface tension is decreased by addition of a detergent or soap. This allows water to flow into crevices and around small particles of soil, thus loosening them.

37. According to the above paragraph, synthetic detergents are made from all of the following EXCEPT

   A. petroleum products
   B. vegetable oils
   C. surface tension oils
   D. animal fats

38. According to the above paragraph, water's poor wetting ability is related to

   A. its low surface tension
   B. its high surface tension
   C. its vegetable oil content
   D. the amount of dirt on the surface to be cleaned

39. According to the above paragraph, synthetic detergents are added to all of the following EXCEPT

   A. alkalines
   B. water
   C. acids
   D. solvents

40. According to the above paragraph, altering a property of a cleaner can give an advantage in meeting a certain cleaning problem.
   The one of the following that is NOT a property altered by synthetic detergents is the cleaner's

   A. flow ability
   B. foaming property
   C. emulsifying property
   D. wetting ability

## KEY (CORRECT ANSWERS)

| | | | | | | | |
|---|---|---|---|---|---|---|---|
| 1. | C | 11. | D | 21. | B | 31. | B |
| 2. | A | 12. | B | 22. | C | 32. | C |
| 3. | B | 13. | A | 23. | C | 33. | C |
| 4. | B | 14. | C | 24. | A | 34. | B |
| 5. | B | 15. | B | 25. | B | 35. | C |
| 6. | A | 16. | D | 26. | C | 36. | A |
| 7. | B | 17. | B | 27. | B | 37. | C |
| 8. | C | 18. | B | 28. | D | 38. | B |
| 9. | D | 19. | C | 29. | D | 39. | C |
| 10. | C | 20. | B | 30. | C | 40. | A |

# EXAMINATION SECTION
# TEST 1

DIRECTIONS: Each question or incomplete statement is followed by several suggested answers or completions. Select the one that BEST answers the question or completes the statement. *PRINT THE LETTER OF THE CORRECT ANSWER IN THE SPACE AT THE RIGHT.*

1. Mineral oils are USUALLY refined from _____ products.  1._____
   - A. lard-beef
   - B. crude petroleum
   - C. cottonseed
   - D. lime soap

2. In general, light-bodied oils are MOST suitable for  2._____
   - A. light loads at high speeds
   - B. heavy loads at slow speeds
   - C. heavy bearing pressures
   - D. chain drives and roller bearings

3. Of the following, a good lubricant should ALWAYS possess  3._____
   - A. high viscosity
   - B. minimum impurities
   - C. animal oils
   - D. mineral oils

4. Of the following oils, the one which is generally considered useless as a lubricant is _____ oil.  4._____
   - A. castor
   - B. tallow
   - C. rape
   - D. linseed

5. The property of a lubricant that a Saybolt viscosimeter measures is called the  5._____
   - A. chill point
   - B. acid point
   - C. degree of fluidity
   - D. specific gravity

6. The texture of calcium-base greases is USUALLY  6._____
   - A. smooth
   - B. fibrous
   - C. spongy
   - D. rubbery

7. The equipment commonly used to separate heavy liquids from lighter liquids is called a  7._____
   - A. centrifuge
   - B. pump
   - C. mechanical lubricator
   - D. strainer

8. Clean storage of lubricants and proper handling methods  8._____
   - A. are too costly for use in small power plants
   - B. are of minor importance in new power plants
   - C. prevent injury and breakdown to machinery
   - D. are not economical over a long period of time

9. As an Oiler, you notice a leak around the piston rod of a double acting water pump. In order to reduce this leak, you should FIRST tighten each hexagon nut on the packing gland one  9._____
   - A. sixth of a turn
   - B. quarter of a turn
   - C. half of a turn
   - D. full turn

10. A lubricant that possesses high adhesion qualities is LESS likely

    A. to run out of a bearing
    B. to become rancid while in use
    C. used with heavy bearing pressures
    D. used with heavy loads at slow speeds

11. Of the following lubricants, the one which is USUALLY NOT attacked by acids is

    A. graphite           B. cottonseed oil
    C. castor oil         D. lard

12. Packing glands of reciprocating pumps or compressors should generally be

    A. left loose when machine is shut down over night
    B. tightened when machine is shut down over night
    C. tightened when machine is ready to start in the morning
    D. adjusted once a month when replacing packing

13. The device that feeds oil in direct proportion to the speed of a steam engine is called a _____ lubricator.

    A. forced feed        B. gravity type
    C. wick type          D. compound

14. When installing four new packing rings in a stuffing box, the joints of the packing should be placed _____ apart.

    A. 90°    B. 120°    C. 220°    D. 270°

15. The valve that allows oil to flow in one direction only is commonly known as a _____ valve.

    A. globe    B. gate    C. check    D. stop

16. The minimum amount of oil required in a system which circulates 30 gallons of oil per minute, with sufficient oil to give a complete oil change each 8 minutes, is MOST NEARLY _____ gallons.

    A. 240    B. 320    C. 360    D. 480

17. If the oil pressure in a continuous lubricating system suddenly decreases, it USUALLY indicates that

    A. the filters are dirty or clogged
    B. there must be a leak in the line
    C. the oil pump is worn
    D. the oil level glass needs adjustment

18. Spontaneous ignition is USUALLY caused by the combination of poor ventilation and a pile of

    A. linen rags           B. oily waste
    C. exposed oil cans     D. exposed grease cans

19. The inside dimensions of a rectangular oil gravity tank are: height 15", width 9", length 10".
    The amount of oil in the tank, in gallons, (231 cu.in. = 1 gallon) when the oil level is 9" high is MOST NEARLY

    A. 2.3    B. 3.5    C. 5.2    D. 5.8

20. If 30 gallons of oil cost $9.60, 45 gallons of oil at the same rate will cost

    A. $11.40    B. $14.40    C. $15.40    D. $16.40

21. If an oiler earns $1800 in the first six months of a year and receives a 10% raise in salary for the next six months of the same year, his total earnings for the year will be

    A. $3600    B. $3750    C. $3780    D. D, $3960

22. If the cost of lubricating oil increases 15%, then a gallon of oil which used to cost $2.00 will now cost MOST NEARLY

    A. A6. $2.10    B. $2.20    C. $2.30    D. $2.40

23. The sum of 7/8", 3/4", 1/2", and 3/8" is MOST NEARLY

    A. 2 1/8"    B. 2 1/4"    C. 2 3/8"    D. 2 1/2"

24. A safe recommendation for the bearing lubricant of a steam engine equipped with oil cups would be a(n) _____ oil.

    A. reasonably heavy      B. light
    C. inexpensive           D. vegetable

25. Crankcase explosions in an internal combustion engine

    A. are prevented by use of oils of proper viscosity
    B. occur when crankcase oil temperature reaches about 150-200° F
    C. are prevented by use of oils of proper type
    D. are preventable by keeping air out of the crankcase when practicable

Questions 26-30.

DIRECTIONS: Questions 26 through 30, inclusive, are related to the sketch that appears on the following page.

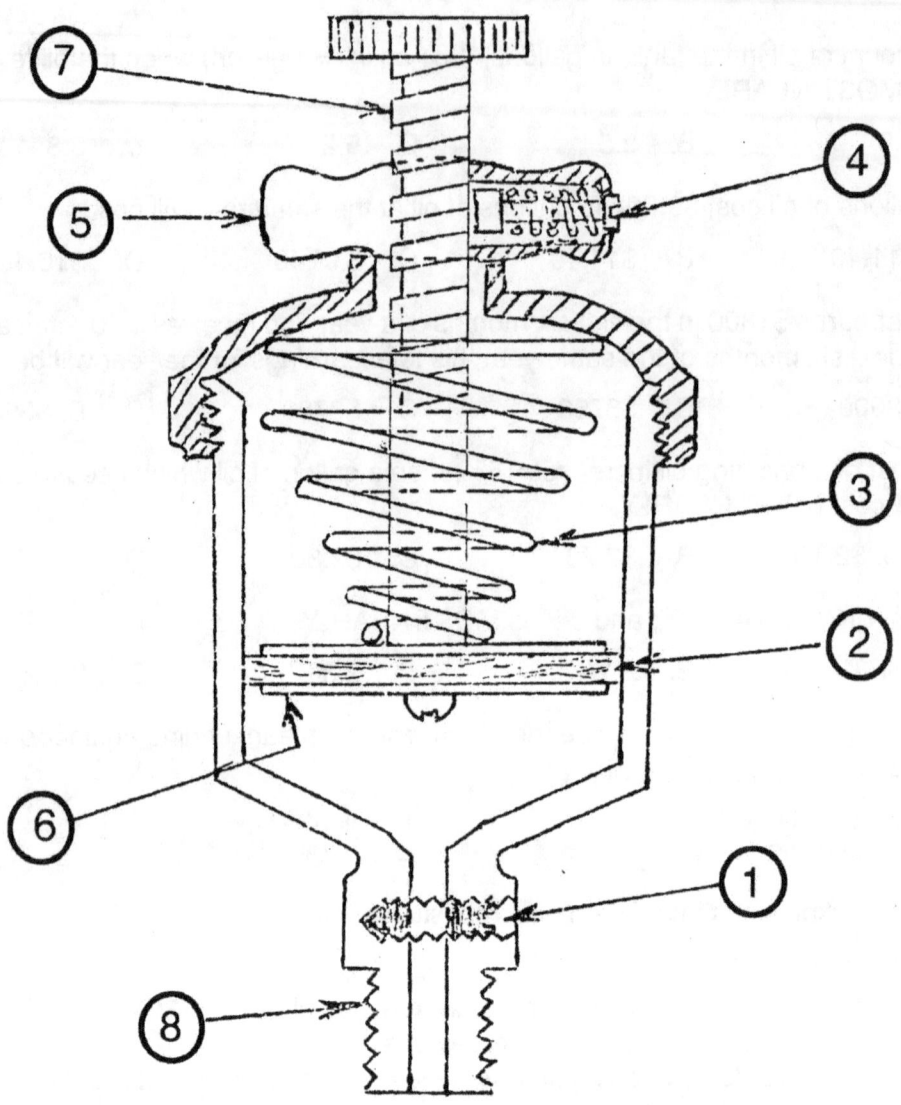

26. The part that prevents a change of plunger adjustment due to vibration is numbered 26.____
    A. 3      B. 4      C. 2      D. 5

27. The leather packed plunger is numbered 27.____
    A. 6      B. 4      C. 7      D. 2

28. The part that controls the flow of lubricant into the bearing is numbered 28.____
    A. 4      B. 5      C. 1      D. 6

29. The plunger stem is numbered 29.____
    A. 8      B. 3      C. 7      D. 6

30. The part that applies the force to automatically feed the lubricant into the bearing is numbered 30.____
    A. 3      B. 1      C. 4      D. 8

31. An oiler has put an excess amount of lube oil into the crankcase of an air conditioning refrigeration compressor.
    The MOST likely effect will be

    A. none other than more oil on the cylinder walls
    B. that the oil carried over will be removed by an oil separator
    C. carbonizing of the piston rings
    D. no carry-over of oil from the suction to the discharge side

32. When operating a freon refrigeration compressor, it is found that

    A. the refrigerant is miscible with the lubricating oil
    B. a lower viscosity oil should be used compared to other comparable refrigeration systems
    C. a chemical reaction between the freon and lube oil occurs
    D. a vegetable oil is preferred for best results

33. In a centrifugal refrigeration compressor,

    A. no auxiliary oil pump is used
    B. the only parts requiring lubrication are the bearings of the rotor and the thrust bearing
    C. auxiliary pumps are manually operated
    D. leakage of refrigerant to the oiling system is common

34. In the operation of heavy duty gears, *thick film* lubrication means that

    A. at times no oil is on the teeth
    B. the film does not separate the tooth contact areas completely
    C. the oil supports the load by hydraulic action
    D. little attention must be paid to the oil viscosity

35. Reduction of ring wear in an engine is one of the jobs of a lubricant.
    The MOST modern method of measuring ring wear is

    A. weighing the rings before and after use
    B. to observe changes in markings on the rings
    C. by chemical tests for iron in the lube oil
    D. by use of radioactive rings

## KEY (CORRECT ANSWERS)

1. B
2. A
3. B
4. D
5. C

6. A
7. A
8. C
9. A
10. A

11. A
12. B
13. A
14. A
15. C

16. A
17. B
18. B
19. B
20. B

21. C
22. C
23. D
24. A
25. D

26. B
27. D
28. C
29. C
30. A

31. B
32. A
33. B
34. C
35. D

# TEST 2

DIRECTIONS: Each question or incomplete statement is followed by several suggested answers or completions. Select the one that BEST answers the question or completes the statement. *PRINT THE LETTER OF THE CORRECT ANSWER IN THE SPACE AT THE RIGHT.*

1. Of the following types of bearings, the one which is NOT commonly used in most electric motors is _____ bearing.

    A. ball
    B. Gibbs thrust
    C. roller
    D. sleeve type

    1.____

2. If an electric motor is regularly overlubricated,

    A. the motor life will be increased
    B. its operating temperature will probably decrease
    C. it may result in oil-soaked insulation
    D. dirt accumulation in the windings will not vary

    2.____

3. The oil feed rate to a steam engine cylinder with a 10-inch diameter piston is APPROXIMATELY a pint each

    A. day   B. hour   C. 12 hours   D. 5 hours

    3.____

4. An oiler, in swabbing the piston rods of a small duplex direct-acting pump, is found to be doing this too often.
   The MOST probable disadvantage is

    A. the water end will be heavily fouled
    B. that the mechanical lubricator will decrease its oil discharge
    C. a waste of time and oil
    D. a severe shortening of packing life

    4.____

5. An oiler has been ordered to lubricate a duplex direct-acting steam pump feeding to a boiler.
   To do the job effectively, he must do the following:

    A. Swab the rods, check discharge water pressure and steam head pressure
    B. Check the hydrostatic lubricator and the steam exhaust pressure
    C. Swab the rods, check hydrostatic lubricator, lubricate water end piston
    D. Swab the rods and check hydrostatic lubricator

    5.____

6. If a large machine is noted to have both a hand oiler and a mechanical feed lubricator, one may reasonably assume that the hand oiler

    A. is for starting
    B. is there to be used in the event of failure of the mechanical system
    C. and the mechanical feed lubricator are used during regular operation
    D. is used to charge the mechanical feed system

    6.____

7. When a compressor is used for compression of natural gas, it is a fact that

    A. the lube oil is not thinned by dissolved gas
    B. the gas will have no sludging effect on the oil

    7.____

C. the gas has no corrosive tendency
D. properly refined straight mineral oils are recommended

8. When lubrication is required for a modern centrifugal blower, as in an air conditioning blower unit,

    A. other parts, aside from the shaft bearings, require lubrication
    B. grease is usually used
    C. ring oil bearings are usually provided
    D. a mineral oil must be used

9. Of the following, the one method of lubrication which is NOT commonly used for an encased chain drive is _____ lubrication.

    A. bath
    B. slinger disc
    C. gravity tank
    D. drip

10. A gear type flexible coupling is used in a gas turbine application.
In this instance,

    A. no lubrication of the coupling is required
    B. the coupling develops heat if misalignment occurs
    C. grease is always used as the lubricant
    D. both oil and grease are commonly used at the same time

11. The oil pressure gage of a diesel engine lubrication system shows a high reading. This may be due to

    A. high oil temperature
    B. decreased engine speed
    C. low viscosity oil
    D. oil gage out of adjustment

12. When large gears are bath lubricated, the oil level should be maintained so that

    A. the casing is half full
    B. the casing is three-quarters full
    C. all gears are covered
    D. the lowest gear teeth dip into the oil

13. Speed reduction gears which operate exposed require

    A. lubricants of heavier body than those which are tightly encased
    B. lubricants with a talc filler
    C. a non-adhesive lubricant
    D. a corrosive lead soap lubricant

14. In a stationary diesel engine, a grade of lube oil is selected based PRINCIPALLY on

    A. first cost as against replacement cost
    B. flash points less than 120° F
    C. minimizing carbon deposits between rings
    D. cetaine number

15. A 3000 horsepower stationary diesel engine running at full load for an hour uses a quantity of lube oil equal to about

    A. one gallon
    B. one quart
    C. five gallons
    D. one pint

15.____

16. The oil cooler for a steam turbine should

    A. not be of the counterflow type
    B. be installed below the oil reservoir
    C. have an oil pressure greater than the water pressure
    D. have an oil pressure equal to the mean operating steam pressure

16.____

17. Of the following, the one procedure which is NOT recommended in caring for a steam turbine is to

    A. practice a regular method of purifying oil in service
    B. clean oil strainers regularly, usually bi-monthly
    C. drain the bottom of the oil reservoir daily
    D. check on water leakage by inspecting oil cooler

17.____

18. In trouble shooting in a dual fuel engine, it should be remembered that high oil

    A. temperature may result from excess oil in the sump or crankcase
    B. temperature may result from sludge in the crankcase
    C. consumption may result from low oil level in the crankcase
    D. consumption may result from low oil pressure

18.____

19. In normal operation, the lubricating oil in a steam turbine will NOT

    A. reduce friction losses in reduction gears
    B. remove bearing heat
    C. affect the leaving steam
    D. act as a fluid to operate governor valves

19.____

20. A gravity feed lube system is used for the crosshead and main bearing of a large horizontal ammonia refrigeration compressor.
This gravity oil tank should be provided with a valve in the feed line at its base so that the oiler can

    A. regulate the oil flow to the main bearing
    B. readily fill the tank
    C. shut off the flow of oil when making repairs
    D. easily and quickly attach an auxiliary lube oil feed line

20.____

Questions 21-24.

DIRECTIONS: Questions 21 through 24 relate to the paragraph which follows below. Your answers to each of these questions are to be based entirely upon the content and meaning of this paragraph.

There are two, unfounded ideas that must be discarded before tackling the *LUBE-SIMPLIFICATION* job. *Oil is oil* was a common expression from the middle of the nineteenth century up to the early 1900s. Then, as the century got well under way, the pendulum swung in a wide arc. At present we find many oils being used, each with supposedly special properties. The large number of lube oils used at present results from the rapid growth at the same time of machine development and oil refining. The refiner acts to market new oils for each machine developed, and the machine manufacturer feels that each new mechanical unit is different from the others and needs a special lube oil. These feelings may be well founded but in many cases they are based on misinformation or blind faith in certain lube oil qualities. At the present time operators and even lube engineers are finding it tough to keep track of all the claimed properties of all the lube oils.

21. It follows from the sense of this paragraph that the idea that *oil is oil* is unfounded because

    A. it was conceived in the middle of the nineteenth century
    B. the basic and varying properties of lube oils have now been shown to exist
    C. lube oil properties, though fully known, were kept secret for economic reasons
    D. there was need for but one basic lube oil in the latter part of the nineteenth century

22. In the above paragraph, the phrase *the pendulum swung in a wide arc* means MOST NEARLY

    A. oil refining was unable to keep up with machinery development
    B. before 1900 lube oil engineers found it difficult to keep track of lube oil characteristics
    C. the simplification of lube oils and their application was developed about 1900
    D. many different lube oils with varying characteristics were marketed

23. As indicated in this paragraph, the simplification of the characteristics and the uses of lube oils is needed because the

    A. manufacturers develop new machines to overcome competition
    B. change in process at the refineries for a new lube oil is costly
    C. present market is flooded with many so-called *special purpose* lube oils
    D. *blind faith* of the operators in lube oil qualities should be rewarded

24. A reason given for the claimed need for special lube oil, as indicated in this paragraph, is that

    A. development of new lube oils created the need for new machine units
    B. lube oil engineers developed new tests and standards
    C. basic crudes, from which lube oil is obtained, allow different refining methods
    D. newly developed machines are so very different from each other

5 (#2)

Questions 25-35.

DIRECTIONS: Questions 25 through 35 relate to the sketches of parts and devices shown on the following page.

25. The tapered roller bearing is the part marked 25.____
    A. K        B. R        C. V        D. T

26. A street ell is the part marked 26.____
    A. P        B. H        C. G        D. N

27. The part that is used to connect two pieces of pipe in a straight line is marked 27.____
    A. G        B. A        C. S        D. V

28. The part that is used along with a worm gear to transmit rotating motion is marked 28.____
    A. E        B. K        C. Y        D. W

29. An Alemite fitting is the part marked 29.____
    A. D        B. L        C. K        D. H

30. A lined bearing is the part marked 30.____
    A. A        B. V        C. Y        D. R

31. A tee pipe fitting is the part marked 31.____
    A. P        B. H        C. G        D. N

32. A roller bearing is the part marked 32.____
    A. R        B. K        C. T        D. A

33. A ring oil bearing is the part marked 33.____
    A. A        B. V        C. K        D. Y

34. The part that is generally and properly used to loosen varying size nuts from machine foundation studs is marked 34.____
    A. C        B. I        C. B        D. O

35. A Stillson wrench is the part marked 35.____
    A. I        B. C        C. W        D. O

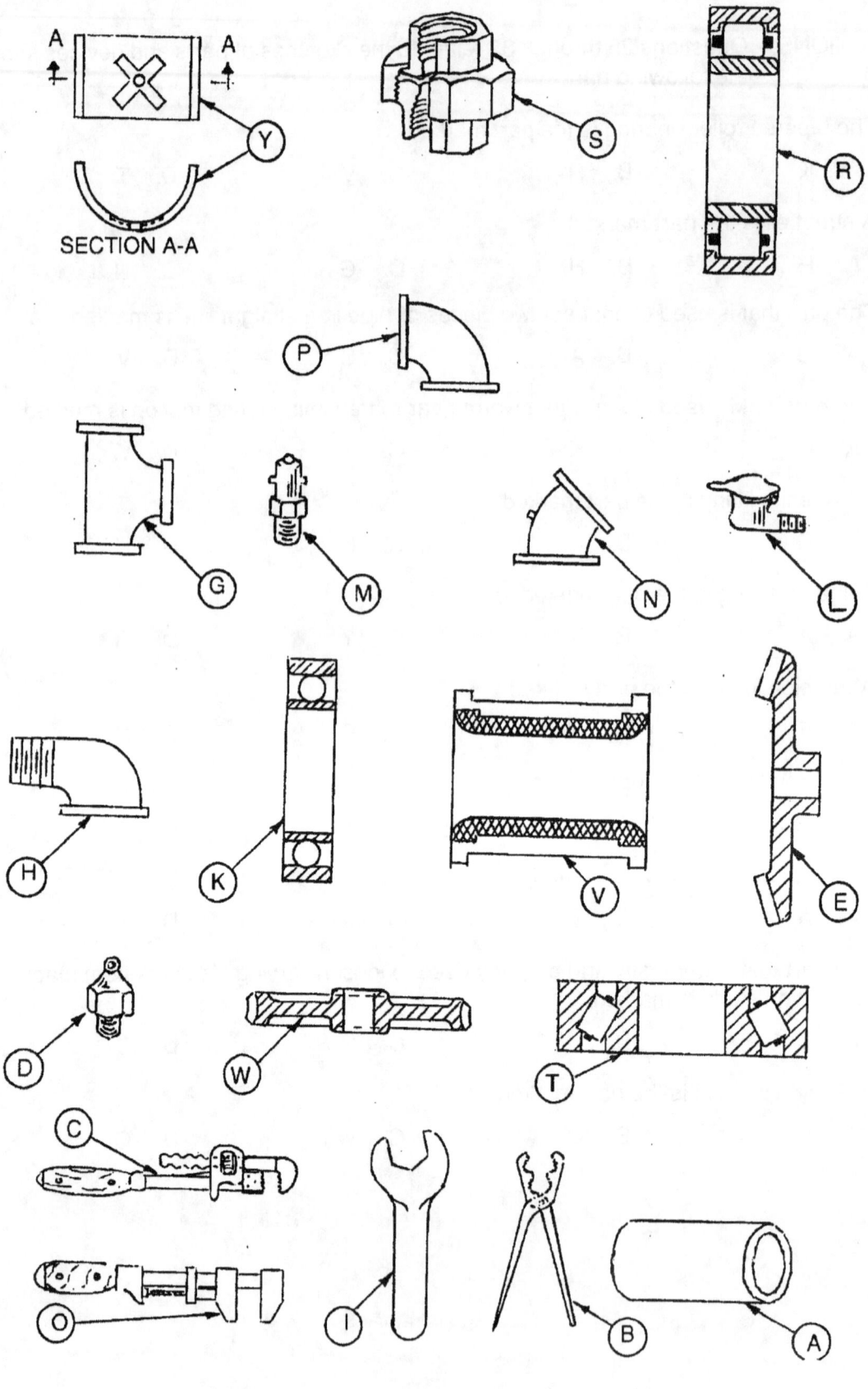

## KEY (CORRECT ANSWERS)

| | | | |
|---|---|---|---|
| 1. | B | 16. | C |
| 2. | C | 17. | B |
| 3. | D | 18. | B |
| 4. | C | 19. | C |
| 5. | D | 20. | C |
| 6. | A | 21. | B |
| 7. | D | 22. | D |
| 8. | B | 23. | C |
| 9. | C | 24. | D |
| 10. | B | 25. | D |
| 11. | D | 26. | B |
| 12. | D | 27. | C |
| 13. | A | 28. | D |
| 14. | C | 29. | A |
| 15. | A | 30. | B |

31. C
32. A
33. D
34. D
35. B

# EXAMINATION SECTION
# TEST 1

DIRECTIONS: Each question consists of a statement. You are to indicate whether the statement is TRUE (T) or FALSE (F). *PRINT THE LETTER OF THE CORRECT ANSWER IN THE SPACE AT THE RIGHT.*

1. The primary purpose of a lubricant is to prevent two rubbing surfaces from coming into direct contact with each other.  1._____

2. An oil that can mix with water is USUALLY used to operate the hydraulic cylinders of turbine governors.  2._____

3. The carbonizing of oil under the action of high temperature improves the lubricating qualities of the oil.  3._____

4. Detergents are sometimes added to lubricants to prevent formation of sludge in gearboxes.  4._____

5. Mineral oils can be manufactured from cotton seed products.  5._____

6. Lubricants that resist the washing action of wet steam in engine cylinders are usually made by compounding mineral oils with graphite.  6._____

7. The specific gravity of a lubricant is USUALLY measured by means of a Saybolt viscosimeter.  7._____

8. A high-viscosity lubricant is one that has high internal fluid friction.  8._____

9. Low-viscosity lubricants are BEST adaptable for low-speed machines.  9._____

10. A centrifuge is USUALLY used to filter the recirculating oil in a pressure lubricating oil system.  10._____

11. A gravity type lubricator USUALLY feeds oil to the piston rod of a steam engine in direct proportion to the speed of the engine.  11._____

12. The temperature at which an oil will vaporize and burn is commonly known as the pour point of the oil.  12._____

13. Electric motors that do not have a pressure relief lubricating system or some means of adding a lubricant must periodically be disassembled, and the bearings repacked.  13._____

14. Wool waste is sometimes placed in oil cups to act as a feed in order to increase the frequency of oiling.  14._____

15. The hydrostatic lubricator is USUALLY used to introduce lubricant into the oil cylinder of a fuel oil pump.  15._____

16. The hydrostatic lubricator is fully automatic and delivers positive oil pressure to the main turbine bearings.  16._____

17. A force-feed lubricator is USUALLY driven by a reciprocating part of the machine it lubricates.  17._____

18. The proper handling and storage of lubricants in power plants is USUALLY of minor importance.  18.___

19. The joints of split packing rings are USUALLY spaced in a stuffing box 120 apart.  19.___

20. A gate valve is properly used in a pipe line only if it is fully opened or fully closed.  20.___

21. Most grease cups operate by means of a spring pressure.  21.___

22. Combustible and flammable cleaning materials should NOT be stored in tightly closed metal containers.  22.___

23. S.A.E. 30 oil is USUALLY the proper viscosity oil to use for machinery bearings operating in $25°$ F. temperature.  23.___

24. Steam-cylinder oils are generally residual, heavy-bodied oils containing 5 to 15% compounds of acidless tallow lard.  24.___

25. Ice-machine oils are USUALLY high-quality, light to-medium-bodied, pure mineral oils.  25.___

26. Engine oils that are used in steam engine external bearings are USUALLY medium-quality, light and medium-bodied oils, and are suited for use in splash and circulating systems.  26.___

27. Grease is USUALLY recommended as a lubricant where leakage is too high to retain liquid lubricants.  27.___

28. Belt dressings are USUALLY made of mixtures of solid fats, waxes, or tallow mixed with castor or fatty oils.  28.___

29. Automotive chassis grease or pressure-gun grease USUALLY consists of lime-aluminum or lime-soda grease.  29.___

30. The texture of a grease refers to its structure such as smooth, fibrous, spongy or rubbery.  30.___

# KEY (CORRECT ANSWERS)

| | | | | |
|---|---|---|---|---|
| 1. | T | | 16. | F |
| 2. | F | | 17. | T |
| 3. | F | | 18. | F |
| 4. | T | | 19. | F |
| 5. | F | | 20. | T |
| 6. | F | | 21. | F |
| 7. | F | | 22. | F |
| 8. | T | | 23. | F |
| 9. | F | | 24. | T |
| 10. | F | | 25. | T |
| 11. | F | | 26. | F |
| 12. | F | | 27. | T |
| 13. | T | | 28. | T |
| 14. | F | | 29. | T |
| 15. | F | | 30. | T |

# TEST 2

DIRECTIONS: Each question consists of a statement. You are to indicate whether the statement is TRUE (T) or FALSE (F). *PRINT THE LETTER OF THE CORRECT ANSWER IN THE SPACE AT THE RIGHT.*

1. The operating temperature of the lubricating oil used in the bearings of a steam condensing engine is USUALLY about 200° F.  1.___

2. The operating oil pressure of a lubrication oil cooler is USUALLY higher than the operating water pressure of the cooler.  2.___

3. Strainers used in a lubricating oil system will USUALLY remove water and foreign particles out of the circulating oil.  3.___

4. Small turbine bearings are USUALLY lubricated by means of sight feed drop oilers.  4.___

5. Excessive lubrication of air compressor valves may cause spontaneous ignition.  5.___

6. Oils used for air compressor lubrication should contain APPROXIMATELY 40% dark cylinder oil.  6.___

7. Under certain conditions water can be used as a lubricant.  7.___

8. The viscosity of an oil used for gear lubrication is NOT very important.  8.___

9. Journal bearings are USUALLY cylindrical in shape, and support a rotating shaft.  9.___

10. Thrust bearings are generally used to prevent lengthwise motion of a rotating shaft.  10.___

11. The temperature of automotive-type bearings is USUALLY held within safe limits by using a pressure-feed oil system.  11.___

12. Hand oiling is USUALLY done with a lower viscosity oil than what is used in automatic lubricating systems.  12.___

13. The grooves often found in plain sleeve bearings are USUALLY deep grooves with vertical sides.  13.___

14. The piston rods of a duplex direct-acting feedwater pump are generally lubricated by means of a bottle oiler.  14.___

15. The reservoir of a mechanical forced-feed lubricator is USUALLY refilled by hand.  15.___

16. If an oiler receives a salary of $450 a month and saves 12% of this every month, in one year his total savings will amount to $648.  16.___

17. The decimal 0.875 written as a fraction would be 15/16.  17.___

18. If it is said that an oil drum is 5/8 empty, it is the same as saying that this drum is 3/8 full.  18.___

19. If an 8" diameter pulley is driven by a 12" diameter pulley which rotates at 100 rpm, the driven pulley will rotate at 150 rpm.  19.___

20. Three pieces of pipe each 2'8" long can be cut from a length of pipe 8' 1 3/8" long if there is a waste of 1/8" per cut.  20.____

21. If 200 feet of a certain size pipe weighs 300 lbs., 60 feet of the same pipe will weigh 100 lbs.  21.____

22. The vacuum reading on a compound pressure gauge is USUALLY measured in inches of mercury.  22.____

23. A flyball governor is USUALLY used on an engine to maintain constant engine speed.  23.____

24. The proper rate of oil feed to a steam cylinder which has a 10-inch diameter piston is APPROXIMATELY one pint per day.  24.____

25. Oil is USUALLY used to lubricate the bearings of a modern centrifugal blower (such as an air conditioning blower unit).  25.____

26. The worm and gear assembly unit of an elevator hoisting machine is USUALLY covered completely with oil for smooth operation.  26.____

27. Bearings that operate at high shaft speeds and low pressure normally require a lubricant that has a fairly low viscosity.  27.____

28. Drip-feed, wick feed and wiper-type lubricating systems USUALLY feed lubricants by means of gravity instead of pressure.  28.____

29. The indirect or atomization method has been generally accepted for introducing oil into the cylinders of steam engines.  29.____

30. A drip-feed lubricator is generally regulated by the size of the wick or the number of strands to be used in the wick.  30.____

# KEY (CORRECT ANSWERS)

| | | | | |
|---|---|---|---|---|
| 1. | F | | 16. | T |
| 2. | T | | 17. | F |
| 3. | F | | 18. | T |
| 4. | F | | 19. | T |
| 5. | T | | 20. | T |
| 6. | F | | 21. | F |
| 7. | T | | 22. | T |
| 8. | F | | 23. | T |
| 9. | T | | 24. | F |
| 10. | T | | 25. | F |
| 11. | T | | 26. | F |
| 12. | F | | 27. | T |
| 13. | F | | 28. | T |
| 14. | F | | 29. | T |
| 15. | T | | 30. | F |

# TEST 3

DIRECTIONS: Each question consists of a statement. You are to indicate whether the statement is TRUE (T) or FALSE (F). *PRINT THE LETTER OF THE CORRECT ANSWER IN THE SPACE AT THE RIGHT.*

1. Oil manifolds, cups and pipes should be cleaned occasionally with a steam hose or with boiling hot soda water.   1.____

2. A temperature of 100° Centigrade is equivalent to a temperature of 212° Fahrenheit.   2.____

3. Globe and angle valves are generally installed where operation is frequent and valve closure must be tight.   3.____

4. Packing glands are USUALLY tightened when machinery is shut down overnight to prevent leakage.   4.____

5. Lubricant impregnated into most asbestos packings by manufacturers is USUALLY all that is needed for steam jobs.   5.____

6. Packing in a centrifugal or reciprocating pump MUST be installed to completely stop leakage.   6.____

7. The first two shaft packing rings nearest the gland of a centrifugal or reciprocating pump USUALLY show the most wear.   7.____

8. Grooved shafts and packing failures are USUALLY caused by NOT loosening packing gland nuts after an overnight shut down.   8.____

9. Labyrinth packing is very often used in steam-turbine practice.   9.____

10. The uniflow steam engine utilizes separate exhaust valves for the head end and crank end.   10.____

11. A low viscosity oil should be used to lubricate the spindle of the throttle valve and connecting levers of the governing mechanism of a steam turbine.   11.____

12. Turbine oils are highly refined, filtered oils with high demulsibility.   12.____

13. Diesel-engine oils are highly filtered, straight mineral oils, USUALLY having a viscosity of SAE 10 to 40.   13.____

14. A "D" type slide valve USUALLY controls the admission and exhaust of steam in a duplex pump.   14.____

15. In a piston type pump, the plunger moves back and forth in a packing gland instead of in a bored cylinder.   15.____

16. A power pump is one in which the piston or plunger is operated by a unit other than the pump itself.   16.____

17. Adjusting the gland nuts on a pump is preferably done while the pump is not running.   17.____

18. If the packing is properly installed and the gland correctly adjusted on a reciprocating pump, the shaft can USUALLY be turned freely by hand.  18.____

19. Grease is a solid lubricant for use where a fluid lubricant is NOT practical or economical.  19.____

20. Compression grease cups are especially suitable for the bearings of machinery that are subjected to dust, dirt and fine abrasive materials.  20.____

21. The viscosity of oil generally decreases with increase of temperature.  21.____

22. The color of lubricating oil USUALLY indicates its quality.  22.____

23. Severe operating conditions will USUALLY change the color of lubricating oil.  23.____

24. The moisture content of refrigeration oil is USUALLY high.  24.____

25. Preventive maintenance implies that equipment MUST be checked when the work load is low.  25.____

26. A tandem-compound engine is one in which the cylinders are USUALLY placed side by side.  26.____

27. A pressure-gage thermometer is a device that measures temperature from a remote point.  27.____

28. On a compound gage, a reading of 20 inches of vacuum indicates APPROXIMATELY a vacuum pressure of 15 p.s.i.  28.____

29. Absolute pressure is the sum of the gage pressure and atmospheric pressure.  29.____

30. An O.S. & Y. globe valve is one having an inside screw, non-rising spindle.  30.____

## KEY (CORRECT ANSWERS)

| | | | |
|---|---|---|---|
| 1. | T | 16. | T |
| 2. | T | 17. | F |
| 3. | T | 18. | T |
| 4. | T | 19. | T |
| 5. | T | 20. | T |
| 6. | F | 21. | T |
| 7. | T | 22. | F |
| 8. | T | 23. | T |
| 9. | T | 24. | F |
| 10. | F | 25. | F |
| 11. | T | 26. | F |
| 12. | T | 27. | T |
| 13. | T | 28. | F |
| 14. | T | 29. | T |
| 15. | F | 30. | F |

36

# EXAMINATION SECTION
## TEST 1

DIRECTIONS: Each question or incomplete statement is followed by several suggested answers or completions. Select the one that BEST answers the question or completes the statement. *PRINT THE LETTER OF THE CORRECT ANSWER IN THE SPACE AT THE RIGHT.*

1. A lubricant for a bearing, if properly selected and used, will do *at least* the following:  1.____

    A. Clean the bearing
    B. Cool the bearing
    C. Prevent **direct** frictional contact between the bearing and the shaft only
    D. Lubricate, clean, and cool the bearing

2. The oil that is *usually* used for lubricating the cylinder and piston of an operating steam engine is a _____ oil.  2.____

    A. paraffin base        B. compounded
    C. vegetable            D. resin

3. If a sudden increase of pressure at the oil pump is noted in a lubricating system, it *usually* indicates that  3.____

    A. a clogging at some point in the system or at the strainer
    B. there is a leak in the cooler
    C. the oil gauge needs adjusting
    D. the oil pump is worn

4. In a force feed lubricating system for marine engines, the temperature, in degrees Fahrenheit, of the oil leaving the cooler *should be*, most nearly,  4.____

    A. 180                      B. between 90 and 115
    C. between 125 and 135      D. 140

5. Lubricating oil coolers are *usually* installed in pairs and operated so that pressure  5.____

    A. in the water side is greater than that in the oil side
    B. in the oil side is greater than that in the water side
    C. of both oil and water is kept the same
    D. of oil in one cooler is always greater than that in the other one

6. Lubricating grease  6.____

    A. is made up of 1/2% to 20% of soap in mineral oil
    B. is thickened by increasing the percentage of oil in it
    C. is only to be used in a grease cup
    D. should be used only where sight feed lubricator is available

7. In 2-cycle and 4-cycle engines, the quantity of lubricating oil used is  7.____

    A. greater in the 4-cycle engine than the 2-cycle engine
    B. the same in both engines
    C. greater in the 2-cycle engine than the 4-cycle engine
    D. controlled by the temperature of the oil

8. A well-designed, properly operated, diesel engine should consume a gallon of lubricating oil for approximately *every* _____ horsepower hours of operation.

   A. 3500   B. 4000   C. 1000   D. 5000

9. In a centrifuge,

   A. the lubricating oil is heated in order to settle out impurities
   B. the oil and water are emulsified
   C. only engine oil is cleaned
   D. heavy liquids are separated from lighter liquids

10. Strainers set in a lubricating oil system

    A. are by-passed when used with purifiers
    B. will remove water and solid particles
    C. will remove only solid particles
    D. should be cleaned only if there should be a sudden increase in oil temperature

11. A 24-strand wick will feed to a large bearing operating at high speed *most nearly* the following quantity of oil, in drops per minute:

    A. 30   B. 60   C. 48   D. 90

12. If wicks are not removed from their oil tubes when the machinery is secured,

    A. the oil pressure in the system will build up
    B. the oil will emulsify
    C. they will wear down
    D. they will continue to deliver oil to the bearings for some time

13. In regard to self-oiling bearings,

    A. the lubricant need never be cleaned out and renewed
    B. the level of lubricant need not be checked
    C. a slight flat on the inside of a ring will not affect the lubricating agent
    D. the level of lubricant in its well should be checked periodically

14. A cylindrical oil cup has an inside diameter of 4 inches and a height of 7 inches. Its contents in cubic inches is, most nearly,

    A. 88   B. 112   C. 44   D. 28

15. The *amount* of oil distributed by a ring oil bearing

    A. gets less as the oil temperature is lowered
    B. is the same regardless of the oil temperature change
    C. gets less as the temperature of oil increases
    D. is the same regardless of width of ring

16. On reciprocating engines,

    A. emulsified lubrication is desired and planned for
    B. if the lubricant is a cream-like lather and of a soapy nature, this indicates poor lubrication

C. if the lubricant is a dark-brown lather, this indicates bearings are running satisfactorily
D. the appearance and texture of the lubricant has no bearing on the effectiveness of lubrication

17. Demulsibility of an oil used for forced-feed lubrication is

    A. not an important characteristic to consider in its selection
    B. the ability of an oil to emulsify with water
    C. a measure of the ability of an oil to separate out from an emulsion
    D. only considered when there is periodic attention to bearings

18. Cooling or circulating water temperature for diesel engine cylinders *should be,* in degrees F, most nearly,

    A. 90    B. 115    C. 130    D. 75

19. The temperature of circulating water in a diesel engine cylinder jacket is kept within the prescribed limits because

    A. low temperatures help combustion
    B. low temperatures increase the horsepower or output
    C. high temperatures make the exhaust gases smoky
    D. high temperatures cause pounding

20. Trapped air pockets in an engine cooling water circulating system

    A. have no effect on temperature of engine
    B. will feel cooler than the surrounding suspected parts
    C. will feel hotter than the surrounding suspected parts
    D. can never occur in the cylinder head or discharge manifold

21. In the splash system of lubrication,

    A. the quantity of oil splashed against the cylinder wall cannot be regulated
    B. there is never too much oil getting into the cylinder
    C. lubricating oil can never get past the piston head and burn with the fuel
    D. rings cannot stick in packing ring grooves

22. Splash lubrication is caused by

    A. emulsifying the oil supply
    B. the proper design of a crosshead
    C. the use of light oils
    D. the action of the crank in the crankcase oil

23. In a common two-part journal bearing,

    A. two or more circumferential grooves around the bearing are better than one groove lengthwise
    B. one groove lengthwise at the top of the bearing is preferred to three circumferential grooves around the bearing
    C. no grooving is required
    D. chamfers have no effect on the distribution of lubricating oil

24. When grooving bearings, the type of groove *most preferable* is

    A. deep U
    B. deep V
    C. shallow U
    D. shallow V

25. Collar thrust bearings

    A. have oil introduced to the periphery of the collar
    B. have oil introduced at the periphery of the shaft between collars
    C. are sometimes called steady bearings
    D. are never water-cooled

Questions 26 - 30.

The following five questions refer to Figure I shown below.

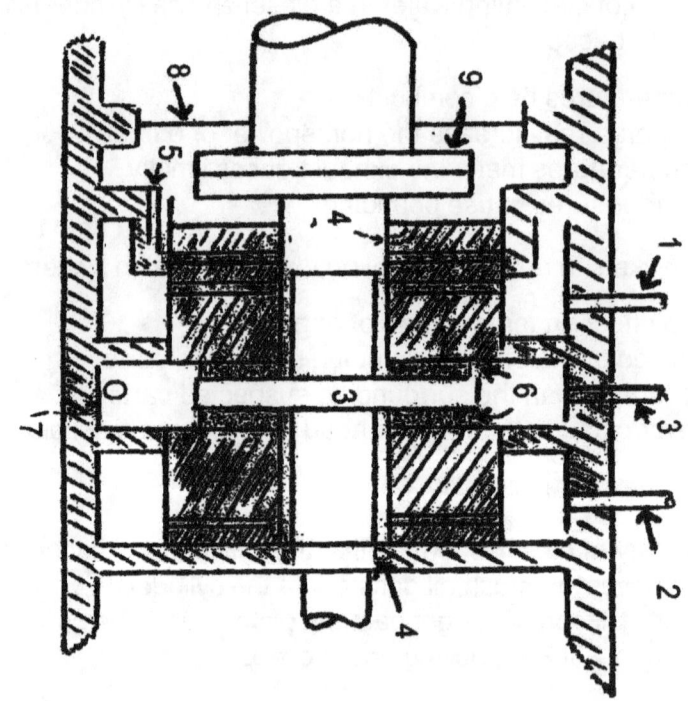

26. Figure I is a sketch of a _____ bearing.

    A. horseshoe thrust
    B. line-shaft steady
    C. Kingsbury thrust
    D. self-aligning

27. Supply of oil enters at

    A. 2
    B. 5
    C. 7
    D. 1

28. Outlet of oil is at

    A. 2
    B. 5
    C. 1
    D. 4

29. Oil is retained in the housing by means of     29.____

    A. 6    B. 4    C. 8    D. 3

30. Thrust collar is indicated in the sketch by number     30.____

    A. 9    B. 6    C. 4    D. 3

31. Anti-friction bearings:     31.____

    A. will stand a good deal of abuse
    B. need very little attention
    C. have greater friction losses than plain bearings of equal capacity
    D. take up more space axially on the shaft, but need less space radially than plain bearings

32. After installing a tapered roller bearing,     32.____

    A. the level of oil in the bearing housing should just cover the lower rollers
    B. the level of oil in the bearing housing should be below the center of the lower rollers
    C. the separate members can be made very tight without causing any damage to the bearing
    D. not much attention need be given to the level of oil in the bearing housing

33. Stern-tube lignum-vitae bearings     33.____

    A. are made with strips of lignum-vitae inserted in circumferential grooves around the bearing
    B. swell when wet and must, therefore, be installed with waterproof stuffing boxes
    C. are made with strips of lignum-vitae inserted in longitudinal grooves in the interior of bearing shell
    D. should be examined very often as they are not durable

34. Water for lubricating purposes     34.____

    A. can be used for certain types of bearings
    B. must be mixed with soapstone
    C. is best for gas engines
    D. is never used

35. In the simple grease cup the lubricant is forced into the part to be lubricated by     35.____

    A. the vibration of the engine
    B. removing the cap
    C. screwing down on the cap
    D. unscrewing the cap

# KEY (CORRECT ANSWERS)

| | | | | |
|---|---|---|---|---|
| 1. | D | | 16. | A |
| 2. | B | | 17. | C |
| 3. | A | | 18. | B |
| 4. | B | | 19. | D |
| 5. | B | | 20. | C |
| 6. | A | | 21. | A |
| 7. | C | | 22. | D |
| 8. | C | | 23. | B |
| 9. | D | | 24. | C |
| 10. | C | | 25. | B |
| 11. | A | | 26. | C |
| 12. | D | | 27. | D |
| 13. | D | | 28. | A |
| 14. | A | | 29. | B |
| 15. | C | | 30. | D |

31. B
32. A
33. C
34. A
35. C

# TEST 2

DIRECTIONS: Each question or incomplete statement is followed by several suggested answers or completions. Select the one that BEST answers the question or completes the statement. *PRINT THE LETTER OF THE CORRECT ANSWER IN THE SPACE AT THE RIGHT.*

Questions 1-5.

The following five questions refer to Figure II shown below.

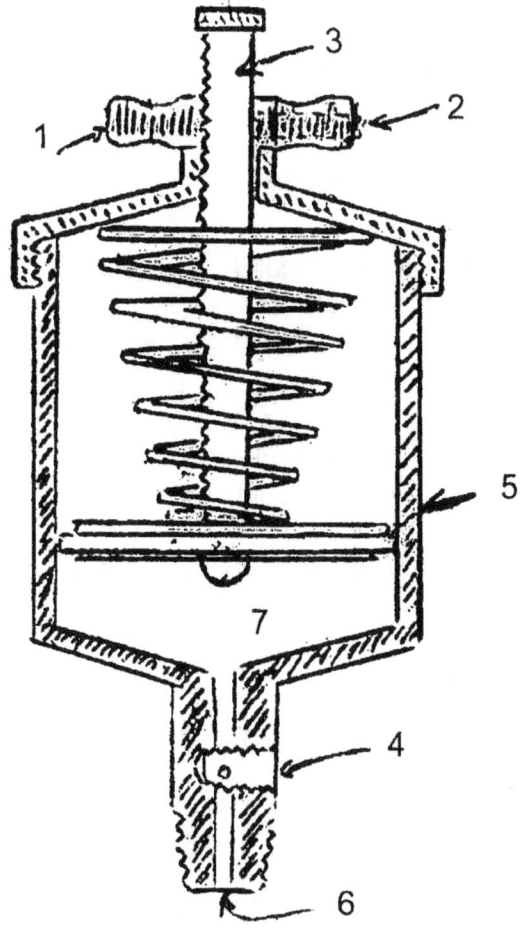

Figure II

1. Figure II is a sketch of a(n)

    A. push-type grease gun
    B. screw-down grease cup
    C. *marline-type* cup
    D. automatic compression grease cup

1.____

2. Refilling is done

   A. through 6
   B. by turning 4
   C. by first raising 5
   D. through 2

3. The feed is regulated by means of

   A. 4   B. 2   C. 3   D. 1

4. The spring and piston are controlled by

   A. 3   B. 1   C. 2   D. 7

5. The piston and spring setting is locked by

   A. 3   B. 1   C. 4   D. 2

6. The spring-loaded compression grease cup

   A. keeps a continuous pressure on the grease
   B. must be continually adjusted to feed the grease
   C. is less efficient than the simple grease cup
   D. is refilled by means of a high pressure grease gun

7. In gear lubrication,

   A. churning is a sign of good lubrication
   B. the level of oil in gear casing should completely immerse gear teeth
   C. emulsification is never encountered
   D. immersion of gear teeth causes sudden increase in temperature of lubricant

8. For lubrication of valve stems and piston rods, one *should use*

   A. pure graphite
   B. oil of vegetable or animal origin
   C. tallow
   D. practically no oil at all

9. Oil coolers *should be*

   A. cut in before oil pumps have been started
   B. secured after first securing oil pumps
   C. cut in after oil pumps have been started
   D. checked once a week

10. An oil sight gauge is a device to

    A. show oil level in a bearing housing or crankcase
    B. register pressure in oil system
    C. show the rate of oil fed to a bearing
    D. register the amount of grease in a grease cup

11. The water cylinder of a duplex direct-acting steam-driven feed-water pump is lubricated by

    A. oil injections into the suction pipe
    B. the water being pumped

C. an oil injector to the cylinder
D. means of graphite packing

12. The eccentrics on a compound marine steam engine are lubricated by

    A. siphon feeder wicks
    B. means of tallow cocks
    C. individual cups on the eccentric rods
    D. a pressure lubricating system

13. In a mechanical force feed lubricator,

    A. the reservoir does not require refilling
    B. there is never more than one pump
    C. it is impossible to get too high a pressure on the oil service lines
    D. the oil feed can be regulated to the required drops per minute

14. A mechanical force feed lubricator on a steam engine

    A. gives only one feed regardless of engine speed
    B. delivers oil in proportion to engine speed changes
    C. can automatically feed before engine is started
    D. always has one pump regardless of number of oil lines fed

15. The one NOT considered in determining characteristics of air compressor oils is

    A. dew point
    B. viscosity
    C. flash and fire points
    D. tendency to form carbon deposits

16. A little oil in compressed air leaving low-pressure cylinder and going to the high-pressure cylinder of a multi-stage air compressor

    A. cannot do any harm
    B. raises efficiency of the inter-cooler
    C. may be dangerous in the high pressure cylinder
    D. is good practice

17. Fires or explosions in air compressor systems

    A. are NOT caused by feeding excess amount of oil
    B. occur when lubricating oil vapor is ignited
    C. are prevented by using low flash point oils
    D. are only caused by using a vegetable oil

18. At intervals carbon deposits are washed out of the air compressor of a diesel-driven installation by using

    A. kerosene
    B. a solution of soap and water fed through the lubricator
    C. a highly volatile liquid because it dissolves the carbon
    D. soap suds into air intake fed at same rate as the usual oil supply

4 (#2)

19. Filtering oil through cotton waste, felt, or cloth filters

    A. is not facilitated when the oil is warmed
    B. does not remove excess water from oil
    C. does not remove fine impurities from oil
    D. removes water from oil

20. The power in kilowatts consumed by an electrical heater used to raise the temperature of 20 gallons of oil per hour 100 degrees F. is, most nearly, (assume 0.0013 K.W.H. will raise 1 gal. of oil 1 degree F., disregarding heat-transfer losses)

    A. 26      B. 2.6      C. 0.13      D. 1.3

21. In a gravity oiling system which circulates 150 gallons of oil per minute, with the cycle repeated at 5 min. intervals, the amount of oil required in the system should be, most nearly, _____ gallons.

    A. 9000      B. 1800      C. 1500      D. 750

22. Gravity system of lubrication is sometimes preferred to the direct pressure system because

    A. smaller pipe size can be used
    B. pipe lines from the gravity tank to the equipment need not be direct
    C. there will still be a few minutes supply of oil in tank in case of pump failure
    D. it is cheaper to install

23. Direct pressure system of lubrication is sometimes preferred to gravity system because

    A. pressure system works efficiently even with too small a quantity of oil in the system
    B. there is always a steady, uninterrupted flow of oil even if a reciprocating pump is used
    C. any air in the pressure system has better chance of escaping than in the gravity system
    D. it is cheaper to install since less equipment is required

24. Interval or cylinder lubrication of vertical marine steam engines are commonly accomplished by means of

    A. a mechanical force feed lubricator
    B. a splash system from crankcase
    C. an oil cup on engine cylinder
    D. hand swabbing of piston rods

25. The *best* location for the atomizer feeding oil to a steam engine cylinder is

    A. after the steam throttle valve
    B. governed by viscosity of oil used
    C. through the cylinder wall
    D. dependent on grade of oil used

Questions 26 - 31.

The following six questions refer to Figure III shown below.

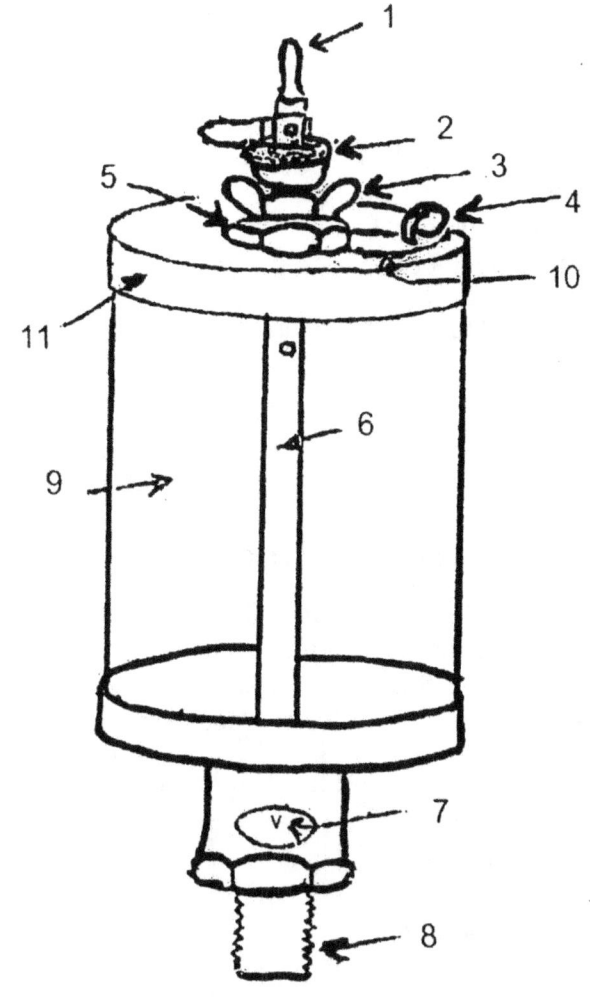

Figure III

26. Figure III is a sketch of a

    A. snap lever sight feed oil cup
    B. friction screw sight feed lubricator
    C. snap lever without sight feed lubricator
    D. friction screw without sight feed lubricator

26.____

27. Rate of oil feed is changed by adjusting part number

    A. 3      B. 1      C. 2      D. 4

27.____

28. To quickly start or stop the oil feed, use part number

    A. 3      B. 1      C. 4      D. 2

28.____

29. The rate of oil feed is kept from changing by using part number  29.___

    A. 5    B. 2    C. 4    D. 3

30. Adjustment of oil feed when this lubricator is in operation can be observed at  30.___

    A. 6    B. 7    C. 9    D. 8

31. Refilling is done  31.___

    A. by removing part number 11
    B. through number 10
    C. by removing part number 2
    D. by removing part number 5

32. A *common* method used to determine when an accessible bearing is running too hot is to  32.___

    A. watch for smoke
    B. check oil pressure only
    C. feel the bearing
    D. listen for noises

33. In the reciprocating steam engine, the piston-type steam valve  33.___

    A. is difficult to lubricate due to inequalities of pressure upon valve seat
    B. can only be used under low steam pressures
    C. stem packing is subjected to high steam pressures
    D. can be operated under high steam pressures

34. If a journal has a diameter of 7" and turns at rate of 600 rpm, the rubbing speed of bearing in feet per min., is, most nearly,  34.___

    A. 1100    B. 25000    C. 3500    D. 500

35. The oil used in a ring-oiled bearing  35.___

    A. usually runs at a somewhat lower temperature than if used in force feed lubrication
    B. can be chosen regardless of its viscosity
    C. usually runs at a somewhat higher temperature than if used in force feed lubrication
    D. can be chosen regardless of clearance

# KEY (CORRECT ANSWERS)

| | | | |
|---|---|---|---|
| 1. | D | 16. | C |
| 2. | C | 17. | B |
| 3. | A | 18. | B |
| 4. | B | 19. | B |
| 5. | D | 20. | B |
| 6. | A | 21. | D |
| 7. | D | 22. | C |
| 8. | D | 23. | D |
| 9. | C | 24. | A |
| 10. | A | 25. | A |
| 11. | B | 26. | A |
| 12. | C | 27. | C |
| 13. | D | 28. | B |
| 14. | B | 29. | D |
| 15. | A | 30. | B |

31. B
32. C
33. D
34. A
35. C

# EXAMINATION SECTION
## TEST 1

DIRECTIONS: Each question or incomplete statement is followed by several suggested answers or completions. Select the one that BEST answers the question or completes the statement. *PRINT THE LETTER OF THE CORRECT ANSWER IN THE SPACE AT THE RIGHT.*

1. The characteristic of a lubricating oil that varies with changes in operating temperatures is *commonly* called its      1.____

   A. pour point  
   B. flash point  
   C. viscosity  
   D. fire point

2. The specific gravity of lubricating oils is *usually* measured by means of a      2.____

   A. venturi meter  
   B. calorimeter  
   C. purifier  
   D. hydrometer

3. A compounded lubricating oil is *usually* a mineral oil to which a quantity of _____ has been added.      3.____

   A. lard oil  
   B. petroleum oil  
   C. petroleum jelly  
   D. caustic soda

4. A lubricating oil made from either animal, vegetable, or fish is *generally* known as a(n) _____ oil.      4.____

   A. steam cylinder  
   B. fixed  
   C. compounded  
   D. engine

5. Of the following, the grease that does NOT contain any soap base is      5.____

   A. fiber  
   B. gear  
   C. petroleum  
   D. graphite

6. Ice machine cylinder oils differ from engine oils in that the ice machine cylinder oils must be      6.____

   A. heavy viscosity oils  
   B. dark in color  
   C. mineral oil plus 20% tallow oil  
   D. low-pour test oils

7. The *two* general classes of oils that are used to lubricate steam engines are      7.____

   A. fixed and neutral  
   B. neutral and mineral  
   C. compounded and mineral  
   D. animal and compounded

8. Internal or cylinder lubrication of reciprocating steam engines can be accomplished BEST by means of      8.____

   A. hydrostatic lubricators  
   B. hand pumps  
   C. sight feed cups  
   D. mechanical force feed oiler

51

9. The steam cylinder of a double-acting steam uniflow engine is *usually* lubricated by means of an oil line located at the

   A. relief valve
   B. throttle valve
   C. exhaust valve
   D. air ejector

10. Some of the major parts of a typical pressure oiling system, as found in an engine room, are:

   A. Pumps, filters, crosshead, and piping
   B. Drain tanks, pumps, coolers, and strainers
   C. Storage tank, turbine, bearings, cooler, and purifier
   D. Eccentric, split-bearing, piping, valves, and cooler

11. In the lubrication of the steam cylinder of a marine reciprocating steam engine, the lubricant *must*

   A. blend with the air
   B. be atomized by the steam
   C. foam on contact with the steam
   D. not adhere to wet surfaces

12. When the oil pressure suddenly increases in a lubricating line to a bearing, the *one* of the following faults which would *most generally* cause this is:

   A. Oil temperature too high
   B. Oil temperature too low
   C. Water in the system
   D. Clogged strainers

13. The wick used in a gravity oil feed system is *usually* made of

   A. worsted yarn
   B. asbestos
   C. nylon
   D. wood pulp

14. The shape of the bottom of an overhead gravity supply oil tank should be

   A. flat
   B. conical
   C. square and flat
   D. the same as the top

15. In a wick lubricator, the wick should be removed from the tube from time to time *and* rinsed in

   A. machine oil
   B. naphtha
   C. kerosene
   D. hot water

16. The temperature of the oil leaving reciprocating engine and turbine bearings, *usually* has a range of

   A. 300° F to 225° F
   B. 210° F to 190° F
   C. 180° F to 110° F
   D. 60° F to 90° F

17. When oiling an air compressor cylinder, it is BEST to use *only*　　17.____

    A. sufficient oil to keep the walls covered with a thin oil film
    B. an oil of light viscosity and medium color
    C. compounded oil to obtain a heavy wall film
    D. heavy viscous oil to insure mixture with air

18. The procedure to follow in the lubrication of the machinery aboard ship is to lubricate　　18.____

    A. when the bearings begin to warm up
    B. when you have time to spare
    C. while the ship is in port
    D. at regularly scheduled intervals

19. The Stephenson double bar link motion is the *usual* type of mechanism employed for　　19.____

    A. force - feed lubricators
    B. wick feed lubricators
    C. gravity feed lubricators
    D. reversing reciprocating engines

20. Lignum vitae is *usually* found in the　　20.____

    A. stern tubes
    B. thrust bearings
    C. cylinder liners
    D. oil ring bearings

21. The mechanism that is used to rotate the crankshaft of a marine engine a fraction of a revolution when making repairs to the engine, is called a　　21.____

    A. thrust bearing
    B. jacking engine
    C. stern bearing
    D. centrifugal jack

22. While under way, the sight glass shows that no oil is flowing to the main bearings of a turbine.　　22.____
    In this case, you immediately tell your supervisor about it so that he may FIRST

    A. shut down the engines
    B. notify the bridge
    C. praise you for the discovery
    D. shut down the boilers

23. The *most important* precaution to take in giving first aid to an injured man, in case of severe injury and where there is a possibility of broken bones, is to　　23.____

    A. raise him to a sitting position and give him a drink of brandy
    B. move him no more than necessary and call a doctor
    C. lower his arms and feet to make him comfortable
    D. bundle him into an automobile and get him to a hospital as fast as possible

24. A well-established lubricating program aboard ship *usually* results in　　24.____

    A. less work for the engine and maintenance crews
    B. increased costs when tied up
    C. greater lube oil and steam costs
    D. the need for periodic inspection of main bearings only

25. When the head of a cold chisel becomes mushroomed, it is *advisable* NOT to use it because

    A. the chisel has lost its temper
    B. chips might fly from the head
    C. the chisel may not cut squarely
    D. the head cannot be hit squarely

26. A thrust bearing is *least likely* to be found on a(n)

    A. impulse turbine
    B. reciprocating pump
    C. reaction turbine
    D. auxiliary turbine driving a pump

27. A turbine driven generator is equipped with a pressure lubricator and a hand operated oil pump.
    This arrangement is *advisable* so that

    A. shafts can be lubricated with heavy oil
    B. in the event of failure of the pressure lubricator, the hand pump can be used
    C. lubrication is available on starting
    D. the oil pressure can be increased at higher speeds

28. Strainers installed in an oil service system *should be* of the duplex design so that

    A. the flow of oil can thereby be increased at higher steaming rates
    B. both strainers can be cleaned at the same time
    C. the oil can be strained twice before being used
    D. the flow of oil will not be interrupted when it becomes necessary to clean either of the strainers

29. Filters in the lubricating system of a vertical steam engine are *generally* used to

    A. remove dust from the entrained air
    B. do away with all foaming or priming
    C. settle the water out of the oil
    D. remove solid particles from the oil

30. The slide valve gear is *generally* used to control the flow of steam in

    A. centrifugal pumps
    B. impulse turbines
    C. Diesel engines
    D. reciprocating engines

31. Centrifugal purifiers are *generally* used to separate

    A. condensate from steam headers
    B. heavy liquids from light liquids
    C. scale from condensate
    D. non-condensable gases from condensate

32. Of the following actions, the one which is *least advisable* to follow in the event that the temperature of a bearing begins to increase above normal, is to    32.____

    A. see that the bearing is getting oil and examine the oil
    B. increase the supply of oil by increasing oil temperature
    C. increase the cooling water by increasing water pressure
    D. reduce speed of the shaft on advice from your supervisor

33. A "shrink fit" collar is to be removed from a shaft.    33.____
    One *good* way to do this would be to drive out the shaft *after*

    A. heating both shaft and collar
    B. chilling both shaft and collar
    C. chilling the collar only
    D. heating the collar only

34. The time required to cut off a 1" diameter rod, 6" long, from a length of stock, is LEAST affected by the    34.____

    A. material of which the rod is made
    B. number of teeth on the cutting blade
    C. length of the rod
    D. diameter of the rod

35. When it becomes necessary to use "V" blocks to hold stock when drilling holes therein, it can *usually* be said that this stock is    35.____

    A. round                B. flat
    C. square               D. plate

36. The sum of the fractions 3 1/4, 4 1/8, 6 3/8, and 12 5/8 is, most nearly,    36.____

    A. 25 1/4               B. 25 5/8
    C. 26 3/8               D. 27 1/4

37. The weight, per linear foot, of a steel bar which is 12' 6" long and weighs 40 lbs., is, most nearly, _____ lbs.    37.____

    A. 3.2                  B. 3.3
    C. 3.4                  D. 3.5

38. It takes 8 men, working 6 hours a day, 5 days to complete a particular repair job in the engine room.    38.____
    The number of days it will take 4 men, working 10 hours a day, to do the same job, assuming all work at the same rate of speed, is

    A. 5                    B. 5 1/2
    C. 6                    D. 7 1/2

39. A rectangular gravity feed tank measures 27" high, 30" long, and 28" wide.    39.____
    Its capacity, in gallons, when full, is, most nearly, (231 cubic inches per gallon)

    A. 3.5                  B. 3.65
    C. 93.65                D. 98.4

40. If a man earns $187.00 a day, the number of months it will take him to earn $55,000 is, most nearly, (assume 21 working days per month)  40._____

   A. 14
   B. 15
   C. 16
   D. 17

## KEY (CORRECT ANSWERS)

| | | | |
|---|---|---|---|
| 1. C | 11. B | 21. B | 31. B |
| 2. D | 12. D | 22. B | 32. B |
| 3. A | 13. A | 23. B | 33. D |
| 4. B | 14. B | 24. A | 34. C |
| 5. C | 15. C | 25. B | 35. A |
| 6. D | 16. C | 26. B | 36. C |
| 7. C | 17. A | 27. C | 37. A |
| 8. D | 18. D | 28. D | 38. C |
| 9. B | 19. D | 29. D | 39. D |
| 10. B | 20. A | 30. D | 40. A |

# TEST 2

DIRECTIONS: Each question or incomplete statement is followed by several suggested answers or completions. Select the one that BEST answers the question or completes the statement. *PRINT THE LETTER OF THE CORRECT ANSWER IN THE SPACE AT THE RIGHT.*

1. A valve that allows oil to flow in one direction only is *generally* called a _____ valve.  1._____

    A. stop
    B. glove
    C. gate
    D. check

2. The *proper* method an oiler should use to lubricate a duplex direct-acting steam pump feeding water to a boiler is to  2._____

    A. check the water pressure and swab the rods
    B. swab the rods, check hydrostatic lubricator, lubricate water piston
    C. swab the rods and check hydrostatic lubricator
    D. check steam pressure and swab the rods

3. When installing three (3) new packing rings in a stuffing box, the joints of the packing should be placed _____ apart.  3._____

    A. 360°
    B. 270°
    C. 180°
    D. 120°

4. Where the bearings are ring-oiled, as in the case of certain types of auxiliaries, it may be said that  4._____

    A. the bearing temperature may run higher than with force feed lubrication
    B. the viscosity of the oil in the bearing is unimportant
    C. lighter-bodied oil may be used regardless of bearing load and speed
    D. this type of bearing is less likely to burn out

5. To do a *satisfactory* lubricating job, a turbine oil *must*  5._____

    A. have the proper viscosity
    B. prime at operating temperatures
    C. be non-resistant to foaming
    D. oxidize at operating temperatures

6. Oxidation of lubricants usually requires the presence of  6._____

    A. water
    B. steam
    C. air
    D. bronze

7. Spontaneous fires are usually caused by poor ventilation and exposed  7._____

    A. oily rags
    B. grease cans
    C. clean waste
    D. oil cans

8. Of the following, the substance that is NOT commonly used in fire fighting equipment is  8._____

    A. soda-acid
    B. water
    C. $CO_2$
    D. sodium chloride

Questions 9-23.

The following 15 question, 9 to 23 inclusive, relate to sketches of parts, fittings, tools, and devices shown below.

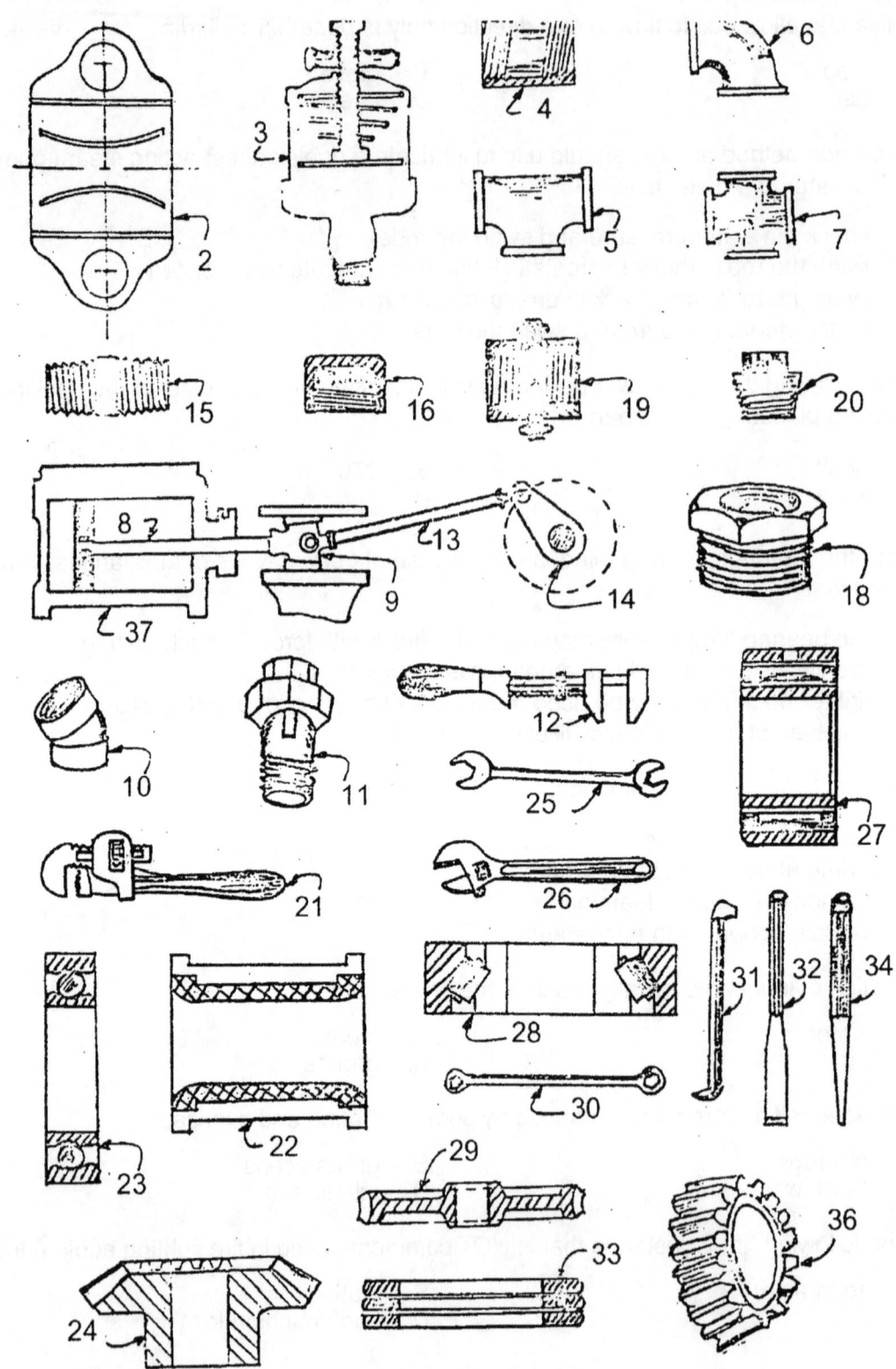

9. The fitting that is used to connect two pieces of pipe and provide a 45 degree offset is numbered                9.____

   A. 11      B. 5      C. 10      D. 6

10. A marine type crosshead bearing is the part numbered                10.____

    A. 33     B. 2      C. 27      D. 9

11. The tool used for lining up holes when assembling angles and plates is numbered                11.____

    A. 31     B. 26     C. 32      D. 34

12. A union coupling is the fitting numbered                12.____

    A. 11     B. 19     C. 4       D. 15

13. The part that can be used to take off power at a 90° angle from the end of a driving shaft is numbered                13.____

    A. 36     B. 25     C. 24      D. 29

14. The fitting that is used to close the end of a piece of threaded pipe is numbered                14.____

    A. 6      B. 20     C. 21      D. 16

15. The device that is used to take up the horizontal thrust on a rotating shaft is numbered                15.____

    A. 33     B. 22     C. 23      D. 24

16. A monkey wrench is the tool numbered                16.____

    A. 26     B. 30     C. 21      D. 12

17. A worm wheel is the device numbered                17.____

    A. 29     B. 24     C. 36      D. 2

18. A connecting rod is the part numbered                18.____

    A. 14     B. 30     C. 13      D. 8

19. A roller bearing is the device numbered                19.____

    A. 23     B. 33     C. 27      D. 28

20. A piston rod is the part numbered                20.____

    A. 14     B. 8      C. 13      D. 31

21. A bushing is the fitting numbered                21.____

    A. 11     B. 4      C. 15      D. 18

22. The crosshead is the part numbered                22.____

    A. 14     B. 2      C. 9       D. 37

23. The fitting that is used along with fitting numbered 4 to connect two pipes of different sizes is the fitting numbered

    A. 18   B. 19   C. 20   D. 15

24. It is important to CONVEY TO new members of the crew the fundamental methods of lubrication.
    As used in this sentence, the words CONVEY TO mean, most nearly,

    A. prove to
    C. make known to
    B. suggest to
    D. assign to

25. If a marine oiler is engaged in a HAZARDOUS job, he is doing a job which is

    A. dangerous
    C. long
    B. difficult
    D. demanding

26. If a marine oiler is ADEPT at his job, he is one who is

    A. honest
    C. developed
    B. skilled
    D. cooperative

27. A marine oiler who makes a SIGNIFICANT error, makes one which is

    A. doubtful
    C. accidental
    B. meaningless
    D. important

28. A marine oiler who is working on a repair job which is to be EXPEDITED, is working on a job which is to be done

    A. as quickly as possible
    C. slowly
    B. carefully
    D. safely

Questions 29 - 30.

Questions 29 and 30 are based on the paragraph below. Use only this information in answering these 2 questions.

To determine whether an oil will corrode a particular bearing metal, specimens of the metal are exposed to the oil for a few hours, the oil is agitated, and is usually maintained at temperatures around 350° F. If under these conditions there is no appreciable loss of weight of the bearing specimen, it can be rather safely assumed that the oil will be non-corrosive in service. If, however, there is some corrosion by the laboratory tests, the oil may or may not cause corrosion in actual service, depending upon the severity of operating conditions. The Underwood and the MacCoull Corrosion Tests are the two most prominent being used at the present time.

29. According to above paragraph, the one of the following statements that is *most nearly true* is that:

    A. If there is a loss of weight of the oil, the oil is corrosive in service
    B. If there is a very small loss of weight of the bearing metal, the oil will be non-corrosive
    C. If there is some loss of weight of the bearing metal, the oil will always be corrosive in service
    D. Operating conditions have little effect on the corrosion of the oil

30. According to the paragraph, the *one* of the following statements that is *most nearly true* is that:

    A. The bearing metal must be exposed to the oil for a period of 6 hours
    B. The bearing metal must be agitated and kept at 360° C
    C. The oil must be agitated and kept at 350° F
    D. The Underwood Tests are the only ones used for this purpose

31. Large diesels of the crosshead type *usually* have their cylinders lubricated by

    A. mechanical forced feed lubricators
    B. the splash method
    C. hydrostatic lubricators
    D. the sight feed gravity system

32. On most diesels there are two separate and distinct lubricating systems designated as the high and low pressure systems.
    The high pressure system is *generally* used to lubricate the

    A. cylinders
    B. connecting rod bearings
    C. piston pins
    D. main bearings

33. In comparing a four-cycle diesel to a single acting two-cycle diesel, of the same capacity, it may be said that

    A. the quality of the lubricating oil required for each diesel varies considerably
    B. the two-cycle engine uses more lubricating oil
    C. more heat is developed in the four-cycle engine cylinders
    D. both engines have scavenging ports

34. Excessive lubrication of diesel cylinders may cause _____ in the cylinders.

    A. condensation              B. emulsification
    C. dangerous vapors          D. carbon deposits

35. In marine service, the bearings of auxiliary generators are *usually* oiled by means of the _____ method.

    A. ring or chain             B. hydrostatic
    C. splash                    D. wick

36. "Additives" are *sometimes* added to lubricating oil to

    A. increase compression ratio
    B. hold to a minimum the oxidation of the oil
    C. lower the exhaust gas temperature
    D. neutralize the viscosity of the oil

37. In a diesel engine the fuel is ignited by means of the

    A. spark plugs               B. hot points
    C. heat of compression       D. hot bulbs

38. In a 4-stroke cycle full diesel engine, the fuel is ignited by means of

    A. special spark plugs
    B. hot exhaust gases
    C. highly compressed air in the cylinder
    D. glow plugs in the cylinder heads

39. The S.A.E. numbers, as used in a classification of lubricants, *generally* indicate the

    A. pour point
    B. flash point
    C. viscosity
    D. color grades

40. In a typical lube-oil system aboard ship, the oil purifier is *usually* located

    A. in-line with the condensate pumps
    B. in-line with the fuel oil tanks
    C. below the overhead settling tank
    D. ahead of the oil heater

## KEY (CORRECT ANSWERS)

| | | | |
|---|---|---|---|
| 1. D | 11. D | 21. D | 31. A |
| 2. C | 12. A | 22. C | 32. A |
| 3. D | 13. C | 23. A | 33. B |
| 4. A | 14. D | 24. C | 34. D |
| 5. A | 15. A | 25. A | 35. A |
| 6. C | 16. D | 26. B | 36. B |
| 7. A | 17. A | 27. D | 37. C |
| 8. D | 18. C | 28. A | 38. C |
| 9. C | 19. C | 29. B | 39. C |
| 10. B | 20. B | 30. C | 40. C |

# EXAMINATION SECTION
## TEST 1

DIRECTIONS: Each question or incomplete statement is followed by several suggested answers or completions. Select the one that BEST answers the question or completes the statement. *PRINT THE LETTER OF THE CORRECT ANSWER IN THE SPACE AT THE RIGHT.*

1. Of the following lubricating greases, the one that is generally known as a heat-resisting grease is _____ grease.  1.____

   A. soda (sodium) soap
   B. lime (calcium) soap
   C. aluminum soap
   D. mixed (soda and lime)

2. The chassis grease recommended for MOST pieces of construction equipment is generally  2.____

   A. lime base-water resistant
   B. SAE-140 E.P.
   C. number 3 cup
   D. number 2 cup

3. The PRIMARY advantage that a friction clutch has over a positive clutch is that the friction clutch  3.____

   A. runs at lower speeds
   B. requires less maintenance
   C. can be engaged at either low or high speeds
   D. runs at high speeds

4. Of the following makes of power plants for cranes, the one which uses diesel fuel is the  4.____

   A. Allis-Chalmers L-525
   B. G.M. 4055-C
   C. Waukesha 140 GKU
   D. Waukesha 140 GKU (with torque converter)

5. In a 2-stroke cycle diesel engine, the cylinder is scavenged by  5.____

   A. the combustion air
   B. the exhaust gases
   C. the injected fuel oil
   D. a mixture of fuel oil and air

6. In a 6 x 19 Seale wire rope, the wires in one strand are  6.____

   A. always of the same size
   B. of different diameters
   C. meshed with soft cores
   D. of the flattened strand type

7. Of the following metals, the one that is USUALLY used for socketing wire ropes is  7.____

   A. lead
   B. tin
   C. zinc
   D. 50-50 solder

63

8. On the suction stroke of a four-stroke cycle full diesel engine, _____ drawn into the cylinder.

    A. fuel oil only is
    B. air and a full charge of fuel oil are
    C. air only is
    D. air and a one-half charge of fuel oil are

9. The PRIMARY purpose of crossing a belt when connecting two pulleys is to

    A. rotate the shafts in opposite directions
    B. decrease the belt friction contact
    C. be able to use a thinner belt
    D. increase the overall belt efficiency

10. Double-base safety clips having corrugated jaws when used on wire rope in making up an eye develops approximately _____ of the strength of the rope.

    A. 60%    B. 70%    C. 80%    D. 95%

11. The number of ropes usually used on the movable block of a 4 part fall is MOST NEARLY

    A. 6    B. 4    C. 3    D. 2

12.

In the above sketch, the left $P$, in pounds, required to raise the 1200 pound block from the ground is MOST NEARLY

    A. 200    B. 160    C. 144    D. 96

13. In the common rail system of solid fuel injection in a diesel engine, a control wedge is generally used to

    A. control the lift of the mechanically operated spray valve
    B. meter the fuel oil at the transfer pump
    C. control the fuel oil level in the fuel tank
    D. fix the fuel oil pressure in the *common rail*

14. In the fuel system for a 4-stroke cycle full diesel engine, the oil travels in sequence from the fuel tank to the

    A. filters, transfer pump, pre-combustion chamber, injection pump, and injection valve
    B. filters, transfer pump, pre-combustion chamber, injection valve, and injection pump
    C. transfer pump, filters, injection pump, injection valve, and pre-combustion chamber
    D. filters, injection pump, transfer pump, injection valve, and pre-combustion chamber

15. The camshaft operating the valves of a 4-stroke cycle diesel engine rotates at _____ speed of the crankshaft.

    A. the same           B. half the
    C. double the         D. four times the

16. The speed of a crane trolley motor is 1200 r.p.m.
    If the motor pinion has 24 teeth and the driven gear has 92 teeth, the speed of the gear shaft is MOST NEARLY

    A. 250      B. 300      C. 350      D. 3600

17. In a 4-stroke cycle full diesel engine, the fuel is ignited by means of

    A. special spark plugs
    B. hot exhaust gases
    C. highly compressed air in the cylinder
    D. glow plugs in the cylinder heads

18. The proper gap on a spark plug can be MOST accurately set by use of a _____ gage.

    A. dial                   B. conventional flat feeler
    C. square wire feeler     D. round wire feeler

19. A considerable amount of water in the crankcase of a gasoline engine would NOT be likely due to

    A. a cylinder head crack      B. cylinder head gasket leaks
    C. cylinder block cracks      D. condensation

20. A good program of preventive maintenance would NOT require

    A. having the work done in an off shift
    B. periodic inspection
    C. cleaning the equipment before servicing
    D. accurate records of the servicing done

21. The MAXIMUM ampere rating of the fuse to be used in an existing circuit depends upon the

    A. size of wire in the circuit    B. connected load
    C. voltage of the line            D. rating of the switch

22. On a truck mounted portable air compressor, the differential assembly is located in the

    A. truck transmission housing    B. air compressor crankcase
    C. truck rear housing            D. air regulating equipment

23. In operation, a gasoline driven air compressor is said to be unloaded when the

    A. air compressor is driven at low speed
    B. discharge valves on the air compressor are held in the open position
    C. safety valve on the air compressor is engaged in the open position
    D. inlet valves on the air compressor are held in the open position

24. In reference to air controlled machines operating in mid-winter, the reservoir of the anti-freezer or evaporator should be filled with

    A. methyl alcohol
    B. ethyl alcohol
    C. an alcohol containing an inhibitor
    D. prestone

25. A grade of 1 in 20 is approximately the same as a _____ rise in a _____ run.

    A. 1 foot; 200 inch        B. 1 yard; 125 yard
    C. 10 inch; 200 yard       D. 12 inch; 7 yard

26. The minimum factor of safety of a wire rope that is used for grab buckets should be NOT less than

    A. 4        B. 6        C. 8        D. 10

27. Whenever possible, it is BEST to remove a gear from a shaft by means of

    A. heating the gear with a flame
    B. heavy but uniform blows with a hammer
    C. cooling the shaft with dry ice
    D. an appropriate wheel puller

28. For digging open cuts, drainage ditches, and gravel pits, where the material is to be moved from 20 to 3000 feet before dumping, one would use a _____ Excavator.

    A. Crawler Crane           B. Gantry Crane
    C. Drag-line               D. Diesel Shovel

29. If a bucket capable of carrying 5 3/4 cubic yards is loaded to 3/4 of its capacity, it will be carrying, in cubic yards, APPROXIMATELY

    A. 3 1/2     B. 4 1/4     C. 4 7/8     D. 5 1/4

30. A guy line is generally used with a

    A. diesel driven scraper       B. stiff leg derrick
    C. truck mounted clamshell     D. gantry crane

31. The point shaft on a boom is usually located near the

    A. top of the boom             B. bottom of the boom
    C. dead end cable socket       D. hoist drum

32. Assume that a horizontal roller chain drive is used to transmit power to the jack shaft of a crane.
    For proper tension in the roller chain,
    A. there should be a small amount of sag in the chain
    B. the sag should bring the chain down to the center line of the driving sprocket
    C. there should be no sag in the chain
    D. the chain should make an angle of at least 50 when leaving the driving sprocket

33. In reference to the above sketch, in order to balance the 100 lbs. belt pull on the 6" diameter pulley, a belt pull of approximately 67 lbs. should be attached to which one of the following pulleys?

    A. 16"    B. 12"    C. 9"    D. 8"

34. Of the following statements concerning torque converter equipped machines, the one which is MOST NEARLY CORRECT is that
    A. the torque converter is a transmission with a limited number of ratios
    B. at normal speeds, the line pulls are less than on a standard mechanical drive machine
    C. the shock loading is increased during shovel operations
    D. at stall conditions, the engine is *putting out* its maximum power

35. To transmit power between two shafts that are in the same plane but 90° to each other, it is BEST to use _____ gear(s).
    A. spur              B. worm and spur
    C. bevel             D. herringbone

36. Under normal operations, the oil pressure regulating valve piston on a torque converter should be removed and cleaned once
    A. a day             B. a week
    C. a month           D. every three months

37. The operating oil pressure in a torque converter usually has a range of approximately _____ to _____ psi.
    A. 15; 20    B. 35; 40    C. 50; 65    D. 70; 85

38. For successful operation of a machine equipped with a torque converter, the operator should

    A. watch the load or bucket
    B. listen to the engine
    C. vary the output, shaft governor setting
    D. vary the engine governor setting

39. The clutch torque delivered by a fluid coupling is APPROXIMATELY _____ the engine torque.

    A. the same as
    B. twice that of
    C. three times that of
    D. four times that of

40. The type of knot that can be used for shortening a rope which does not have free ends, without cutting the rope, is called a

    A. sheet bend
    B. hawser bend
    C. sheepshank
    D. clove hitch

## KEY (CORRECT ANSWERS)

| | | | |
|---|---|---|---|
| 1. A | 11. B | 21. A | 31. A |
| 2. A | 12. C | 22. C | 32. A |
| 3. C | 13. A | 23. D | 33. C |
| 4. B | 14. C | 24. A | 34. D |
| 5. A | 15. B | 25. D | 35. C |
| 6. B | 16. B | 26. B | 36. B |
| 7. C | 17. C | 27. D | 37. B |
| 8. C | 18. D | 28. C | 38. A |
| 9. A | 19. D | 29. B | 39. A |
| 10. D | 20. A | 30. B | 40. C |

# TEST 2

DIRECTIONS: Each question or incomplete statement is followed by several suggested answers or completions. Select the one that BEST answers the question or completes the statement. *PRINT THE LETTER OF THE CORRECT ANSWER IN THE SPACE AT THE RIGHT.*

1. The purpose of the hand-operated choke on a gasoline engine is to

   A. provide an excess amount of air for easy starting
   B. provide a rich mixture for starting
   C. increase the jet opening for more gasoline
   D. provide a lean mixture for starting

   1.____

2. In reference to gasoline engines, a common cause of engine back pressure is a

   A. corroded muffler           B. corroded exhaust pipe
   C. loose muffler              D. clogged muffler passage

   2.____

3. A *right* lang lay wire rope has

   A. wires and strands laid opposite to one another
   B. the wires laid left and the strands laid right
   C. both wires and strands laid to the right
   D. the wires laid right and the strands laid left

   3.____

4. An ambidextrous operator during his working hours will MOST likely

   A. handle his controls with ease
   B. handle his controls slowly
   C. be handicapped in lifting loads
   D. understand instructions easily

   4.____

5. Assume that a two leg bridle sling with hooks and 5/8 inch diameter ropes has a safe load capacity of 4.4 tons when the legs are in a vertical position.
   If the legs are set at 90% to each other, the safe load capacity, in tons, of this sling is MOST NEARLY

   A. 6.2      B. 4.4      C. 3.1      D. 2.2

   5.____

6. Fires in and around electrical equipment are BEST extinguished by using

   A. water
   B. sand
   C. carbon dioxide
   D. soda acid chemical solution

   6.____

7. A dipper trip assembly is USUALLY found on a _____ boom.

   A. shovel            B. crane
   C. drag-line         D. clamshell

   7.____

8. A convenient practical method of checking if the spark plugs in a gasoline engine are firing is to

    A. use a high tension voltmeter
    B. short them with an insulated handle screwdriver
    C. replace the spark plugs one at a time in the order of firing
    D. use a high tension ammeter across each spark plug

9. In a two-stage air compressor, if numbers are given to components as follows: 1st stage cylinder (1), 2nd stage cylinder (2), receiver tank (3), and intercooler (4); the path of the air when compressor is operating would be

    A. 1, 2, 4, 3
    B. 4, 1, 2, 3
    C. 1, 3, 2, 4
    D. 1, 4, 2, 3

10. When a lead acid type battery is fully charged, the hydrometer reading should be APPROXIMATELY

    A. 1.280    B. 1.190    C. 1.150    D. 1.000

11. If battery acid comes into contact with the skin, the BEST thing to do is

    A. wipe the contact area with a piece of cloth
    B. wash away with large quantities of water
    C. wash away with a salt solution
    D. place a tourniquet above the contact area

12.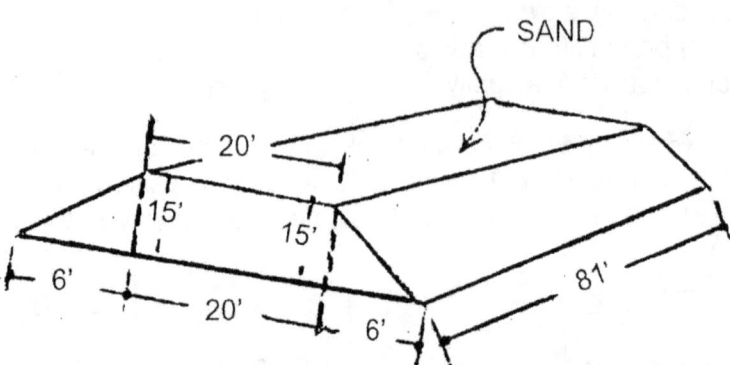

    Assume that a section of a sand barge is uniformally loaded with sand as shown above.
    The total number of cubic yards of sand in this section is MOST NEARLY

    A. 120    B. 790    C. 1170    D. 2260

13. With reference to a gasoline-driven air compressor, the tern *CFM* refers to the

    A. gasoline consumption of the engine
    B. type of unloader used on the compressor
    C. capacity of the compressor
    D. maximum revolutions of the compressor

14. Backfiring through the carburetor of a gasoline engine may MOST likely be caused by    14.____

    A. an advanced spark
    B. a blown cylinder head gasket
    C. poor combustion
    D. a defective condenser

15. Vapor-lock in a gasoline engine is MOST likely due to    15.____

    A. fuel forming bubbles in the gas line
    B. the carburetor being clogged with dirt
    C. an over rich gas-air mixture
    D. a break in the fuel pump diaphragm

16. Of the following lubricating greases, the one that is water-resistant and can be used    16.____
    where the operating temperature does not exceed 175° F is _____ grease.

    A. lime (calcium) soap           B. soda (sodium) soap
    C. aluminum soap                 D. mixed (soda and lime)

17. The speed regulation of an A.C. wound rotor induction motor is BEST obtained by    17.____

    A. using a diverter
    B. varying the resistance in the rotor circuit
    C. varying the stator voltage
    D. rotating the brushes on the slip rings

18. The type of A.C. motor commonly used for powering electric cranes is the _____ motor.    18.____

    A. slip ring type induction
    B. synchronous
    C. squirrel-cage type induction
    D. universal

19. A dash pot arrangement on a circuit breaker or motor starter USUALLY provides for    19.____

    A. under-voltage protection
    B. short-circuit protection
    C. absorbing mechanical stresses or vibration when the device is closed
    D. delayed-time action

20. The PRIMARY importance of outrigging on a truck crane is    20.____

    A. to prevent the load from swinging
    B. to operate the bucket
    C. for lateral support of truck body
    D. to hold the boom in position

21. A shovel equipped with a dual crowd will MOST likely    21.____

    A. handle more cubic yards of material per hour
    B. require superior operators
    C. stall under harder digging
    D. have less tension in the crowd cable

22. The quotation, *When an assembly is removed from a crane for replacement of a bushing, gear, or any individual part, it is an excellent practice to completely recondition the entire assembly.*
Following the advice in this quotation, the crane engineman will MOST likely learn that

   A. it is cheaper to buy two or more different parts
   B. repetition of work on repairs can be eliminated
   C. replacement parts will wear less than original parts
   D. replacement of one part in an assembly is less costly in the long run

23. In reference to overhead traveling bucket cranes, the term dynamic braking means MOST NEARLY

   A. actuating a trustor brake
   B. energizing a magnetic type brake
   C. closing a magnetic contactor which permits the brake to close
   D. a method of reducing the speed of hoisting motors when lowering a load

24. The type of lubricant commonly used for a bridge motor gear case at low temperature (below 32° F) is

   A. S.A.E. 90
   B. S.A.E. 160
   C. S.A.E. 250
   D. dip-gear grease

25. A gear-type transfer pump is one that USUALLY contains

   A. hydraulic plungers
   B. rollers and pinions
   C. twin gear elements
   D. poppet type valves

26. On a shovel boom, the shipper shaft is USUALLY located near the

   A. top of the boom
   B. bottom of the boom
   C. jack shaft drum
   D. mid-point of the boom

27. The characteristic of a series motor which makes its use desirable for cranes is that a large increase in torque is obtained

   A. with a large increase in voltage
   B. with a moderate increase in current
   C. when lowering a load
   D. with a moderate decrease in current

28. The compression ratio of a modern diesel engine has an approximate range of (with no starting ignition device)

   A. 3-5
   B. 6-8
   C. 9-11
   D. 12-22

29. If you were to instruct an oiler to do a sequence of jobs and operations, he would MOST likely do them

   A. in any order
   B. without regards to specifications
   C. when the machine is down
   D. in the prescribed order

30. The lifting ability of a crawler-mounted crane PRIMARILY depends upon the

   A. gearing
   B. engine power
   C. balance of the crane
   D. strength of the cables

31. The breaking strength of a new 1/2" diameter 6 x 19 fiber core wire rope made of plow steel is APPROXIMATELY _____ tons.

   A. 2    B. 3    C. 5    D. 10

32. Of the following tools for cutting wire rope used on construction equipment, the one that is BEST is a(n)

   A. hacksaw
   B. standard bolt cutter
   C. oxyacetylene torch
   D. cold chisel

33. The purpose of adding a jib boom to the regular boom of a crane is to

   A. act as a counterweight when lifting
   B. prevent overloading
   C. shift the center of gravity
   D. obtain greater reach

34. When a crane is equipped with a jib boom, the lifting capacity of the boom is APPROXIMATELY _____ the crane load.

   A. 1/2 of
   B. 3/4 of
   C. the same as
   D. 1 1/2 times

35. Of the following bell or whistle hoist signals, the one that is customarily used to signal the lowering of a load is _____ quick signal(s).

   A. two
   B. three
   C. one
   D. a series of

36. An authorized signalman working in conjunction with the crane operator has his arm extended, fingers clenched, and thumb upward while moving his hand up and down. The signalman is signalling the crane operator to

   A. lift the boom up
   B. lower the load
   C. hoist the load
   D. stop immediately (emergency)

Questions 37-40.

DIRECTIONS: Questions 37 through 40, inclusive, are to be answered in accordance with the paragraph below.

*Operators spotting loads with long booms and working around men need the smooth, easy operation and positive control of uniform pressure swing clutches. There are no jerks or grabs with these large disc-type clutches because there is always even pressure over the entire clutch lining surface. In the conventional band-type swing clutch, the pressure varies between dead and live ends of the band. The uniform pressure swing clutch has excellent provision for heat dissipation. The driving elements, which are always rotating, have a great number of fins cast in them. This gives them an impeller or blower action for cooling, resulting in longer life and freedom from frequent adjustment.*

37. According to the above paragraph, it may be said that conventional band-type swing clutches have

    A. even pressure on the clutch lining
    B. larger contact area
    C. smaller contact area
    D. uneven pressure on the clutch lining

37.____

38. According to the above paragraph, machines equipped with uniform pressure swing clutches will

    A. give better service under all conditions
    B. require no clutch adjustment
    C. give positive control of hoist
    D. provide better control of swing

38.____

39. According to the above paragraph, it may be said that the rotation of the driving elements of the uniform pressure swing clutch is always

    A. continuous            B. constant
    C. varying               D. uncertain

39.____

40. According to the above paragraph, freedom from frequent adjustment is due to the

    A. operator's smooth, easy operation
    B. positive control of the clutch
    C. cooling effect of the rotating fins
    D. larger contact area of the bigger clutch

40.____

## KEY (CORRECT ANSWERS)

| | | | |
|---|---|---|---|
| 1. B | 11. B | 21. A | 31. D |
| 2. D | 12. C | 22. B | 32. C |
| 3. C | 13. C | 23. D | 33. D |
| 4. A | 14. B | 24. A | 34. A |
| 5. C | 15. A | 25. C | 35. B |
| 6. C | 16. D | 26. D | 36. A |
| 7. A | 17. B | 27. B | 37. D |
| 8. B | 18. A | 28. D | 38. D |
| 9. D | 19. D | 29. D | 39. A |
| 10. A | 20. C | 30. C | 40. C |

# EXAMINATION SECTION

## TEST 1

DIRECTIONS: Each question or incomplete statement is followed by several suggested answers or completions. Select the one that BEST answers the question or completes the statement. *PRINT THE LETTER OF THE CORRECT ANSWER IN THE SPACE AT THE RIGHT.*

1. The MAIN advantage of a rotary pump over a centrifugal pump is that it
   A. has more velocity
   B. has greater speed
   C. delivers more gallons per minute
   D. is self-priming and requires no valves

2. Pump efficiency can be termed
   I. hydraulic    II. volumetric    III. thermal    IV. mechanical

   The CORRECT answer is:
   A. I, II    B. I, III, IV    C. I, II, IV    D. I, II, III, IV

3. A superheater vent valve is installed on a boiler to
   A. insure a flow of steam through the superheater when steam is being raised on the boiler
   B. insure that some of the excess steam is released
   C. lower the steam temperature
   D. none of the above

4. Which of the following is a wearing ring on a centrifugal pump?
   A. Lantern    B. Turbine    C. Impeller    D. Thrust

5. Worn sealing rings can cause the
   A. capacity to increase
   B. discharge to flow back into the inlet
   C. priming to stop
   D. shaft to throw out of alignment

6. Vibration is caused by
   A. packing too tight    B. water hammer
   C. shaft alignment    D. worn bearings

7. A condensate pump helps to
   A. create vacuum in the system
   B. induce the steam to circulate rapidly
   C. return the condensate back to the boiler
   D. reduce the back pressure on the engine

8. Important pumps on a feedwater line are the
   I. rotary    II. vacuum    III. turbine    IV. centrifugal
   The CORRECT answer is:
   A. I, II    B. II, III, IV    C. I, II, III    D. I, II, III, IV

75

9. Which of the following is a reciprocating pump?  9._____
   A. Two stage   B. Turbine
   C. Simplex   D. All of the above

10. Which cylinder is larger on a duplex pump?  10._____
    A. Water   B. Air
    C. Steam   D. All are the same size

11. The FEWEST number of valves on a duplex pump is  11._____
    A. 4   B. 8   C. 12   D. 16

12. A pump may fail to discharge when the  12._____
    A. pump is not properly primed
    B. inlet valve is stuck
    C. valve seats are in bad condition
    D. all of the above

13. A pump may pound and vibrate because of  13._____
    A. air in the liquid
    B. a leaky inlet line
    C. excessive speed
    D. all of the above

14. If a pump races while increasing its output, the cause may be  14._____
    A. a leaky plunger
    B. a broken or stuck water valve
    C. an air leak
    D. not enough steam to move the piston

15. If the piston strikes the head of the cylinder, the cause would MOST probably be  15._____
    A. improper adjustment of the cushion valve
    B. cylinder rings are worn
    C. too much lap on the valves
    D. none of the above

16. To adjust the cushion valve, you should  16._____
    A. run the pump at full speed
    B. cut down the steam supply
    C. run the pump with a full load
    D. run the pump without a water load

17. If the pump lacks a cushion valve, you should  17._____
    A. lower the steam pressure
    B. adjust the lost motion enough to permit the pump to make a full stroke without striking
    C. adjust the piston rings
    D. adjust the back pressure valve

18. What condition would cause a piston to stop on dead center?  18.____
    A. The slide valve is worn
    B. There is not enough steam pressure
    C. There is too high of a head
    D. The cylinder shoulders are worn

19. Positive suction head is a condition present when the  19.____
    A. pump is located below the liquid supply
    B. pump is located between the boiler and the feedwater tank
    C. pump is located above the liquid supply
    D. water pressure is greater than the suction pressure

20. A centrifugal pump will most likely fail if  20.____
    A. the suction side of the pump is defective
    B. the discharge valve is closed
    C. wearing rings are worn
    D. strainer is clogged

21. The pump may fail to discharge if there is  21.____
    A. not enough water pressure
    B. improper priming
    C. air trapped at the top of the casing causing the pump to lose its discharge
    D. too high of a head

22. The failure of a pump to discharge can be rectified by  22.____
    A. increasing the water pressure
    B. reducing the pipe size
    C. decreasing the water pressure
    D. repriming the pump

23. To prevent a pump from failing to discharge, you should  23.____
    A. install a lantern ring
    B. replace the impeller
    C. install a bigger motor
    D. remove some packing

24. Reduction in both capacity and head is caused by  24.____
    A. too much air leaking through the packing
    B. reverse rotation of the motor
    C. a closed suction valve
    D. a clogged strainer

25. Small by-pass lines are installed around a large gate valve in order to  25.____
    A. equalize the pressure on the globe valve
    B. balance the pressure on the gate valve when the valve is being opened
    C. increase the velocity of the steam
    D. eliminate the sudden change in temperature of the steam

## KEY (CORRECT ANSWERS)

| | | | |
|---|---|---|---|
| 1. | D | 11. | B |
| 2. | D | 12. | D |
| 3. | A | 13. | D |
| 4. | C | 14. | D |
| 5. | B | 15. | A |
| 6. | D | 16. | D |
| 7. | C | 17. | B |
| 8. | D | 18. | A |
| 9. | C | 19. | A |
| 10. | C | 20. | A |
| | | 21. | B |
| | | 22. | D |
| | | 23. | A |
| | | 24. | B |
| | | 25. | B |

# TEST 2

DIRECTIONS: Each question or incomplete statement is followed by several suggested answers or completions. Select the one that BEST answers the question or completes the statement. *PRINT THE LETTER OF THE CORRECT ANSWER IN THE SPACE AT THE RIGHT.*

1. The purpose of a volume casing on a centrifugal pump is to
   A. convert velocity into vacuum
   B. convert velocity into pressure
   C. prevent cavitation of the pump
   D. increase the velocity of the water

   1.____

2. How many type of feedwater heaters are currently in existence
   A. 1    B. 2    C. 4    D. 5

   2.____

3. Which of the following are types of feedwater heaters?
   A. Economizer    B. Closed    C. Deaerator    D. All of the above

   3.____

4. When the temperature leaving the feedwater heater is too low, the MAIN problem is probably that
   A. steam pressure is too low
   B. back pressure is too low
   C. steam is of poor quality
   D. too much condensate is in the steam

   4.____

5. The advantage of a feedwater heater is:
   A. Hotter feedwater
   B. Less fuel consumption
   C. Less air in the feedwater
   D. All of the above

   5.____

6. To increase the back pressure, you should
   A. install a bigger back pressure valve
   B. put a heavier spring on the valve
   C. close the back pressure valve
   D. increase the line pressure

   6.____

7. Which of the following is NOT a use of a feedwater heater? To
   A. pre-heat the feedwater
   B. eliminate scale foaming substances by precipitation
   C. utilize some of the steam going to waste
   D. store generated steam

   7.____

8. In relation to the feedwater pump, the feedwater heater should be located
   in another part of the building
   A. in the basement of the plant
   B. about 10 or 12 feet above the pump

   8.____

79

9. An open feedwater heater is a heater
   A. open at one end
   B. with steam coils
   C. where water and steam are in actual contact
   D. with 2/3 steam space

10. The MAIN advantage of an open heater is that it
    A. can separate scale forming substances from the feed-water by precipitation
    B. produces hotter water
    C. can hold more steam
    D. is cheap to operate

11. How much steam supply is sufficient for an open heater?
    A. 3 to 5 lbs.   B. 5 to 7 lbs.   C. 8 to 10 lbs.   D. All of the above

12. _____ A(n) should be installed on an open feedwater heater
    A. exhaust or vent pipe          B. oil separator
    C. steam gauge                   D. all of the above

13. A closed feedwater heater is a heater in which
    A. steam travels through coils or tubes and water on the outside of the coils
    B. water runs through a tube with steam on the outside heating the water
    C. feedwater is heated and passed back to the deaerator
    D. none of the above

14. At what pressure should a feedwater heater operate?
    A. 1-15 lbs.   B. 15-20 lbs.   C. 20-25 lbs.   D. 25-30 lbs.

15. The safety device normally installed on a feedwater heater is a _____ valve.
    A. pneumatic                     B. pressure relief
    C. safety                        D. by-pass

16. The FIRST indication of a broken coil on a feedwater heater would be the
    A. heater filling up with water
    B. relief valve opening
    C. steam pressure increasing
    D. water pressure rising

17. On a double-acting reciprocating pump, what is installed on the discharge side of the pump? A(n)
    A. air chamber and gauge
    B. pressure gauge and relief valve.
    C. pressure gauge and safety valve
    D. air chamber and a gate valve

18. What types of lubricators are MOST commonly used today?
    I. Hydrokinetic          II. Force feed pump
    III. Splash system       IV. Gravity

    The CORRECT answer is:
    A. I, II        B. II, III, IV        C. I, III, IV        D. I, II, III, IV

19. What type of lubricant is used on piston rods and valve stems on a reciprocating pump?  19._____
    Mineral oil
    A. Compress oil
    B. Oil with high velocity
    C. Cylinder oil and graphite mixed together
    D. A reciprocating pump contains the following notation:

20. What is the diameter of the liquid cylinder? 7 x 6 x 4.  20._____
    A. 6"                           B. 4"
    C. 7"                           D. none of the above

21. What types of pumps are used in a heating system?  21._____
    I. Reciprocating                II. Condensate
    III. Centrifugal                IV. Vacuum

    The CORRECT answer is:
    A. I, II                        B. I, III
    C. II, IV                       D. III, IV

22. The purpose of a steam loop, or thermal pump, is to  22._____
    A. deliver steam to the engine
    B. protect water from entering the steam gauge
    C. return condensate back to the boiler
    D. trap steam from high pressure lines into a low-pressure line

23. What effect does a short stroke have on a reciprocating pump? It  23._____
    A. increases the pump capacity
    B. increases the steam capacity, and decreases the pump consumption
    C. increases the steam Consumption, and decreases the pump capacity
    D. relieves the pressure in the air chamber

24. A pump with two liquid cylinders, and one steam cylinder is called a ___ pump.  24._____
    A. triplex                      B. duplex
    C. tandem                       D. double tandem

25. The air chamber on a reciprocating pump is located on the  25._____
    A. discharge side of the feed pump
    B. discharge side of the reciprocating pump
    C. discharge side of all pumps
    D. suction side of a reciprocating pump

## KEY (CORRECT ANSWERS)

| | |
|---|---|
| 1. A | 11. D |
| 2. B | 12. D |
| 3. D | 13. A |
| 4. B | 14. A |
| 5. D | 15. B |
| 6. C | 16. B |
| 7. D | 17. B |
| 8. D | 18. D |
| 9. C | 19. D |
| 10. C | 20. A |

21. C
22. C
23. B
24. C
25. B

# EXAMINATION SECTION
# TEST 1

DIRECTIONS: Each question or incomplete statement is followed by several suggested answers or completions. Select the one that BEST answers the question or completes the Statement. *PRINT THE LETTER OF THE CORRECT ANSWER IN THE SPACE AT THE RIGHT.*

1. What type of pump has a diffusion *ring*?  1._____
   - A. Centrifugal
   - B. Duplex double acting
   - C. Helical gear
   - D. Spur gear

2. A cause of excessive oil consumption in an air compressor is  2._____
   - A. oil with improper viscosity
   - B. defective discharge valve
   - C. oil level too high in oil sump
   - D. loose unloader unit

3. How does cylinder oil compare with engine oil at engine room temperature? Cylinder oil  3._____
   - A. is lighter in color
   - B. has a higher viscosity
   - C. has a lower viscosity
   - D. is lighter when put in front of a light

4. On a boiler-feed centrifugal pump, to maintain a certain speed, 60 horsepower is used. To double that speed, so as to obtain double the output, how much horsepower is needed?  4._____
   - A. 120   B. 240   C. 360   D. 480

5. The *slip* of a pump refers to  5._____
   - A. lost motion on the steam slide valve
   - B. leakage past the plunger on an outside packed pump
   - C. recirculation of liquid from discharge side back to suction side
   - D. clearance when piston is slipped inside cylinder

6. On a reciprocating vacuum pump, the diameter of the steam piston is _____ the liquid piston.  6._____
   - A. larger than
   - B. smaller than
   - C. the same size as
   - D. twice the diameter of

7. How many valves are there on the water end of a duplex double-acting feed pump?  7._____
   - A. 8   B. 6   C. 4   D. 2

8. Which of the following would you find on a duplex pump?

    A. Springs and packing
    B. Gears and impeller
    C. Flywheel and crank
    D. Crankshaft and air chamber

9. The function of the air chamber on a duplex, double-acting pump is to

    A. prevent hammering
    B. increase capacity of pump
    C. aerate the water
    D. prevent cavitation

10. The valve discs on the water end of a duplex pump are USUALLY made of

    A. wood
    B. steel
    C. rubber
    D. cast iron

11. A direct-acting, duplex steam pump *short strokes* when it returns from overhaul. The PROBABLE cause is

    A. feed water too cold
    B. steam pressure too low
    C. steam valves not properly set
    D. water discharge pressure too high

12. A heavy duty pump is one which

    A. is designed for the pumping of heavy liquids
    B. pumps large quantities of water
    C. has a high thermal efficiency
    D. is made of extra heavy material for high head pressure

13. When a punch is used in making holes for rivets or boiler tubes, the diameter of the punch shall be _____ the desired hole.

    A. three-quarters of the diameter of
    B. slightly smaller than
    C. exactly the same size as
    D. slightly larger than

14. On a _____ pump, you would find a *volute*.

    A. reciprocating
    B. centrifugal
    C. jet
    D. direct-pressure

15. In starting a centrifugal boiler feed pump with 300 lbs. water pressure on the line, the valves should be set with suction _____ and discharge _____.

    A. open; open
    B. open; closed
    C. closed; closed
    D. closed; open

16. On a centrifugal boiler feed pump, the regulating valve functions to maintain

    A. speed constant
    B. pressure constant
    C. variable speed
    D. water level

3 (#1)

17. With centrifugal pumps, the head varies directly as the 17.____

    A. speed                    B. speed squared
    C. speed cubed              D. diameter squared

18. An intercooler is used on a 18.____

    A. compound engine          B. two-stage air compressor
    C. two-stage turbine        D. two-stage evactor

19. The unloader on an air compressor is provided for 19.____

    A. reducing pressure        B. easy starting
    C. high-starting pressure   D. reducing temperature

20. A duplex center outside a packed feed water pump has 20.____

    A. yoke rod                 B. two water plungers
    C. compound steam glands    D. four water pistons

21. A centrifugal pump operates with a high suction lift, which would require _____ line. 21.____

    A. lift check at bottom of suction
    B. swing check in discharge
    C. stop valve in discharge
    D. lift check at top of suction

22. Diffuser vanes will MOST generally be found in a _____ pump. 22.____

    A. centrifugal turbine      B. centrifugal volute
    C. rotary                   D. reciprocating

23. A sewer ejector would be located 23.____

    A. on the roof of a building
    B. in the basement
    C. in the sub-basement
    D. in the sewer

24. How many pots are there on a double-acting water pump? 24.____

    A. 1        B. 2        C. 3        D. 4

25. What is the amount of steam consumption of a simple, duplex steam pump, in lbs./H.P. hour? 25.____

    A. 5-20     B. 25-35    C. 50-90    D. 120-200

# KEY (CORRECT ANSWERS)

1. A
2. C
3. B
4. D
5. B

6. B
7. A
8. A
9. A
10. C

11. C
12. D
13. D
14. B
15. A

16. D
17. B
18. B
19. A
20. B

21. A
22. A
23. C
24. D
25. A

# TEST 2

DIRECTIONS: Each question or incomplete statement is followed by several suggested answers or completions. Select the one that BEST answers the question or completes the statement. *PRINT THE LETTER OF THE CORRECT ANSWER IN THE SPACE AT THE RIGHT.*

1. The type of valve on a duplex steam pump is  1.____

   A. sleeve  B. piston
   C. D-slide valve  D. poppet

2. The slide valve on a Knowles pump is operated by  2.____

   A. linkage attached to the piston rod
   B. rocker arm of opposite steam slide
   C. an auxiliary piston
   D. discharge water pressure

3. A duplex, double-acting pump with the valves properly adjusted will  3.____

   A. not start sometimes
   B. always start
   C. jig
   D. start when off dead center

4. If one valve stem of a duplex, double-acting pump broke, the pump would  4.____

   A. increase in speed  B. run slower
   C. stop  D. run on one side only

5. The diameter of the steam cylinders of an 18 x 16 x 24 duplex, direct-acting steam pump is _____ inches.  5.____

   A. 18  B. 16  C. 24  D. 30

6. On a boiler feed pump, the  6.____

   A. steam cylinder is always larger than the water cylinder
   B. water cylinder is always larger than the steam cylinder
   C. cylinders are of equal size
   D. water discharge pipe is always larger than the suction pipe

7. Flax packing is used for  7.____

   A. steam end of pump
   B. water end of pump
   C. between flanges of pipe lines
   D. high temperature

8. Water is dripping out of the gland of a centrifugal pump used to pump feed water. You should  8.____

   A. renew the packing at the first opportunity
   B. pull up the gland as tight as possible with an ordinary 6 inch pipe wrench

87

C. pull up the gland just to the point where water does not leak out
D. do nothing

9. On the initial tightening of a jam-type gland on a boiler-feed water pump to stop excessive leakage, you would pull up alternately on the hexagonal nuts _____ turn.

   A. 1/6  B. 1/2  C. 3/4  D. 1 full

10. Diffuser vanes will MOST generally be found in a _____ pump.

    A. centrifugal turbine
    B. centrifugal volute
    C. rotary
    D. reciprocating

11. If the consumption of lubricating oil in an air compressor is excessive, it is MOST likely due to

    A. using too high viscosity oil
    B. a defective discharge valve
    C. a loose unloader unit
    D. oil too high in sump

12. Which of the following statements is CORRECT about a Worthington steam-driven duplex double-acting boiler feed pump?

    A. Will always start in position in which it was stopped
    B. Will not start if stopped with one piston at extreme head end and other at dead center
    C. Speed is controlled by inertia type governor
    D. Dust of f must always be 25%

13. Centrifugal boiler feed pumps for large boilers with fluctuating loads are usually fitted with a system for recirculating or recycling.
    This is done to prevent

    A. excessive head pressure
    B. loss of suction
    C. excessing governor action
    D. overheating with consequent flashing and seizing of the pump

14. In the operation of a turbo-driven centrifugal pump, the delivery of the pump would PROPERLY be controlled by

    A. throttling the discharge
    B. throttling the suction
    C. using a bypass
    D. throttling the steam supply

15. Assume that it is necessary to pump 40 M.G.D. against a 65 ft. head.
    If the pump efficiency is 65%, the B.H.P. of this pump is MOST NEARLY

    A. 920  B. 700  C. 460  D. 176

16. Assume that a pump had to be shut down temporarily due to trouble which was first reported by an oiler.
The one of the following entries in the log concerning this occurrence which is LEAST important is

 A. time of the shutdown
 B. period of time the pump was out of service
 C. cause of the trouble
 D. time the oiler came on shift

17. At sea level, the theoretical maximum distance, in feet, the water can be lifted by suction *only* is MOST NEARLY

 A. 12.00  B. 14.70  C. 33.57  D. 72.00

18. While a lubricating oil is in use, for good performance, its neutralization number should

 A. keep rising
 B. remain about the same
 C. be greater than 0.1
 D. be greater than 2.0

19. The parts of a large sewage pump that would MOST likely need repairs after the fewest number of hours of operation are the

 A. pump casings
 B. impellers
 C. wearing rings
 D. outboard bearings

20. Flexible coupling used to connect a pump to an electric motor valve is USUALLY rated in horsepower per

 A. 100 rpm of shaft
 B. 300 rpm of shaft
 C. square inch of shaft area
 D. inch of shaft diameter

## KEY (CORRECT ANSWERS)

| | | | |
|---|---|---|---|
| 1. | C | 11. | D |
| 2. | B | 12. | A |
| 3. | B | 13. | D |
| 4. | C | 14. | D |
| 5. | A | 15. | B |
| 6. | A | 16. | D |
| 7. | B | 17. | C |
| 8. | D | 18. | B |
| 9. | A | 19. | C |
| 10. | A | 20. | A |

# READING COMPREHENSION
## UNDERSTANDING AND INTERPRETING WRITTEN MATERIAL
# EXAMINATION SECTION
## TEST 1

DIRECTIONS: Each question or incomplete statement is followed by several suggested answers or completions. Select the one that BEST answers the question or completes the statement. *PRINT THE LETTER OF THE CORRECT ANSWER IN THE SPACE AT THE RIGHT.*

Questions 1-2.

DIRECTIONS: Questions 1 and 2 are to be answered SOLELY on the basis of the following paragraph.

When fixing an upper sash cord, you must also remove the lower sash. To do this, the parting strip between the sash must be removed. Now remove the cover from the weight box channel, cut off the cord as before, and pull it over the pulleys. Pull your new cord over the pulleys and down into the channel where it may be fastened to the weight. The cord for an upper sash is cut off 1" or 2" below the pulley with the weight resting on the floor of the pocket and the cord held taut. These measurements allow for slight stretching of the cord. When the cord is cut to length, it can be pulled up over the pulley and tied with a single common knot in the end to fit into the socket in the sash groove. If the knot protrudes beyond the face of the sash, tap it gently to flatten. In this way, it will not become frayed from constant rubbing against the groove.

1. When repairing the upper sash cord, the FIRST thing to do is to
    A. remove the lower sash
    B. cut the existing sash cord
    C. remove the parting strip
    D. measure the length of new cord necessary

2. According to the above paragraph, the rope may become frayed if the
    A. pulley is too small     B. knot sticks out
    C. cord is too long         D. weight is too heavy

Questions 3-4.

DIRECTIONS: Questions 3 and 4 are to be answered SOLELY on the basis of the following paragraph.

Repeated burning of the same area should be avoided. Burning should not be done on impervious, shallow, unstable, or highly erodible soils, or on steep slopes—especially in areas subject to heavy rains or rapid snowmelt. When existing vegetation is likely to be killed or seriously weakened by the fire, measures should be taken to assure prompt revegetation of the burned area. Burns should be limited to relatively small proportions of a watershed unit so that the stream channels will be able to carry any increased flows with a minimum of damage.

3. According to the above paragraph, planned burning should be limited to small areas of the watershed because
   A. the fire can be better controlled
   B. existing vegetation will be less likely to be killed
   C. plants will grow quicker in small areas
   D. there will be less likelihood of damaging floods

4. According to the above paragraph, burning USUALLY should be done on soils that
   A. readily absorb moisture
   B. have been burnt before
   C. exist as a thin layer over rock
   D. can be flooded by nearby streams

Questions 5-11.

DIRECTIONS: Questions 5 through 11 are to be answered SOLELY on the basis of the following paragraph.

## FUSE INFORMATION

Badly bent or distorted fuse clips cannot be permitted. Sometimes, the distortion or bending is so slight that it escapes notice, yet it may be the cause for fuse failures through the heat that is developed by the poor contact. Occasionally, the proper spring tension of the fuse clips has been destroyed by overheating from loose wire connections to the clips. Proper contact surfaces must be maintained to avoid faulty operation of the fuse. Maintenance men should remove oxides that form on the copper and brass contacts, check the clip pressure, and make sure that contact surfaces are not deformed or bent in any way. When removing oxides, use a well-worn file and remove only the oxide film. Do not use sandpaper or emery cloth as hard particles may come off and become embedded in the contact surfaces. All wire connections to the fuse holders should be carefully inspected to see that they are tight.

5. Fuse failure because of poor clip contact or loose connections is due to the resulting
   A. excessive voltage         B. increased current
   C. lowered resistance        D. heating effect

6. Oxides should be removed from fuse contacts by using
   A. a dull file               B. emery cloth
   C. fine sandpaper            D. a sharp file

7. One result of loose wire connections at the terminal of a fuse clip is stated in the above paragraph to be
   A. loss of tension in the wire
   B. welding of the fuse to the clip
   C. distortion of the clip
   D. loss of tension of the clip

8. Simple reasoning will show that the oxide film referred to is undesirable CHIEFLY because it
   A. looks dull
   B. makes removal of the fuse difficult
   C. weakens the clips
   D. introduces undesirable resistance

8._____

9. Fuse clips that are bent very slightly
   A. should be replaced with new clips
   B. should be carefully filed
   C. may result in blowing of the fuse
   D. may prevent the fuse from blowing

9._____

10. From the fuse information paragraph, it would be reasonable to conclude that fuse clips
    A. are difficult to maintain
    B. must be given proper maintenance
    C. require more attention than other electrical equipment
    D. are unreliable

10._____

11. A safe practical way of checking the tightness of the wire connection to the fuse clips of a live 120-volt lighting circuit is to
    A. feel the connection with your hand to see if it is warm
    B. try tightening with an insulated screwdriver or socket wrench
    C. see if the circuit works
    D. measure the resistance with an ohmmeter

11._____

Questions 12-13.

DIRECTIONS: Questions 12 through 13 are to be answered SOLELY on the basis of the following paragraph.

For cast iron pipe lines, the middle ring or sleeve shall have *beveled* ends and shall be high quality cast iron. The middle ring shall have a minimum wall thickness of 3/8" for pipe up to 8", 7/16" for pipe 10" to 30", and 1/2" for pipe over 30", nominal diameter. Minimum length of middle ring shall be 5" for pipe up to 10", 6" for pipe 10" to 30", and 10" for pipe 30" nominal diameter and larger. The middle ring shall not have a center pipe stop, unless otherwise specified.

12. As used in the above paragraph, the word *beveled* means MOST NEARLY
    A. straight    B. slanted    C. curved    D. rounded

12._____

13. In accordance with the above paragraph, the middle ring of a 24" nominal diameter pipe would have a minimum wall thickness and length of _____ thick and _____ long.
    A. 3/8"; 5:
    B. 3/8"; 6"
    C. 7/16"; 6"
    D. 1/2"; 6"

13._____

Questions 14-17.

DIRECTIONS: Questions 14 through 17 are to be answered SOLELY on the basis of the following paragraph.

Operators spotting loads with long booms and working around men need the smooth, easy operation and positive control of uniform pressure swing clutches. There are no jerks or grabs with these large disc-type clutches because there is always even pressure over the entire clutch lining surface. In the conventional band-type swing clutch, the pressure varies between dead and live ends of the band. The uniform pressure swing clutch has excellent provision for heat dissipation. The driving elements, which are always rotating, have a great number of fins cast in them. This gives them an impeller or blower action for cooling, resulting in longer life and freedom from frequent adjustment.

14. According to the above paragraph, it may be said that conventional band-type swing clutches have
    A. even pressure on the clutch lining
    B. larger contact area
    C. smaller contact area
    D. uneven pressure on the clutch lining

14._____

15. According to the above paragraph, machines equipped with uniform pressure swing clutches will
    A. give better service under all conditions
    B. require no clutch adjustment
    C. give positive control of hoist
    D. provide better control of swing

15._____

16. According to the above paragraph, it may be said that the rotation of the driving elements of the uniform pressure swing clutch is ALWAYS
    A. continuous        B. constant
    C. varying           D. uncertain

16._____

17. According to the above paragraph, freedom from frequent adjustment is due to the
    A. operator's smooth, easy operation
    B. positive control of the clutch
    C. cooling effect of the rotating fins
    D. larger contact area of the bigger clutch

17._____

Questions 18-22.

DIRECTIONS:   Questions 18 through 22 are to be answered SOLELY on the basis of the following paragraphs.

Exhaust valve clearance adjustment on diesel engines is very important for proper operation of the engine. Insufficient clearance between the exhaust valve stem and the rocker arm causes a loss of compression and, after a while, burning of the valves and valve seat inserts. On the other hand, too much valve clearance will result in noisy operation of the engine.

Exhaust valves that are maintained in good operating condition will result in efficient combustion in the engine. Valve seats must be true and unpitted, and valve stems must work smoothly within the valve guides. Long valve life will result from proper maintenance and operation of the engine.

Engine operating temperatures should be maintained between 160°F and 185°F. Low operating temperatures result in incomplete combustion and the deposit of fuel lacquers on valves.

18. According to the above paragraphs, too much valve clearance will cause the engine to operate
    A. slowly   B. noisily   C. smoothly   D. cold

    18._____

19. On the basis of the information given in the above paragraphs, operating temperatures of a diesel engine should be between
    A. 125°F and 130°F   B. 140°F and 150°F
    C. 160°F and 185°F   D. 190°F and 205°F

    19._____

20. According to the above paragraphs, the deposit of fuel lacquers on valves is caused by
    A. high operating temperatures
    B. insufficient valve clearance
    C. low operating temperatures
    D. efficient combustion

    20._____

21. According to the above paragraphs, for efficient operation of the engine, valve seats must
    A. have sufficient clearance
    B. be true and unpitted
    C. operate at low temperatures
    D. be adjusted regularly

    21._____

22. According to the above paragraphs, a loss of compression is due to insufficient clearance between the exhaust valve stem and the
    A. rocker arm          B. valve seat
    C. valve seat inserts  D. valve guides

    22._____

Questions 23-25.

DIRECTIONS: Questions 23 through 25 are to be answered SOLELY on the basis of the following excerpt:

A SPECIFICATION FOR ELECTRIC WORK FOR THE CITY

Breakers shall be equipped with magnetic blowout coils...Handles of breakers shall be trip-free...Breakers shall be designed to carry 100% of trip rating continuously; to have inverse time delay tripping above 100% of trip rating...

23. According to the above paragraph, the breaker shall have provision for
    A. resetting           B. arc quenching
    C. adjusting trip time D. adjusting trip rating

    23._____

24. According to the above paragraph, the breaker
    A. shall trip easily at exactly 100% of trip rating
    B. shall trip instantly at a little more than 100% of trip rating
    C. should be constructed so that it shall not be possible to prevent it from opening on overload or short circuit by holding the handle in the ON position
    D. shall not trip prematurely at 100% of trip rating

    24._____

25. According to the above paragraph, the breaker shall trip
    A. instantaneously as soon as 100% of trip rating is reached
    B. instantaneously as soon as 100% of trip rating is exceeded
    C. more quickly the greater the current, once 100% of trip rating is exceeded
    D. after a predetermined fixed time lapse, once 100% of trip rating is reached

25._____

## KEY (CORRECT ANSWERS)

| | | | |
|---|---|---|---|
| 1. | C | 11. | B |
| 2. | B | 12. | B |
| 3. | D | 13. | C |
| 4. | A | 14. | D |
| 5. | D | 15. | D |
| 6. | A | 16. | A |
| 7. | D | 17. | C |
| 8. | D | 18. | B |
| 9. | C | 19. | C |
| 10. | B | 20. | C |

21. B
22. A
23. B
24. C
25. C

# TEST 2

DIRECTIONS: Each question or incomplete statement is followed by several suggested answers or completions. Select the one that BEST answers the question or completes the statement. *PRINT THE LETTER OF THE CORRECT ANSWER IN THE SPACE AT THE RIGHT.*

Questions 1-4.

DIRECTIONS: Questions 1 through 4 are to be answered SOLELY on the basis of the following paragraph.

    A low pressure hot water boiler shall include a relief valve or valves of a capacity such that with the heat generating equipment operating at maximum, the pressure cannot rise more than 20 percent above the maximum allowable working pressure (set pressure) if that is 30 p.s.i. gage or less, nor more than 10 percent if it is more than 30 p.s.i. gage. The difference between the set pressure and the pressure at which the valve is relieving is known as *over-pressure or accumulation*. If the steam relieving capacity in pounds per hour is calculated, it shall be determined by dividing by 1,000 the maximum BTU output at the boiler nozzle obtainable from the heat generating equipment, or by multiplying the square feet of heating surface by five.

1. In accordance with the above paragraph, the capacity of a relief valve should be computed on the basis of
   - A. size of boiler
   - B. maximum rated capacity of generating equipment
   - C. average output of the generating equipment
   - D. minimum capacity of generating equipment

    1._____

2. In accordance with the above paragraph, with a set pressure of 30 p.s.i. gage, the overpressure should not be more than _____ p.s.i.
   - A. 3    B. 6    C. 33    D. 36

    2._____

3. In accordance with the above paragraph, a relief valve should start relieving at a pressure equal to the
   - A. set pressure
   - B. over pressure
   - C. over pressure minus set pressure
   - D. set pressure plus over pressure

    3._____

4. In accordance with the above paragraph, the steam relieving capacity can be computed by
   - A. *multiplying* the maximum BTU output by 5
   - B. *dividing* the pounds of steam per hour by 1,000
   - C. *dividing* the maximum BTU output by the square feet of heating surface
   - D. *dividing* the maximum BTU output by 1,000

    4._____

Questions 5-8.

DIRECTIONS: Questions 5 through 8 are to be answered SOLELY on the basis of the following paragraph.

Air conditioning units requiring a minimum rate of flow of water in excess of one-half (1/2) gallon per minute shall be metered. Air conditioning equipment with a refrigeration unit which has a definite rate of capacity in tons or fractions thereof, the charge will be at the rate of $30 per annum per ton capacity from the date installed to the date when the supply is metered. Such units, when equipped with an approved water-conserving device, shall be charged at the rate of $4.50 per annum per ton capacity from the date installed to the date when the supply is metered.

5. A man who was in the market for air conditioning equipment was considering three different units. Unit 1 required a flow of 28 gallons of water per hour; Unit 2 required 30 gallons of water per hour; Unit 3 required 32 gallons of water per hour. The man asked the salesman which units would require the installation of a water meter. According to the above passage, the salesman SHOULD answer:
   A. All three units require meters
   B. Units 2 and 3 require meters
   C. Unit 3 only requires a meter
   D. None of the units require a meter

6. Suppose that air conditioning equipment with a refrigeration unit of 10 tons was put in operation on October 1; and in the following year on July 1, a meter was installed. According to the above passage, the charge for this period would be _____ the annual rate.
   A. twice              B. equal to
   C. three-fourths      D. one-fourth

7. The charge for air conditioning equipment which has no refrigeration unit
   A. is $30 per year
   B. is $25.50 per year
   C. is $4.50 per year
   D. cannot be determined from the above passage

8. The charge for air conditioning equipment with a seven-ton refrigeration unit equipped with an approved water-conserving device
   A. is $4.50 per year
   B. is $25.50 per year
   C. is $31.50 per year
   D. cannot be determined from the above passage

Questions 9-14.

DIRECTIONS: Questions 9 through 14 are to be answered SOLELY on the basis of the following paragraph.

The city makes unremitting efforts to keep the water free from pollution. An inspectional force under a sanitary expert is engaged in patrolling the watersheds to see that the department's sanitary regulations are observed. Samples taken daily from various points in the water supply system are examined and analyzed at the three laboratories maintained by the department. All water before delivery to the distribution mains is treated with chlorine to destroy bacteria. In addition, some water is aerated to free it from gases and, in some cases, from microscopic organisms. Generally, microscopic organisms which develop in the reservoirs and at times impart an unpleasant taste and odor to the water, though in no sense harmful to health, are destroyed by treatment with copper sulfate and by chlorine dosage. None of the supplies is filtered, but the quality of the water supplied by the city is excellent for all purposes, and it is clear and wholesome.

9. According to the above paragraph, microscopic organisms are removed from the water supplied to the city by means of
    A. chlorine alone
    B. chlorine, aeration, and filtration
    C. chlorine, aeration, filtration, and sampling
    D. copper sulfate, chlorine, and aeration

9._____

10. Microscopic organisms in the water supply GENERALLY are
    A. a health menace      B. impossible to detect
    C. not harmful to health      D. not destroyed in the water

10._____

11. The MAIN function of the inspectional force, as described in the above paragraph, is to
    A. take samples of water for analysis
    B. enforce sanitary regulations
    C. add chlorine to the water supply
    D. inspect water-use meters

11._____

12. According to the above paragraph, chlorine is added to water before entering the
    A. watersheds      B. reservoirs
    C. distribution mains      D. run-off areas

12._____

13. Of the following suggested headings or titles for the above paragraph, the one that BEST tells what the paragraph is about is
    A. QUALITY OF WATER      B. CHLORINATION OF WATER
    C. TESTING OF WATER      D. BACTERIA IN WATER

13._____

14. The MOST likely reason for taking samples of water for examination and analysis from various points in the water supply system is:
    A. The testing points are convenient to the department's laboratories
    B. Water from one part of the system may be made undrinkable by a local condition
    C. The samples can be distributed equally among the three laboratories
    D. The hardness or softness of water varies from place to place

14._____

Questions 15-17.

DIRECTIONS:      Questions 15 through 17 are to be answered SOLELY on the basis of the following paragraph.

A building measuring 200' x 100' at the street is set back 20' on all sides at the 15th floor, and an additional 10' on all sides at the 30th floor. The building is 35 stories high.

15. The floor area of the 16th floor is MOST NEARLY _____ sq. ft.      15._____
    A. 20,000    B. 14,400    C. 9,600    D. 7,500

16. The floor area of the 35th floor is MOST NEARLY _____ sq. ft.      16._____
    A. 20,000    B. 13,900    C. 7,500    D. 5,600

17. The floor area of the 16th floor, compared to the floor area of the 2nd floor, is    17._____
    MOST NEARLY _____ as much.
    A. three-fourths (3/4)      B. two-thirds (2/3)
    C. one-half (1/2)           D. four-tenths (4/10)

Question 18.

DIRECTIONS:   Question 18 is to be answered SOLELY on the basis of the following paragraph.

Experience has shown that, in general, a result of the installation of meters on services not previously metered is to reduce the amount of water consumed, but is not necessarily to reduce the peak load on plumbing systems. The permissible head loss through meters at their rated maximum flow is 20 p.s.i. The installation of a meter may therefore appreciably lower the pressures available in fixtures on a plumbing system.

18. According to the above paragraph, a water meter may      18._____
    A. limit the flow in the plumbing system of 20 p.s.i.
    B. reduce the peak load on the plumbing system
    C. increase the overall amount of water consumed
    D. reduce the pressure in the plumbing system

Question 19.

DIRECTIONS:   Question 19 is to be answered SOLELY on the basis of the following paragraph.

Spring comes without trumpets to a city. The asphalt is a wilderness that does not quicken overnight; winds blow gritty with cinders instead of merry with the smells of earth and fertilizer. Women wear their gardens on their hats. But spring is a season in the city, and it has its own harbingers, constant as daffodils. Shop windows change their colors, people walk more slowly on the streets, what one can see of the sky has a bluer tone. Pulitzer prizes awake and sing and matinee tickets go-a-begging. But gayer than any of these are the carousels, which are already in sheltered places, beginning to turn with the sound of springtime itself. They are the earliest and the truest and the oldest of all the urban signs.

19. In the passage above, the word *harbingers* means      19._____
    A. storms    B. truths    C. virtues    D. forerunners

Questions 20-22.

DIRECTIONS:   Questions 20 through 22 are to be answered SOLELY on the basis of the following paragraph.

Gas heaters include manually operated, automatic, and instantaneous heaters. Some heaters are equipped with a thermostat which controls the fuel supply so that when the water falls below a predetermined temperature, the fuel is automatically turned on. In some types, the hot-water storage tank is well-insulated to economize the use of fuel. Instantaneous heaters are arranged so that the opening of a faucet on the hot-water pipe will increase the flow of fuel, which is ignited by a continuously burning pilot light to heat the water to from 120° to 130°F. The possibility that the pilot light will die out offers a source of danger in the use of automatic appliances which depend on a pilot light. Gas and oil heaters are dangerous, and they should be designed to prevent the accumulation, in a confined space within the heater, of a large volume of an explosive mixture.

20. According to the above passage, the opening of a hot-water faucet on a hot-water pipe connected to an instantaneous hot-water heater will the pilot light.
    A. *increase* the temperature of
    B. *increase* the flow of fuel to
    C. *decrease* the flow of fuel to
    D. *have a marked effect* on

21. According to the above passage, the fuel is automatically turned on in a heater equipped with a thermostat whenever
    A. the water temperature drops below 120°F
    B. the pilot light is lit
    C. the water temperature drops below some predetermined temperature
    D. a hot water supply is opened

22. According to the above passage, some hot-water storage tanks are well-insulated to
    A. accelerate the burning of the fuel
    B. maintain the water temperature between 120° and 130°F
    C. prevent the pilot light from being extinguished
    D. minimize the expenditure of fuel

Question 23.

DIRECTIONS: Question 23 is to be answered SOLELY on the basis of the following paragraph.

Breakage of the piston under high-speed operation has been the commonest fault of disc piston meters. Various techniques are adopted to prevent this, such as *throttling* the meter, cutting away the edge of the piston, or reinforcing it, but these are simply makeshifts.

23. As used in the above paragraph, the word *throttling* means MOST NEARLY
    A. enlarging          B. choking
    C. harnessing         D. dismantling

Questions 24-25.

DIRECTIONS: Questions 24 and 25 are to be answered SOLELY on the basis of the following paragraph.

One of the most common and objectionable difficulties occurring in a drainage system is trap seal loss. This failure can be attributed directly to inadequate ventilation of the trap and the subsequent negative and positive pressures which occur. A trap seal may be lost either by siphonage and/or back pressure. Loss of the trap seal by siphonage is the result of a negative pressure in the drainage system. The seal content of the trap is forced by siphonage into the waste piping of the drainage system through exertion of atmospheric pressure on the fixture side of the trap seal.

24. According to the above paragraph, a positive pressure is a direct result of     24._____
    A. siphonage
    B. unbalanced trap seal
    C. poor ventilation
    D. atmospheric pressure

25. According to the above paragraph, the water in the trap is forced into the drain pipe by     25._____
    A. atmospheric pressure
    B. back pressure
    C. negative pressure
    D. back pressure on fixture side of seal

## KEY (CORRECT ANSWERS)

| | | | | |
|---|---|---|---|---|
| 1. | B | | 11. | B |
| 2. | B | | 12. | C |
| 3. | D | | 13. | A |
| 4. | D | | 14. | B |
| 5. | C | | 15. | C |
| 6. | C | | 16. | D |
| 7. | D | | 17. | C |
| 8. | C | | 18. | D |
| 9. | D | | 19. | B |
| 10. | C | | 20. | B |

21. C
22. D
23. B
24. C
25. A

# ARITHMETICAL REASONING

## EXAMINATION SECTION
## TEST 1

DIRECTIONS: Each question or incomplete statement is followed by several suggested answers or completions. Select the one that BEST answers the question or completes the statement. *PRINT THE LETTER OF THE CORRECT ANSWER IN THE SPACE AT THE RIGHT.*

1. Assume that a certain state set aside 40% of the state gasoline tax for use by its cities in solving traffic problems. This year, there were 800,000,000 gallons of gasoline used in that state, and the tax was 12 cents per gallon.
   The amount which the cities received as their share this year was

   A. $3,840,000     B. $9,600,000
   C. $38,400,000     D. $96,000,000

   1.___

2. Suppose that a radio motor patrol car costs the municipality $11,075 less a discount of 15%. After five years, it is sold at public auction for $1,750.
   The annual cost of the car to the municipality, excluding other costs, was *most nearly*

   A. $1,500  B. $1,750  C. $2,000  D. $2,250

   2.___

3. A police car on a special assignment made a round trip to another city 186 miles away. For the entire trip, it used 24.8 gallons of gasoline, costing $3.70 a gallon.
   The cost for gasoline per mile was *most nearly*

   A. $.09  B. $.18  C. $.24  D. $.31

   3.___

4. The city has been testing various types of gasoline for economy and efficiency. It has been found that a police radio patrol car can travel 18 miles on a gallon of gasoline Brand A costing $4.50 a gallon and 15 miles on a gallon of gasoline Brand B costing $3.96 a gallon.
   For a trip of 900 miles, Brand B will cost _____ Brand A.

   A. $12.60 more than    B. $12.60 less than
   C. $126.00 more than    D. the same as

   4.___

5. A Police Department helicopter has been flying for 3 hours at an average speed of 40 miles per hour in search of an overturned boat. The helicopter started out with 210 gallons of fuel, used an average of 60 gallons of fuel per hour, and is now twenty miles from the airport.
   The MAXIMUM amount of time that the pilot can spare in his search before returning to the airport is

   A. 1 hour  B. 1 1/2 hours  C. 2 hours  D. no more time

   5.___

6. There were 25% more arrests for shoplifting in a congested business area in 2004 than in 2006, and 10% less in 2006 than in 2002.
   If the number of such arrests in 2002 was 150, then the number of such arrests in 2004 was *most nearly*

   A. 160  B. 170  C. 180  D. 205

   6.___

7. The cost of operating 20 radio patrol cars assigned to a certain district was carefully checked during the past year. The cost of running 4 of the cars was $525 each, the cost of running 5 of the cars was $750 each, the cost of running 7 of the cars was $975 each, and the remainder cost $1,125 each to run.
   The AVERAGE operating cost per car was *most nearly*

   A. $820   B. $840   C. $860   D. $880

   7._____

8. A suspect arrested in New Jersey is being turned over by New Jersey authorities to two Nassau County police officers for a crime committed in Nassau County. The Nassau County, N.Y. officers receive their prisoner at a point 18 1/2 miles from their precinct station house, and travel directly toward their destination at an average speed of 40 miles an hour, except for a delay of 10 minutes at one point because of a traffic tie-up. The time it should take the officers to reach their destination is *most nearly* _____ minutes.

   A. 18   B. 22   C. 32   D. 38

   8._____

9. A parking lot is to be set up near a new baseball stadium with provision for 3,750 cars. Each car requires 160 square feet of parking space; also, additional space equal to 30% of car space requirements is needed for driveways. Four sites for the lot are being considered. Site A is 1,000 feet long and 800 feet wide. Site B is 900 feet long and 875 feet wide. Site C is 800 feet long and 925 feet wide. Site D is 950 feet long and 850 feet wide. On the basis of the above information, the SMALLEST site which will provide sufficient space is Site

   A. A   B. B   C. C   D. D

   9._____

10. As a result of a series of robberies of small jewelry establishments, an intensified check of 364 pawn shops has been ordered. Four detectives have been assigned to this detail. At the end of 3 days of 7 hours each, they have checked 168 pawn shops. In order to speed up the investigation, three more detectives are assigned at this point.
    If they worked at the same rate, the number of ADDITIONAL 7-hour days it would take to complete the job is *most nearly* _____ days.

    A. 2   B. 4   C. 6   D. 8

    10._____

## KEY (CORRECT ANSWERS)

1. C
2. A
3. C
4. A
5. D

6. B
7. C
8. D
9. B
10. A

# SOLUTIONS TO PROBLEMS

1. ANSWER: C.
   800,000,000 × .12 = $96,000,000
   $96,000,000 × .40 = $38,400,000

2. ANSWER: A. $1,500

   $11,075
   × .15
   ―――――
   55375
   11075
   ―――――
   $1661.25 (discount)

   $11075 - $1661.25 = $9413.75 (original cost of car)
   $9413.75 - $1750 = $7663.75 (cost of car after 5 years)
   $7663.75 ÷ 5 = $1532.75 (annual cost of car)

3. ANSWER: C. $.24
   24.8 × $3.70 = $91.76 (total cost of gasoline)
   186 × 2 = 372 miles (total distance round trip)
   ∴ $91.76 ÷ 372 = $.24 (cost for gasoline per mile)

4. ANSWER: A. $12.60 more than Brand A
   Brand A: 900 ÷ 18 × 4.50 = $225.00
   Brand B: 900 ÷ 15 × 3.96 = $237.60
   ∴ Brand B will cost $12.60 more than Brand A

5. ANSWER: D. no more time
   Helicopter has already used up 180 gallons of the 210 gallons
   (3 hours at 60 gallons of fuel per hour)
   Since its average speed is 40 m.p.h., it will take one-half hour
   to complete the 20 miles to the airport.
   In 1/2 hour, it will use up another 30 gallons of fuel or the
   remainder of the 210 gallons.
   Therefore, the pilot can spare no more time.

6. ANSWER: B. 170
   2002: 150
   2006: 150 - 15 (10% of 150) = 135
   2004: 135 + 1/4 × 135 (25% more than in 2006)
   135 + 33 3/4 = 168 3/4

4 (#1)

7. ANSWER: C. $860

    4 at $525 =                $2100
    5 at $750 =                3750
    7 at $975 =                6825
    4 (20 - 16 = 4,
    remainder) at $1125   =   4500
                                  $17,175 (total operating cost)

$17,175 (total operating cost)
$17,175 ÷ 20 = average operating cost per car
               = $858.75

8. ANSWER: D. 38 minutes
Average speed of 40 miles an hour   = 2/3 mile per minute
                                                (40 mph 60 min.)

Distance ÷ Rate                    = Time
18 1/2 (miles) ÷ 2/3 (mile per minute = 37/2 ÷ 2/3
                                      = 37/2 x 3/2 = 111/4 = 27 3/4 minutes

27 3/4 + 10 (delay) = 37 3/4 minutes

9. ANSWER: B. Site B

3750 x 160 =        600,000 sq. ft. (parking space)
600,000 x .30 =    180,000 sq. ft. (driveways)
                      780,000 sq. ft. (total needed for parking lot)

Site A:      1000     x     800    =    800,000    sq. ft.
Site B:      900      x     875    =    787,500    sq. ft.
Site C:      800      x     925    =    740,000    sq. ft.
Site D:      950      x     850    =    807,500    sq. ft.

10. ANSWER: A. 2 days

$168 ÷ 3 (days) = 56 checked per day (by 4 detectives)
4 detectives do 1 day's work = 56
3 detectives added do 1 3/4 day's work = 56 x 7/4 = 98 (in one day by all seven working together)
  364 - 168 = 196 (remain to be checked)
  ∴ 196 ÷ 98 = 2 days

# TEST 2

DIRECTIONS: Each question or incomplete statement is followed by several suggested answers or completions. Select the one that BEST answers the question or completes the statement. *PRINT THE LETTER OF THE CORRECT ANSWER IN THE SPACE AT THE RIGHT.*

1. During the first nine months of this year, an officer spent an average of $270 a month. In October and November, he spent an average of $315 a month. In December, he spent $385.
   His average monthly spending during the year was *most nearly*

   A. $254    B. $287    C. $323    D. $3,000

2. In 2005, there were 8,270 arrests in a certain city. In 2006, the number of arrests increased by 12 1/2%. In 2007, the number of arrests decreased 5% from the 2006 figures. The number of arrests in 2007 was *most nearly*

   A. 8,840    B. 9,770    C. 6,870    D. 7,600

3. Assume that parking space is to be provided for 25% of the tenants in a new housing development. The project will have five 6-story buildings, having seven tenants on each floor, and eight 11-story buildings, having eight tenants on each floor.
   The number of parking spaces needed is *most nearly*

   A. 215    B. 230    C. 700    D. 895

4. A stolen vehicle traveling at 60 miles per hour passes by a police car which is standing still with the engine running. The police car immediately starts out in pursuit, and one minute later, having covered a distance of half a mile, it reaches a speed of 90 miles per hour and continues at this speed.
   After the stolen vehicle passes the police car, the police car will overtake it in _____ minute(s).

   A. 1    B. 1 1/2    C. 2    D. 3

5. A police officer found his 42-hour work week was divided as follows: 1/6 of his time in investigating incidents on his patrol post; 1/2 of his time patrolling his post; and 1/8 of his time in special traffic duty. The rest of his time was devoted to assignments at precinct headquarters. The percentage of his work week which was spent at precinct headquarters is *most nearly*

   A. 10%    B. 15%    C. 20%    D. 25%

6. In 2006, the Department of Sanitation towed away 8,430 cars which were abandoned or illegally parked on city streets. If the value of the abandoned cars was $1,038,200 and that of the illegally parked cars was $6,234,800, then the AVERAGE value of one of the towed-away cars was *most nearly*

   A. $400    B. $720    C. $860    D. $1,100

7. Two percent of all school children are problem children. Some 80% of these problem children become delinquents, and about 80% of the delinquent children become criminals. If the school population is 1,000,000 children, the number of this group who will eventually become criminals, according to this analysis, is

   A. 12,800    B. 1,280    C. 640    D. 128

8. A patrol car began a trip with 12 gallons of gasoline in the tank and ended with 74 gallons. The car travelled 17.3 miles for each gallon of gasoline. During the trip, gasoline was bought for $20.88 at $2.61 per gallon.
The TOTAL NUMBER of miles travelled during this trip was, *most nearly*

   A.  79  B.  196  C.  216  D.  229

8.____

9. A radio motor patrol car finds it necessary to travel at 90 miles per hour for a period of 1 minute and 40 seconds. The NUMBER of miles which the car travels during this period is

   A.  1 5/6  B.  2  C.  2 1/2  D.  3 3/4

9.____

10. A radio motor patrol car has to travel a distance of 15 miles in an emergency. If it does the first two-thirds of the distance at 40 m.p.h. and the last third at 60 m.p.h., the TOTAL NUMBER of minutes required for the entire run is *most nearly*

   A.  15  B.  20  C.  22 1/2  D.  25

10.____

## KEY (CORRECT AMSWERS)

| | | | |
|---|---|---|---|
| 1. | B | 6. | C |
| 2. | A | 7. | A |
| 3. | B | 8. | C |
| 4. | C | 9. | C |
| 5. | C | 10. | B |

# SOLUTIONS TO PROBLEMS

1. ANSWER: B. $287

   First 9 months at $270 = $ 2430
   October     at   315 =    315
   November    at   315 =    315
   December    at   385 =    385
                           $ 3445 (total for year)

   ∴ $3445 12 = $287.08 (average monthly spending during the year)

2. ANSWER: A. 8840
   <u>Given</u>   2005   8270
            2006   + 12 1/2% of 2005
            2007   - 5% of 2006
   <u>Solving</u> 12 1/2% = 1/8; 1/8 x 8270       = 1035
            2005 = 1035 + 8270              = 9305
            .05 x 9305 = 465.25
            2006 = 9305 - 465.25            = 8839.75

3. ANSWER: B. 230
   5 six-story buildings at 7 tenants each floor = 5x6x7 = 210
   8 eleven-story buildings at 8 tenants each floor = 8 x 11 x 8 = 704
   210 + 704 = 914 (total number of tenants)
   ∴ 1/2 (25%) x 914 = 228.5 (number of parking spaces needed)

4. ANSWER: C. 2 minutes

   <u>Given</u>       Stolen car:    travels 60 miles per hour; will have travelled 1 mile in 1 minute (60(miles) ÷ 60 (minutes)

                  Police car:    travels 1/2 mile in first minute; thereafter, travels at rate of 1 1/2 miles per minute (90 miles per hour (rate) ÷ 60 (minutes)

   Solution       Stolen car:    in 3 minutes will have travelled 3 miles (3x1 mph)

                  Police car:    in first minute covers distance of 1/2 mile; in next two minutes will have covered an additional 3 miles (2 x 1 1/2 miles)

5. ANSWER: C. 20%

   $42 \times 1/6 = 7$ hrs.
   $42 \times 1/2 = 21$ hrs.
   $42 \times 1/8 = 5\frac{1}{4}$ hrs.
   $\phantom{42 \times 1/8 = } 33\frac{1}{4}$ hrs.

   42 - 33 1/4 = 8 3/4 hrs. (time spent at precinct headquarters)

   ∴ 8 3/4 ÷ 42 = 35/4 ÷ 42 = 35/4 x 1/42 = 35/168 = .20+

6. ANSWER: C. $860
   $1,038,200 + $6,234,800 = $7,273,000
   $7,273,000 ÷ 8430 = $862+

7. ANSWER: A. 12,800
   | $1,000,000 | x | .02 | = | 20,000 | (number of problem children) |
   | 20,000 | x | .80 | = | 16,000 | (number of delinquent children) |
   | 16,000 | x | .80 | = | 12,800 | (number of criminals) |

8. ANSWER: C. 216
   Patrol car began trip with 12 gallons
   Added to tank, while on trip, 8 gallons ($20.88 ÷ $2.61(per gallon) Therefore, the patrol car had a total of 20 gallons for the trip. If 7 1/2 gallons remained at end of trip, therefore
   ∴ 12 1/2 gallons had been used up on the trip.
   12 1/2 (gallons) x 17.3 (miles for each gallon) = total number of miles travelled = 216.25

9. ANSWER: C. 2 1/2
   Rate of 90 = 1 1/2 miles per minute (90 (miles) 4 ÷ 60 (minutes)
   1 minute and 40 seconds = 1 2/3 minutes
   ∴ 1 1/2 x 1 2/3 = 3/2 x 5/3 = 15/6 = 2 1/2

10. ANSWER: B. 20
    40 m.p.h. = 2/3 mile per minute (40 (miles) 60 (minutes)
    ∴ 2/3 x 15 ÷ 2/3 = 10 ÷ 2/3 = 10 x 3/2 = 15 minutes
    60 m.p.h. = 1 mile per minute (60 (miles) ÷ 60 (minutes)
    ∴ 1/3 x 15 1 = 5 minutes
    15 minutes + 5 minutes = 20 minutes

# TEST 3

DIRECTIONS: Each question or incomplete statement is followed by several suggested answers or completions. Select the one that BEST answers the question or completes the statement. *PRINT THE LETTER OF THE CORRECT ANSWER IN THE SPACE AT THE RIGHT.*

1. A patrol car had 11 1/2 gallons of gasoline at the beginning of a trip of 196 miles and 5 1/2 gallons at the end of the trip. During the trip, gasoline was bought for $19.53 at a cost of $3.90 per gallon.
   The AVERAGE number of miles driven per gallon of gasoline is *most nearly*

   A. 14  B. 14.5  C. 18  D. 25.5

   1.____

2. There are 15 police cadets assigned to a certain operation. One-third earn $21,000 per year, three earn $22,050 per year, one earns $24,675 per year, and the rest earn $27,905 per year.
   The AVERAGE annual salary of these policemen is *most nearly*

   A. $23,750  B. $24,000  C. $24,250  D. $24,500

   2.____

3. In 2006, the cost of patrol car maintenance and repair was $2,500 more than in 2005, representing an increase of 10%.
   The cost of patrol car maintenance and repair in 2006 was *most nearly*

   A. $2,750  B. $22,500  C. $25,000  D. $27,500

   3.____

4. A police precinct has an assigned strength of 180 men. Of this number, 25% are not available for duty due to illness, vacations, and other reasons. Of those who are available for duty, 1/3 are assigned outside of the precinct for special emergency duty.
   The ACTUAL available strength of the precinct in terms of men immediately available for precinct duty is

   A. 45  B. 60  C. 90  D. 135

   4.____

5. Five police officers are taking target practice. The number of rounds fired by each and the percentage of perfect shots is as follows:
   Officer  R  80  rounds fired;  30%  perfect shots
            S  70  rounds fired;  40%  perfect shots
            T  75  rounds fired;  60%  perfect shots
            U  92  rounds fired;  25%  perfect shots
            V  96  rounds fired;  66 2/3% perfect shots
   The AVERAGE number of perfect shots fired by them is *most nearly*

   A. 30  B. 36  C. 42  D. 80

   5.____

6. A dozen five-gallon cans of paint weigh 492 pounds. Each can, when empty, weighs 3 pounds.
   The weight of one gallon of paint is *most nearly* _____ lbs.

   A. 5  B. 6 1/2  C. 7 1/2  D. 8

   6.____

111

7. A parade is marching up an average of 60 city blocks. A sample count of the number of people watching the parade on one side of the street in the block is taken, first, in a block near the end of the parade, and then in a block at the middle; the former count is 4000, the latter is 6000. If the average for the entire parade is assumed to be the average of the two samples, then the ESTIMATED number of persons watching the entire parade is *most nearly*

    A. 240,000    B. 300,000    C. 480,000    D. 600,000

8. Suppose that the revenue from parking meters in the city was 5% greater in 2005 than in 2004, and 2% less in 2006 than in 2005.
If the revenue in 2004 was $1,500,000, then the revenue in 2006 was

    A. $1,541,500    B. $1,542,000
    C. $1,542,500    D. $1,543,000

9. A radio motor patrol car completes a ten-mile trip in twenty minutes.
If it does one-half the distance at a speed of twenty miles an hour, its speed, in miles per hour, for the remainder of the distance must be

    A. 30    B. 40    C. 50    D. 60

10. A public beach has two parking areas. Their capacities are in the ratio of two to one and, on a certain day, are filled to 60% and 40% of capacity, respectively. The entire parking facilities of the beach on that day are *most nearly* _____ filled.

    A. 38%    B. 43%    C. 48%    D. 53%

## KEY (CORRECT ANSWERS)

1. C
2. C
3. D
4. C
5. B

6. C
7. D
8. D
9. D
10. D

# SOLUTIONS TO PROBLEMS

1. ANSWER: C. 18
   Gasoline:   At beginning of trip -11 1/2 gallons
   Bought gasoline for $19.53 at $3.90 per gallon; or
   19.53 ÷ 3.90 = 5 gal.
   11 1/2 + 5 = 16 1/2 gallons (total)
   16 1/2 - 51/2 = 11 (number of gallons used up on the trip)
   ∴ 196 ÷ 11 = 17.8 = 18 (average number of miles
   driven per gallon.

2. ANSWER: C.   $24,250
   5 (1/3 x 15)   at   $21,000   =   $105,000
   3              at    22,050   =     66,150
   1              at    24,675   =     24,675
   6 (rest)       at    27,905   =    167,430
   ∴ $363,255 ÷ 15 = $24,250+ (average annual salary)

3. ANSWER: D. $27,500
   In 2006, the cost of $2,500 = an increase of 10% over 2005.
   Therefore, the cost of maintenance and repair in 2005 = $25,000 ($2,500 is 10% of $25,000).
   Hence, the cost in 2006 was $25,000 + $2,500 = $27,500.

4. ANSWER: C. 90
   Not available for duty: 1/4 (25%) x 180 = 45
   Available for duty: 1/3 x 135 (180 - 45) = 45
   ∴ 45 + 45 = 90 (actual available strength of the precinct)

5. ANSWER: B. 36
   R   =   .30 x 80          =   24
   S   =   .40 x 70          =   28
   T   =   .60 x 75          =   45
   U   =   .25 x 92          =   23
   V   =   2/3(.66 2/3) x 96 =   64
                                184 (total perfect shots)
   ∴ 184 ÷ 5 = 35 4/5 (average number of perfect shots)

6. ANSWER: C. 7 1/2 lbs.
   12 x 3 = 36 pounds (weight of a dozen 5-gallon cans when empty)
   Hence, 492 - 36 = 456 lbs. (weight of the paint only in the
   dozen 5-gallon cans)
   ∴ 456 ÷ 60 (number of gallons in a dozen 5-gallon cans)
   = 7.6 lbs. (weight of one gallon of paint)

7. ANSWER: D. 600,000
   4000 + 6000 = 10,000 (total for one side of the street)
   10,000 ÷ 2 = 5,000 (average for one side of the street)
   5,000 x 2 = 10,000 (average for both sides of the street)
   ∴ 60 (blocks) x 10,000 (people) = 600,000

8. ANSWER: D. $1,543,500
   2004:   $1,500,000
   2005:   $1,500,000 + .05 x $1,500,000      = $1,500,000 + $75,000 =
                                                                $1,575,000
   2006:   $1,575,000 - .02 x $1,575,000      = $1,575,000 - $31,500 =
                                                                $1,543,500

9. ANSWER: D. 60
   10 miles are completed in a total of 20 minutes. 5 miles (1/2 of 10 miles) at 20 miles an hour = 1 mile in 3 minutes or
   5 miles in 15 minutes
   ∴ the remaining 5 miles must be completed in 5 minutes, or a rate of one mile a minute, which is equal to a speed of 60 miles per hour

10. ANSWER: D. 53% filled
    If the capacities of the parking areas are in the ratio of 2:1, then one has 2/3 of the total capacity, and the other has 1/3.
    Then, 2/3 x .60 = .40
          1/3 x .40 = .13 1/3
                     .53 1/3

# BASIC FUNDAMENTALS OF LUBRICATION AND ASSOCIATED EQUIPMENT

## CONTENTS

| | | Page |
|---|---|---|
| I. | Friction | 1 |
| II. | Fluid Lubrication | 1 |
| III. | Langmuir Theory | 2 |
| IV. | Factors Affecting Lubrication | 2 |
| V. | Lubricants | 3 |
| VI. | Lubricating Oil Characteristics | 4 |
| VII. | Lubricating Systems | 5 |
| VIII. | Forced-Feed Lubrication Systems | 5 |
| IX. | Gravity-Feed Lubrication Systems | 10 |
| X. | Grease Lubrication Systems | 11 |
| XI. | Ball and Roller Bearing Lubrication | 11 |
| XII. | Lube Oil Purification | 12 |
| XIII. | Types of Centrifugal Purifiers | 13 |
| XIV. | General Notes on Purifier Operations | 15 |

# BASIC FUNDAMENTALS OF LUBRICATION AND ASSOCIATED EQUIPMENT

Lubrication reduces friction between moving parts by substituting fluid friction for solid friction. Without lubrication, it is difficult to move a hundred-pound weight across a rough surface; with lubrication, and with proper attention to the design of bearing surfaces, it is possible to move a million-pound load with a motor that is small enough to be held in the hand. By reducing friction, lubrication reduces the amount of energy required to perform mechanical actions and also reduces the amount of energy that is dissipated as heat.

Lubrication is a matter of vital importance throughout the shipboard engineering plant. Moving surfaces must be steadily supplied with the proper kinds of lubricants. Lubricants must be maintained at specified standards of purity, and at designed pressures and temperatures in the lubrication systems. Without adequate lubrication, a good many units of shipboard machinery would quite literally grind to a screeching halt.

The lubrication requirements of shipboard machinery are met in various ways, depending upon the nature of the machinery. This chapter deals with the basic principles of lubrication, the lubricants used aboard ship, the lubrication systems installed for many shipboard units, and the devices used to maintain lubricating oils in the required condition of purity.

## I. FRICTION

The friction that exists between a body at rest and the surface upon which it rests is called static friction. The friction that exists between moving bodies (or between one moving body and a stationary surface) is called kinetic friction. Static friction, which must be overcome to put any body in motion, is greater than kinetic friction, which must be overcome to keep the body in motion.

There are three types of kinetic friction: sliding friction, rolling friction, and fluid friction. Sliding friction exists when the surface of one solid body is moved across the surface of another solid body. Rolling friction exists when a curved body such as a cylinder or a sphere rolls upon a flat or curved surface. Fluid friction is the resistance to motion exhibited by a fluid.

Fluid friction exists because of the cohesion between particles of the fluid and the adhesion of fluid particles to the object or medium which is tending to move the fluid. If a paddle is used to stir a fluid, for example, the cohesive forces between the molecules of the fluid tend to hold the molecules together and thus prevent motion of the fluid. At the same time, the adhesive forces of the molecules of the fluid cause the fluid to adhere to the paddle and thus create friction between the paddle and the fluid. Cohesion is the molecular attraction between particles that tends to hold a substance or a body together; adhesion is the molecular attraction between particles that tends to cause unlike surfaces to stick together. From the point of view of lubrication, adhesion is the property of a lubricant that causes it to stick (or adhere) to the parts being lubricated; cohesion is the property which holds the lubricant together and enables it to resist breakdown under pressure.

Cohesion and adhesion are possessed by different materials in widely varying degrees. In general, solid bodies are highly cohesive but only slightly adhesive. Most fluids are quite highly adhesive but only slightly cohesive; however, the adhesive and cohesive properties of fluids vary considerably.

## II. FLUID LUBRICATION

Fluid lubrication is based on the actual separation of surfaces so that no metal-to-metal contact occurs. As long as the lubricant film remains unbroken, sliding friction and rolling friction are replaced by fluid friction.

In any process involving friction, some power is consumed and some heat is produced. Overcoming sliding friction consumes the greatest amount of power and produces the greatest amount of heat. Overcoming rolling friction consumes less power and produces less heat. Overcoming fluid friction consumes the least power and produces the least amount of heat.

## III. LANGMUIR THEORY

A presently accepted theory of lubrication is based on the Langmuir theory of the action of fluid films of oil between two surfaces, one or both of which are in motion. Theoretically, there are three or more layers or films of oil existing between two lubricated bearing surfaces. Two of the films are boundary films (indicated as I and V in part A of fig. 1), one of which clings to the surface of the rotating journal and one of which clings to the stationary lining of the bearing. Between these two boundary films are one or more fluid films (indicated as II, III, and IV in part A of fig. 1). The number of fluid films shown in the illustration is arbitrarily selected for purposes of explanation.

When the rotating journal is set in motion (part B of fig. 1), the relationship of the journal to the bearing lining is such that a wedge of oil is formed. The oil films II, III, and IV begin to slide between the two boundary films, thus continuously preventing contact between the two metal surfaces. The principle is again illustrated in part C of figure 1, where the position of the oil wedge W is shown with respect to the position of the journal as it starts and continues in motion.

The views shown in part C of figure 1 represent a journal or shaft rotating in a solid bearing. The clearances are exaggerated in the drawing in order to illustrate the formation of the oil film. The shaded portion represents the clearance filled with oil. The film is in the process of being squeezed out while the journal is at rest, as shown in the stationary view. As the journal slowly starts to turn and the speed increases, oil adhering to the surfaces of the journal is carried into the film, increasing the film thickness and tending to lift the journal as shown in the starting view. As the speed increases, the journal takes the position shown in the running view. Changes in temperature,

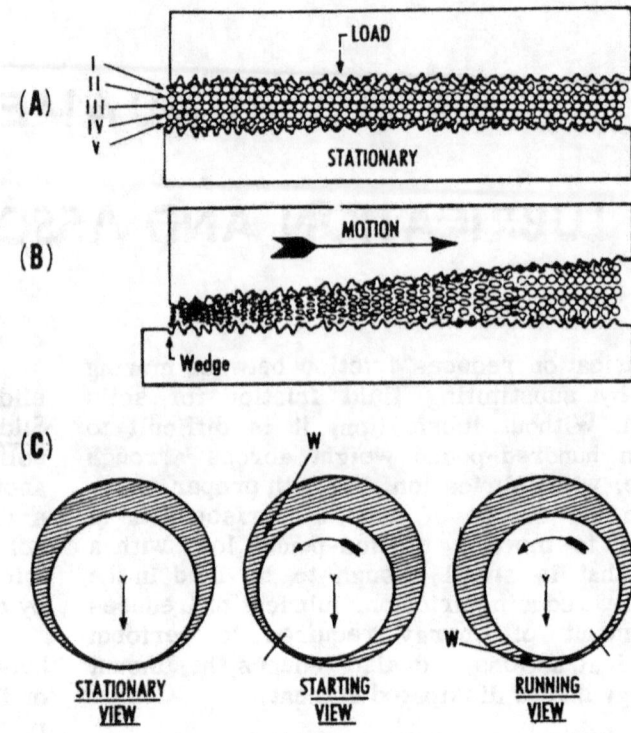

Figure 1.—Oil film lubrication. (A) Stationary position, showing several oil films; (B) surface set in motion, showing principle of oil wedge; (C) principle of (A) and (B) shown in a journal bearing.

with consequent changes in oil viscosity, cause changes in the film thickness and in the position of the journal.

If conditions are correct, the two surfaces are effectively separated, except for a possible momentary contact at the time the motion is started.

## IV. FACTORS AFFECTING LUBRICATION

A number of factors determine the effectiveness of oil film lubrication, including such things as pressure, temperature, viscosity, speed, alignment, condition of the bearing surfaces, running clearances between the bearing surfaces, starting torque, and the nature of purity of the lubricant. Many of these factors are interrelated and interdependent. For example, the viscosity of any given oil is affected by temperature and the temperature is affected by

# LUBRICATION AND ASSOCIATED EQUIPMENT

running speed; hence the viscosity is partially dependent upon the running speed.

A lubricant must be able to stick to the bearing surfaces and support the load at operating speeds. More adhesiveness is required to make a lubricant adhere to bearing surfaces at high speeds than at low speeds. At low speeds, greater cohesiveness is required to keep the lubricant from being squeezed out from between the bearing surfaces.

Large clearances between bearing surfaces require high viscosity and cohesiveness in the lubricant to ensure maintenance of the lubricating oil film. The larger the clearance, the greater must be the resistance of the lubricant to being pounded out, with consequent destruction of the lubricating oil film.

High unit load on a bearing requires high viscosity of the lubricant. A lubricant subjected to high loading must be sufficiently cohesive to hold together and maintain the oil film.

## V. LUBRICANTS

Although there is growing use of synthetic lubricants, the principal source of the oils and greases used is still petroleum. By various refining processes, lubricating stocks are extracted from crude petroleum and blended into a multiplicity of products to meet all lubrication requirements. Various compounds or additives are used in some lubricants (both oils and greases) to provide specific properties required for specific applications.

### Types of Lubricating Oils

Lubricating oils approved for shipboard use are limited to those grades and types deemed essential to provide proper lubrication under all anticipated operating conditions.

For diesel engines, it is necessary to use a detergent-dispersant type of additive oil in order to keep the engines clean. In addition, these lubricating oils must be fortified with oxidation inhibitors and corrosion inhibitors to allow long periods between oil changes and to prevent corrosion of bearing materials.

For steam turbines, it is necessary to have an oil of high initial film strength. This oil is then fortified with anti-foaming additives and additives that inhibit oxidation and corrosion.

In addition, it is necessary to use extreme pressure (EP) additives to enable the oil to carry the extremely high loading to which it is subjected in the reduction gear.

For the hydraulic systems in which petroleum lubricants are used, and for general lubrication use, industry uses a viscosity series of oils reinforced with oxidation and corrosion inhibitors and anti-foam additives. The compounded oils, which are mineral oils to which such products as rape seed, tallow, or lard oil are added, are still used in deck machinery and in the few remaining steam plants that utilize reciprocating steam engines.

A great many special lubricating oils are available for a wide variety of services. These are listed in the Federal Supply Catalog. Among the more important specialty oils are those used for lubricating refrigerant compressors. These oils must have a very low pour point and be maintained with a high degree of freedom from moisture.

The principal synthetic lubricants currently in naval use are (1) a phosphate ester type of fire-resistant hydraulic fluid, used chiefly in the deck-edge elevators of carriers (CVAs); and (2) a water-base glycol hydraulic fluid used chiefly in the catapult retracting gears.

### Classification of Lubricating Oils

Industry identifies lubricating oils by symbols. Each identification number consists of four digits (and, in some cases, appended letters). The first digit indicates the class of oil according to type and use; the last three digits indicate the viscosity of the oil. The viscosity digits are actually the number of seconds required for 60 milliliters of the oil to flow through a standard orifice at a specified temperature. The symbol 3080, for example, indicates that the oil is in the 3000 series and that a 60-ml sample flows through a standard orifice in 80 seconds when the oil is at a specified temperature (210°F, in this instance). To take another example, the symbol 2135 TH indicates that the oil is in the 2000 series and that a 60-ml sample flows through a standard orifice in 135 seconds when the oil is at a specified temperature (130°F, in this case).

The letters H, T, TH, or TEP added to a basic symbol number indicate that the oil contains additives for special purposes.

# VI. LUBRICATING OIL CHARACTERISTICS

Lubricating oils used are tested for a number of characteristics, including viscosity, pour point, flash point, fire point, auto-ignition point, neutralization number, demulsibility, and precipitation number. Standard test methods are used for making all tests. The characteristics of lube oil are briefly explained in the following paragraphs.

The VISCOSITY of an oil is its tendency to resist flow or change of shape. A liquid of high viscosity flows very slowly. In variable climates automobile owners, for example, change oils in accordance with prevailing seasons because heavy oil becomes too sluggish in cold weather, and light oil becomes too fluid in hot weather. The higher the temperature of an oil, the lower its viscosity becomes; lowering the temperature increases the viscosity. The high viscosity or stiffness of the lube oil on a cold morning makes an engine difficult to start.

If an oil of a higher viscosity is used under such conditions, the increased internal friction will raise the temperature and reduce the viscosity of the oil. The viscosity must always be high enough to keep a good oil film between the moving parts—otherwise, there will be increased friction, power loss, and rapid wear on the parts. Oils are graded by their viscosities at a certain temperature—by noting the number of seconds required for a given quantity (60 milliliters) or the oil at the given temperature to flow through a standard orifice. The right grade of oil, therefore, means oil of the proper viscosity.

THE VISCOSITY INDEX of an oil is based on the slope of the temperature-viscosity curve—or on the rate of change in viscosity of a given oil with a change in temperature, with other conditions remaining unchanged. A low index figure denotes a steep slope of the curve, or a great variation of viscosity with a change in temperature; a higher index figure denotes a flatter slope, or lesser variation of viscosity with identical changes in temperatures. If you are using an oil with a high viscosity index, its viscosity or body will change less when the temperature of the engine increases.

The POUR POINT of an oil is the lowest temperature at which the oil will barely flow from a container. At a temperature below the pour point, oil congeals or solidifies. A low pour point is an essential characteristic of lube oils used in cold weather operations. (NOTE: The pour point is closely related to the viscosity of the oil. In general, an oil of high viscosity will have a higher pour point than an oil of low viscosity.)

The FLASH POINT of an oil is the temperature at which enough vapor is given off to flash when a flame or spark is present. The minimum flash points allowed for lube oils are all above 315°F, and the temperatures of the oils are always far below that under normal operating conditions.

The FIRE POINT of an oil is the temperature at which the oil will continue to burn when ignited.

The AUTO-IGNITION POINT of an oil is the temperature at which the flammable vapors given off from the oil will burn without the application of a spark or flame. For most lubricating oils, this temperature is in the range of 465°F to 815°F.

The NEUTRALIZATION NUMBER of an oil is the measure of the acid content and is defined as the number of milligrams of potassium hydroxide (KOH) required to neutralize one gram of the oil. All petroleum products deteriorate (oxidize) in the presence of air and heat; the products of this oxidation include organic acids, which, if present in sufficient concentration, have harmful effects on alloy bearings at high temperatures, galvanized surfaces, and the demulsibility of the oil with respect to fresh and sea water. This last effect, in turbine installations, may result in the formation of sludge and emulsions too stable to be broken by the means available. An increase in acidity is an indication that the lubricating oil is deteriorating.

The DEMULSIBILITY (or emulsion characteristic) of an oil is its ability to separate cleanly from any water present—an important factor in forced-feed systems. It is especially important to keep water (fresh or salt) out of oils.

The PRECIPITATION NUMBER of an oil is a measure of the amount of solids classified as asphalts or carbon residue contained in the oil. The number is reached by diluting a known amount of oil with naphtha and separating the precipitate by centrifuging—the volume of separated solids equals the precipitation number. The test is a quick means of determining the presence of foreign materials in used oils. An

# LUBRICATION AND ASSOCIATED EQUIPMENT

oil with a high precipitation number may cause trouble in an engine by leaving deposits or by plugging up valves and pumps.

## Lubricating Greases

Some lubricating greases are simple mixtures of soaps and lubricating oils. Others are more exotic liquids such as silicones and dibasic acid esters, thickened with metals or inert materials to provide adequate lubrication. Requirements for oxidation inhibition, corrosion prevention, and extreme pressure performance are met by incorporating special additives.

Lubricating greases are supplied in three grades: soft, medium, and hard. The soft greases are used for high speeds and low pressures; the medium greases are used for medium speeds and medium pressures; the hard greases are used for slow speeds and high pressures.

## Classification of Greases

Specifications have been drawn to cover the several grades of lubricating greases, the grades most common in engineroom use are as follows:

Ball and roller bearing grease
    For general use in ball and roller bearings operating at medium speeds and over a temperature range of 125°F to 200°F and for a short intermittent service at 225°F.

Extreme pressure grease
    Has antirust properties and is suitable for the lubrication of semienclosed gears, or any sliding or rolling metal surfaces where loads may be high and where the equipment may be exposed to salt spray or moisture. It is intended for use through a temperature range of 0°F to 140°F.

Graphite Grease
    Graphite grease is intended for use in compression grease cups for bearings operating at temperatures not to exceed 150°F.

| | |
|---|---|
| Grade 1 Soft | For light pressures and high speeds |
| Grade 2 Medium | For medium pressures and medium speeds |
| Grade 3 Medium Hard | For high pressures and slow speeds |

## VII. LUBRICATING SYSTEMS

Main lubricating oil systems on steam-driven ships provide lubrication for the turbine bearing and the reduction gears. The main lubricating oil system generally includes a filling and transfer system, a purifying system, and separate service systems for each propulsion plant. On most ships, each lubricating oil service system includes three positive-displacement lube oil service pumps: (1) a shaft-driven pump, (2) a turbine-driven pump, and (3) a motor-driven pump. The shaft-driven pump, attached to and driven by either the propulsion shaft or the quill shaft of the reduction gear, is used as the main lube oil service pump when the shaft is turning fast enough so that the pump can supply the required lube oil pressure. The turbine-driven pump is used while the ship is getting underway and is then used as standby at normal speeds. The motor-driven pump serves as an emergency pump standby for the other two lube oil service pumps.

Figure 2 illustrates the lube oil supply and lube oil drain piping of the service system.

## VIII. FORCED-FEED LUBRICATION SYSTEMS

The forced-feed lubricating oil systems are used for the lubrication of main engine turbines and reduction gears, turbogenerators, feed pumps and other auxiliary machinery, and in most internal-combustion engines. Each engineroom lube oil system is arranged for independent operation, and generally there is no service connection provided between enginerooms. The main engine lubricating systems include a purifier; whereas the other auxiliary systems must be periodically drained (as the crankcase of an automobile is drained) and replenished with new or purified oil.

The essential parts of a forced lubrication system are as follows:

1. Pumps for delivering the oil to the various parts of the system. If the pump is driven from the unit it serves, additional pumps are provided, where necessary, for supplying oil to the system before the unit is started, during warming up and low speed operation.

2. Oil relief valves are intended primarily to protect the system from excessive pressures that may occur because of a malfunction of an operating part.

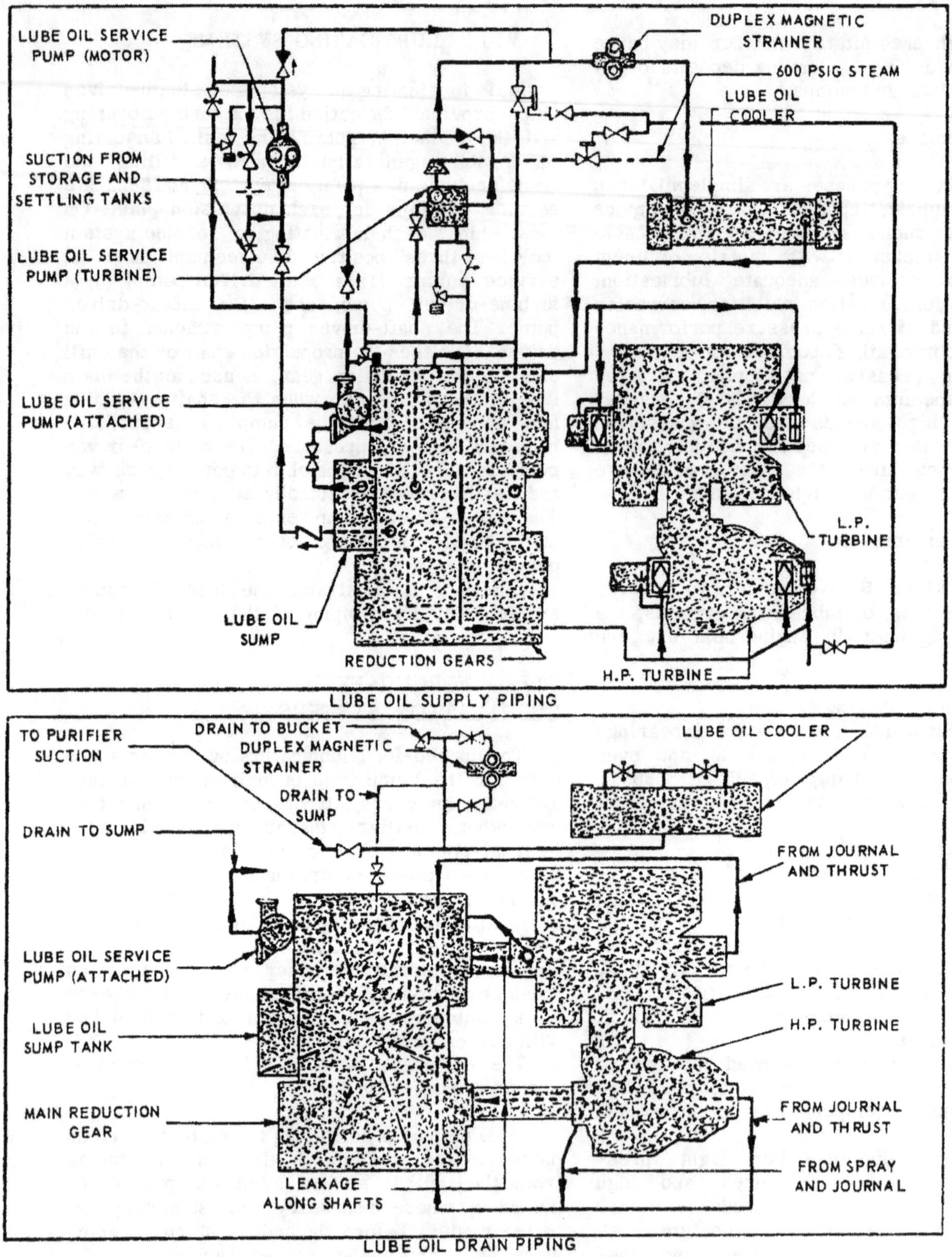

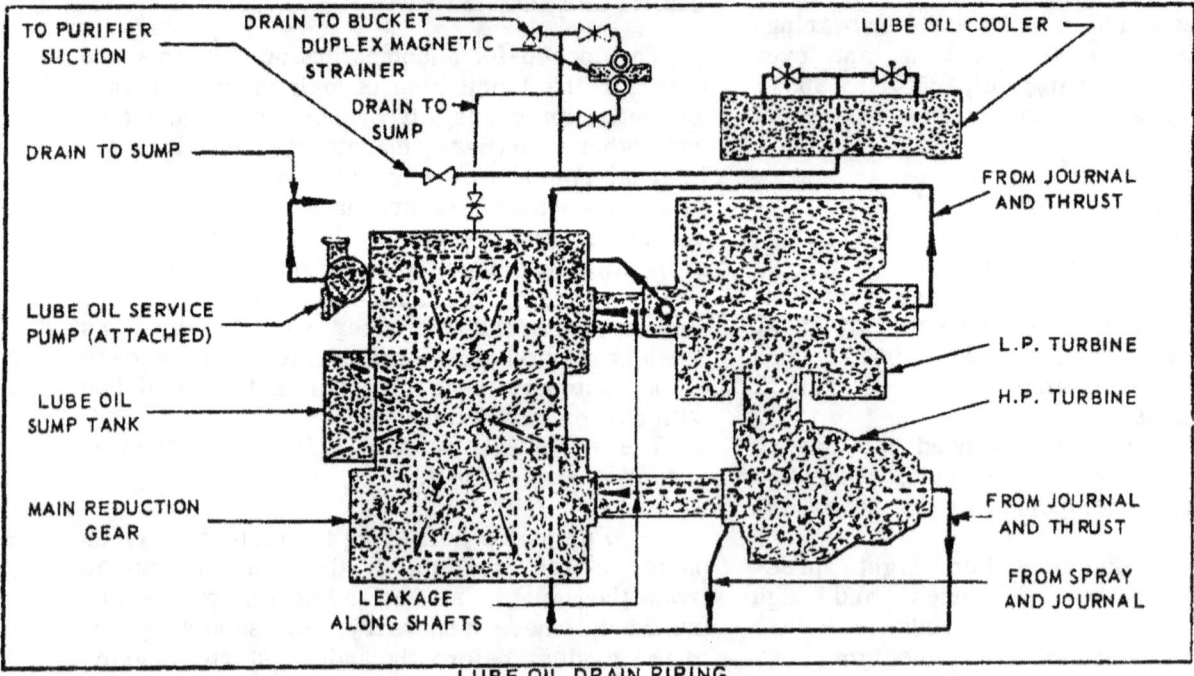

Figure 2.—Lubricating oil service system

# LUBRICATION AND ASSOCIATED EQUIPMENT

3. Oil strainers and filters for removing foreign matter from the oil before it enters the bearings and oil sprays.

4. Integral oil cooler heater, through which the oil passes on its way to the system, keeps the oil at the desired temperature.

5. Oil back pressure regulating valve to automatically control the oil pressure at the most remote bearing by bypassing all excess oil back.

6. Piping, gages, thermometers, and other instruments, used to indicate the operating conditions of the system.

7. Oil drain tanks or sump tanks to which the oil is led after having passed through the various bearings and other parts of the system.

8. Oil purifiers, which are used to remove all water and other impurities from the oil that collects in the oil on a daily basis.

9. Oil heaters, which are used to raise the temperature of the oil entering the centrifugal purifier to facilitate removal of water, and other impurities.

10. Oil-settling tanks in which the water and other impurities are removed by special treatment when they have accumulated in the oil.

A forced-feed lubrication system for a main engine and reduction gear installation is illustrated in figure 3. Three main lube oil service pumps are provided. Shaft or chain driven pumps installed and operating properly, will supply oil at designed pressure while operating at speeds specified by the manufacturer.

Lube oil standby and emergency pumps are generally provided with an automatic cut in device which starts the pumps when the lubricating oil supply line pressure falls below a certain value. The standby turbine-driven lube oil pump, controlled by a governor, assumes or shares the load when the supply from the attached pump is no longer sufficient to maintain the required pressure. If both the attached and standby pump cannot maintain the system pressure, a pressure sensing switch will then start the emergency motor-driven pump. Usually, at the point of lowest pressure in the lube oil supply line to the bearings, a pressure operated switch WARNING SIGNAL is installed. It is set to operate whenever the lube oil supply falls below a predetermined pressure, thereby giving the throttleman (or operators of other machinery) instant warning of low oil pressure.

The OIL COOLER, through which the oil passes on its way to the lubricated parts, is fitted with thermometers and a bypass (bypasses are not fitted on some new ships). Thermometers register the inlet and outlet oil temperatures; the bypass may be used to bypass the cooler in case of tube failure. Valves are also provided in the cooling water supply and discharge lines to and from the cooler to provide for varying the rate of flow of cooling water, which controls the temperature of the lube oil leaving the cooler. From the cooler, the oil passes to individual bearings through NEEDLE VALVES or, on some ships, internal fixed orifices. These valves regulate the oil flow to the individual bearings. From the bearings, the oil is drained back to the main engine sump. Oil is supplied to the teeth of the reduction gears through SPRAY NOZZLES, after which the oil drains to the main engine sump. A FLOAT GAGE on the sump indicates the oil level. As additional oil is required for the system, it is drained or pumped into the sump from the STORAGE TANK.

Figure 4 illustrates a typical main turbine bearing which is lubricated by a forced-feed lube oil service system. Since these bearings are located close to the shaft glands, OIL DEFLECTORS are fitted to prevent leaking gland steam from contaminating the lube oil, and to prevent the oil from escaping.

Oil Purifying
and Settling System

The oil purifying and settling functions of the forced-feed system include a centrifugal OIL PURIFIER (discussed later in the chapter), an OIL HEATER for raising the temperature of the oil entering the purifier (to facilitate removal of water), and SETTLING TANKS fitted with steam heating coils.

The oil is normally purified while the lubricating system is in operation. The purifier takes oil from the main sump tank; after it is purified, the oil is discharged back to the same sump. Oil from the smaller forced-feed systems is drained and put into a settling tank, from which the purifier may take a suction when it is not employed in purifying oil of the main system. The purifier is normally operated 12 hours a day for the main system, while underway.

If the oil becomes badly contaminated by water or other impurities, or if it becomes emulsified, the mixture is pumped up to the SETTLING TANKS. Here the oil is heated by

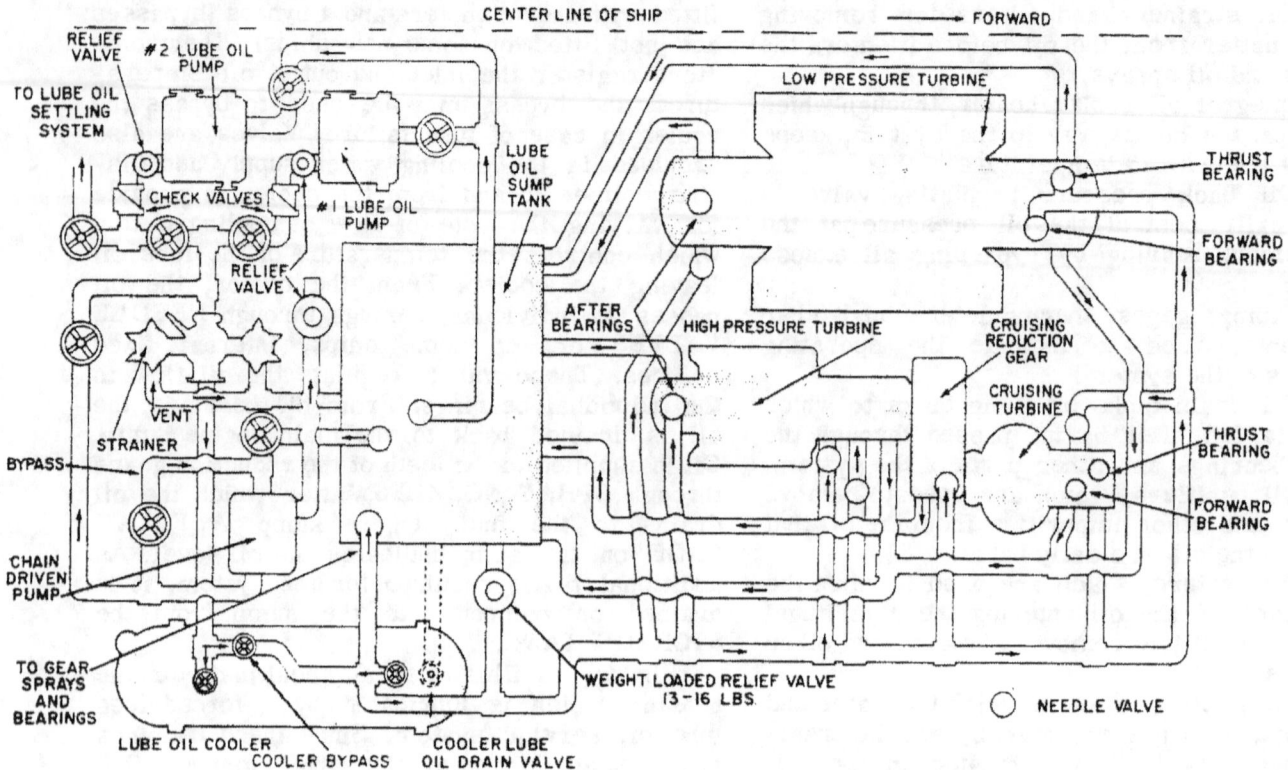

Figure 3.—Diagram of a DD-692 class destroyer forced-feed lubricating system.

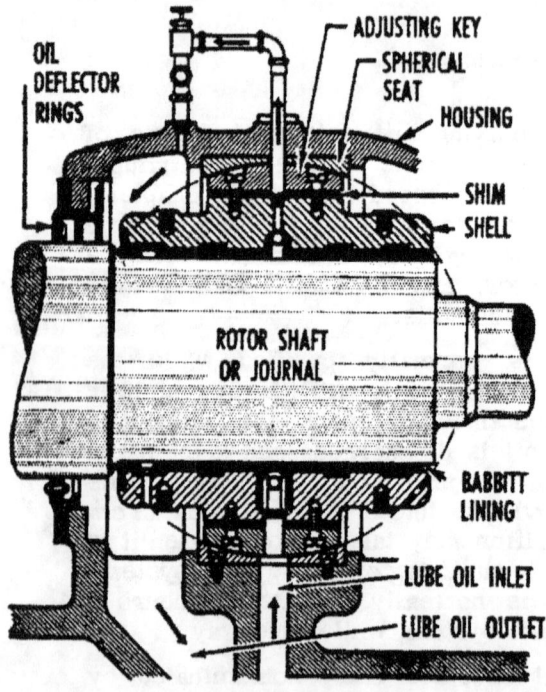

Figure 4.—Adjustable spherical-seated bearing lubricated by forced feed.

the steam-heated coils. After several hours of heating, the impurities will have settled and can be drawn off through the drains at the bottom of the tanks. The remaining oil is then passed through the purifier and discharged back to the sump. Purification of the main sump oil, by heating and settling, can be done only in port, because all the oil must be pumped out of the main engine sump. This should be done as soon as possible after securing. The reason for this action is to take advantage of the heat accumulated by normal engine operation.

Oil Check Fittings

Various means are provided for maintaining a continuous check on the supply of oil to bearings and on the temperature of oil flowing from the bearings. In modern turbines and reduction gears, a THERMOMETER, and a bull's-eye SIGHT-FLOW fitting are installed in the return line leading from the individual bearing. A combined sight-flow and thermometer fitting (fig. 5) is one type normally installed.

# LUBRICATION AND ASSOCIATED EQUIPMENT

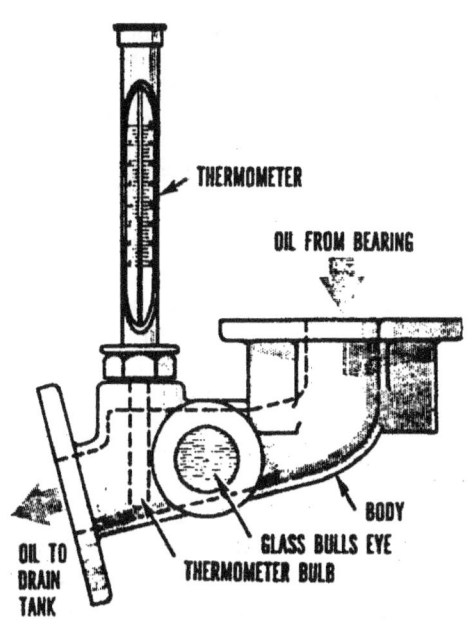

Figure 5.—Combined lube oil sight-flow and thermometer.

A PRESSURE GAGE is also installed outside the gear case—on the header from which oil is fed to the bearings. The thermometers are sometimes of the distant-reading type—with the recording bulbs connected to a dial-type indicator or a temperature monitoring panel.

## Oil Pressures

The pressures to be carried at the various parts of the lubrication system differ with the type of installation. Pressure at the service pumps should be such that the pressure at the most remote bearing will be in accordance with the manufacturer's specification. A higher pressure than this will cause the bearings to become flooded and the oil to foam. Pressures shown by the oil gages on the main gage board should indicate the actual pressure at the low pressure alarm connections to the system. Sudden increases in pressure at the pump (usually due to a clogged strainer or pipeline) should prompt immediate checking of oil flow at the bearings. The trouble should be located and corrected at once.

## Oil Flow

The flow of oil at the bearing, as seen through the sight-flow glass, must be uniform. Frequent inspections should be made during each watch. If the oil supply is interrupted at any time, the main shaft should be stopped and locked. If the oil temperature rises beyond allowable limits, reduce the shaft speed and notify the bridge.

## Oil Temperatures

Bearing temperatures depend on the viscosity of the oil being used, design of the bearing, rpm, and clearances. The manufacturer's technical manual for a unit gives the correct temperatures of lube oil flowing from the bearings. The temperature rise of oil passing through the bearings should not exceed 50° F (difference between discharge of lube oil cooler and the temperature leaving the bearing), even though the maximum allowable temperature is not exceeded. Investigate the cause of any rising temperature that fails to level off, no matter how slowly it is rising.

Since friction loss in a journal bearing is directly proportional to the oil viscosity, and the viscosity depends upon the temperature, the oil leaving the cooler should be between 120° and 130° F. The efficiency of double reduction gears, for example, will be decreased appreciably at cruising speeds, if operated at temperatures lower than those prescribed.

Take PRECAUTIONS WITH THE THERMOMETERS. Make certain that the bulbs are sufficiently immersed in the oil streams to give an accurate reading. In many cases, the thermometers give only the average temperature in the bearing reservoir. Checks on temperature should, therefore, be periodically made by feeling the cap and by inspecting the sight glasses to ensure that there is a flow of oil.

The OIL COOLERS should be put into operation when the temperature of the oil from the cooler reaches 120° F. The temperature from the cooler should be carried at 120° to 130° F. When the system has more than one cooler, the coolers should be used alternately. (The operating principles of the lube oil cooler are discussed in the preceding chapter.)

## Oil Purity

Lubricating oils may be kept in service for long periods of time, provided the purity of the oil is maintained at the required standard. The simple fact is that lubricating oil does not wear out, although it can become unfit for use when it is robbed of its lubricating properties by the presence of water, sand, sludge, fine metallic particles, acid, and other contaminants.

Proper care of lubricating oil requires, then, that the oil be kept as free from contamination as possible and that, once contaminated, the oil must be purified before it can be used again.

Strainers are used in many lubricating systems to prevent the passage of grit, scale, dirt, and other foreign matter. Duplex strainers are used in lubricating systems in which an uninterrupted flow of lubricating oil must be maintained; the flow may be diverted from one strainer basket to the other while one is being cleaned. If pieces of metal are found, determine the character of the metal. Later ships have strainer magnets installed to remove ferrous (iron) particles from the oil. Bits of brass or babbitt metal indicate that there is a damaged, or wiped, bearing in the system, or that the bearing metal is breaking up. If the metal has the appearance of rust, it indicates that corrosion is occurring in the system. Pieces of metal rust will scratch the bearing or mar a thrust shoe. A sudden rise in bearing temperature, followed by a return to normal, usually indicates that some foreign substance reached the bearing, scratched it, and was then washed out by the oil supply. The oil strainers should be removed and cleaned during each watch.

The use of strainers does not solve the problem of water contamination of lubricating oil. Even a very small amount of water in lubricating oil can be extremely damaging to machinery, piping, valves, and other equipment. Water in lubricating oil can cause widespread pitting and corrosion; also, by increasing the frictional resistance, water can cause the oil film to break down prematurely. Every effort must be made to prevent the entry of water into any lubricating system.

Water may actually cause corrosion in the entire system, particularly in those parts which are not covered with oil at all times. Condensation of moisture, which promotes rusting on exposed surfaces such as gear casings, upper portions of drain tanks, etc. should be prevented by eliminating factors which tend to reduce the temperature of the surfaces. All unprotected escape hatches in the vicinity of gear casings must be kept secured at all times when the temperature of the outside air is less than 70°F, except when engines are secured. Air from ventilation ducts should never blow directly or indirectly on the gear casing. When coming to anchor, or securing main propulsion machinery, circulate oil through the system for at least an hour to minimize the effects of an unavoidable amount of fresh-water condensation.

Water enters the lubrication system at the following principal points:

1. Leaky tubes or joints in the oil coolers.
2. Steam-sealed glands or turbines (sometimes because of clogged drain).
3. Vents on tanks and gear casings (as atmospheric moisture, subsequently condensed).
4. Leaks in drain or sump tanks located in bilges.

Lube oil may lose its lubricating qualities if it is contaminated, but if the impurities and water are removed as soon as their presence is noted, the oil can be used over and over indefinitely. To ensure that the oil is kept free of all foreign matter, a sample of lube oil should be drawn from the auxiliary machinery sumps about once a week. Allow this sample to settle and examine for contamination. If the lube oil shows any contamination, drain the oil system of the particular piece of auxiliary machinery, and replenish the system with clean lube oil. The contaminated oil should be placed into one of the settling tanks and purified at some later date.

CENTRIFUGAL PURIFIERS (centrifuges) are used to purify the lube oils. Because of the importance of this purifier, and because it is employed for the purification of lube oil used in other than forced-feed systems, it is treated somewhat fully further on in this chapter. Generally, the oil must be heated to higher than operating temperature before being run through the centrifuge. This results in a greater degree of purification.

## IX. GRAVITY-FEED LUBRICATION SYSTEMS

There are two types of gravity-feed lubricating systems—the gravity force feed and the straight gravity feed. The straight gravity-feed system is further differentiated as being either a DRIP-FEED or a WICK-FEED system. None of these systems will be found to any great extent on the modern naval ships.

# LUBRICATION AND ASSOCIATED EQUIPMENT

## SELF-OILING SPRING BEARINGS

Main shaft spring bearings on the propulsion shaft are lubricated by a self-oiling system. Most of these bearings are ring-oiled, though some are chain-oiled. You must know how to ensure continuous correct lubrication of these important units.

### Ring-Oiled Spring Bearings

The lubrication system for the ring-oiled bearings consists of an OIL SUMP below the bearing journal, and brass OILER RINGS which are hung loosely over the journal and lower half of the bearing. These rings are immersed in the oil and carry a continuous supply of oil over the journal as the rings are dragged around by the rotation of the shaft. The rings must be finished smoothly and fit properly in the guides in the upper half of the bearing shell to prevent hanging and failure to rotate evenly. The upper half of the bearing is cut away in the middle to accommodate the oiler rings. A hinged ACCESS COVER in the upper half of the bearing housing permits inspection of the journal and oiler rings. The OIL DEFLECTOR RINGS, secured to the shaft, keep the oil within the bearing space.

### Care of Spring Bearing Oil

The frequency of changing the oil and cleaning the oil sumps depends upon the service and the mechanism. If the oil doesn't become contaminated by impurities, it can be used for an extended period before the lubricating qualities are reduced. Regardless of condition, the oil should be drained once a quarter and run through the purifier. Whenever the oil is renewed, the sump should be thoroughly cleaned. Be sure to keep inspection openings in operating condition, and closed when not in use.

Samples of the oil in the sump should be examined after each extended run, and after 10 days of periodic service. If the oil shows an increase in viscosity, discoloration, or formation of sludge deposits in the reservoir, immediate renewal is necessary. When underway, the oil level and bearing operations must be inspected and logged hourly.

## X. GREASE LUBRICATION SYSTEMS

Grease lubrication is employed in many locations where the retention of lube oil at the bearing surface would otherwise be difficult. The grease is applied either through the use of grease cups or through pressure fittings, such as the Zerk type.

### Grease Cup Lubrication

Whereas dirt in lube oil will generally settle out, dirt in grease remains mixed with grease and becomes abrasive. For this reason, particular care must be taken to prevent contamination, especially where grease cups are used. Before opening the container, all dirt should be carefully removed from the exterior. No dirt must be allowed to enter either the opening or the grease cups. The cups should be frequently emptied, cleaned, and refilled with fresh grease.

### Pressure Greasing

Pressure fittings form a convenient means of lubricating numerous low-speed, lightly loaded, or widely separated bearings. They are not, however, satisfactory for use on electric generators and motors because of the danger of forcing grease out of the bearing and onto windings. These fittings are similar to those on an automobile, where grease guns are employed for lubrication.

Before applying the grease gun, the pressure fittings should be wiped clean. The gun tip, too, must be clean. The pressure should be applied until grease comes out around the edges of the bearing. In bearings fitted with felt or other seals, care must be taken to avoid breaking the seals by overpressure. Excessive pressure in the lubrication of needle-type roller bearings may unseat the needles.

## XI. BALL AND ROLLER BEARING LUBRICATION

The oil or grease employed for the lubrication of ball and roller bearings (known jointly as ROLLER CONTACT BEARINGS) provides a lubricating film between the balls and rollers and the retainers, and between ends of the rollers and the races; dissipates heat caused by friction; prevents corrosion of the highly polished parts; and aids in excluding dirt, water, and other foreign matter. The lubricant specified for each machine should be used, and excessive lubrication should be avoided.

Oil Lubrication

Where ball or roller bearings are oil lubricated, the lube oil, as speeds increase, begins churning and produces heat. The quantity of oil must, therefore, be reduced accordingly, until at very high speeds only a mist of oil is desirable. It is common practice to fill the bearing housing to a point between the center of the lower ball and the lowest point of the inner ring, depending upon the speed of operation. DRAINS are generally installed to prevent the oil from rising above this point; SIGHT INDICATORS are also provided. For extremely high speeds, the drip-feed or wick-feed gravity lubrication is sometimes used.

Grease Lubrication

To apply grease to ball and roller bearings, proceed as follows:

1. Remove the relief plug at the bottom of the bearing closure and free a hole through the cavity.
2. With the mechanism running, turn down the grease cup slowly until grease begins to push through the relief plug hole.
3. Leave the hole open for 10 to 15 minutes, then free the hole again with a clean rod or knife, and replace the plug.
4. If excessive grease appears when the plug is removed, remove the cover and clean out excessive grease. Add sufficient grease, if necessary, to the bearing closure to make it about 1/3 to 1/2 full. This procedure should be followed after new bearings are installed.

Where a relief pipe is fitted to the bearing closure or grease sump, and the closure is not accessible, the relief pipe should be removed (if possible) and thoroughly cleaned. A stiff, clean wire should be inserted through the pipe, to free an opening through the grease in the sump, before attempting to replenish the lubricant in the bearing.

After relubricating with the relief plug off the relief pipe, and with the motor running, leave the plug open for 10 to 15 minutes, occasionally loosening the excess grease in the pipe with the stiff wire. Then remove the relief pipe and free it of excess grease, attach it to the closure, and place the plug in the end of the relief pipe.

## XII. LUBE OIL PURIFICATION

In the forced-feed lubrication systems on modern naval ships, if the purity of the oil remains intact, the oil may be kept in service for a long period of time. LUBE OIL DOES NOT WEAR OUT; it is merely robbed of its lubricating properties by foreign substances. In other words, improper performance of a correct oil is not due to internal change, but to contamination or to the formation of sludge. No one would ever willfully pour into the lubrication system of his machine a mixture of oil, water, sand, fine metallic particles, sludge, and acid. Yet lubricating systems do contain mixtures of this nature, when preventive measures are not taken. The centrifugal oil purifier is employed on all naval ships to remove the water and other foreign matter from the lube oil. Water is the greatest source of contamination.

Contamination must be removed or the oil will not meet lubrication requirements. Dirt, sludge, and other contaminants will act as abrasives to score and scratch the rubbing metal surfaces within engines, generators, pumps, and blowers. Contaminants interfere with the ability of the oil to maintain a good lubricating film between metal surfaces.

Several different devices are used to keep the oil as clean as possible. Each device is designed to remove certain kinds of contamination and it takes several types of devices in a lubricating system to keep oil in a usable condition. Strainers, filters, settling tanks, and centrifugal purifiers are the devices used to free oil of contamination. Strainers and filters will not be discussed in this chapter — settling tanks and purifiers will be discussed, with emphasis on purifiers.

### SETTLING TANKS

Shipboard lubricating systems include settling tanks which permit used oil to stand while water and other impurities settle out. Settling is due to force of gravity. A number of layers of contamination may form, the number of layers formed depending upon the difference in specific gravity of the various substances. For example, there might be a layer of metal particles on the bottom, then a layer of sludge, then a layer of water, and then the clean oil.

Lubricating oil piping is generally arranged to permit two methods of purification: batch purification and continuous purification. In the batch process, usually done while the ship is

# LUBRICATION AND ASSOCIATED EQUIPMENT

in port, the lubricating oil is transferred from the sump to a settling tank by means of a purifier or a transfer pump. (After the oil is heated and allowed to settle for several hours, water as well as other impurities are removed from the settling tanks. The oil is then centrifuged and returned to the sump from which it was taken.)

## CENTRIFUGAL PURIFICATION

While a ship is at sea or when time does not permit batch purification in the settling tanks the continuous purification process is used. Centrifugal purifiers are also used in this process. The purifier takes the oil from the main sump in a continuous cycle. Before entering the purifier, the oil is heated to facilitate easier removal of the impurities.

Detailed instructions on construction, operation, and maintenance of purifiers are furnished by the 3-M System and the manufacturers. The instructions should be carefully studied and followed by the personnel who are responsible for operation and maintenance of purifiers. The following general information is provided to familiarize you with the methods of purification and the purposes and principles of operation of purifiers.

## PRINCIPLES OF PURIFIER OPERATION

In the purification process, a purifier may be used to remove water and sediment from oil or to remove sediment only. When water is involved in the purification process, the purifier is called a SEPARATOR. When the principal item of contamination is sediment, the purifier is used as a CLARIFIER. When used to purify lubricating oil, a purifier may be used as either a separator or a clarifier. Whether a purifier is used as a separator or a clarifier depends upon the moisture content of the oil to be purified.

If an oil contains no moisture, it needs only to be clarified, since the solids will be deposited in the bowl, and the oil will be discharged in a pure state. If, however, the oil contains some moisture, the continued feeding of "wet" oil to the bowl results eventually in a bowl filled with water, and from then on the centrifuge is not separating any water from the oil. Even before the bowl is completely filled with water, the presence of a layer of water in the bowl reduces the depth of the oil layer. As a result, the incoming oil passes through the bowl at a very high velocity.

This higher velocity means that the liquid is under centrifugal force for a shorter time, and the separation of water from the oil is, therefore, not so complete as it would be if the bowl were without the water layer, or if the water layer were a shallow one. Because of this, the centrifuge should not be operated as a clarifier unless the oil contains very little or no water. A small amount of water can be satisfactorily accumulated, together with the solids, to be drained out when the bowl is stopped for cleaning. However, if there is any appreciable amount of water in the oil, the bowl should be operated as a separator.

## XIII. TYPES OF CENTRIFUGAL PURIFIERS

There are two types of purifiers used in installations. Both types operate on the same principle. The principal difference in the two types of purifiers is in the design of the rotating units. In one type the rotating element is a bowl-like container which encases a stack of disks and in the other type the rotating element is a hollow, tubular rotor; thus, they are known as the DISK-TYPE PURIFIER and the TUBULAR-TYPE PURIFIER.

A sectional view of a disk type centrifugal purifier is shown in figure 6. The bowl is mounted on the upper end of the vertical bowl spindle, which is driven by means of a worm wheel and friction clutch assembly. A radial thrust bearing is provided at the lower end of the bowl spindle to carry the weight of the bowl spindle and to absorb any thrust created by the driving action.

The parts of a disk-type bowl are shown in figure 7. The flow of oil, through the bowl and additional parts, is shown in figure 8.

Contaminated oil enters the top of the revolving bowl through the regulating tube. The oil then passes down the inside of the tubular shaft and out at the bottom into the stack of disks. As the dirty oil flows up through the distribution holes in the disks, the high centrifugal force exerted by the revolving bowl causes the dirt, sludge, and water to move outward and the purified oil inward toward the tubular shaft. The disks divide the space within the bowl into many separate narrow passages or

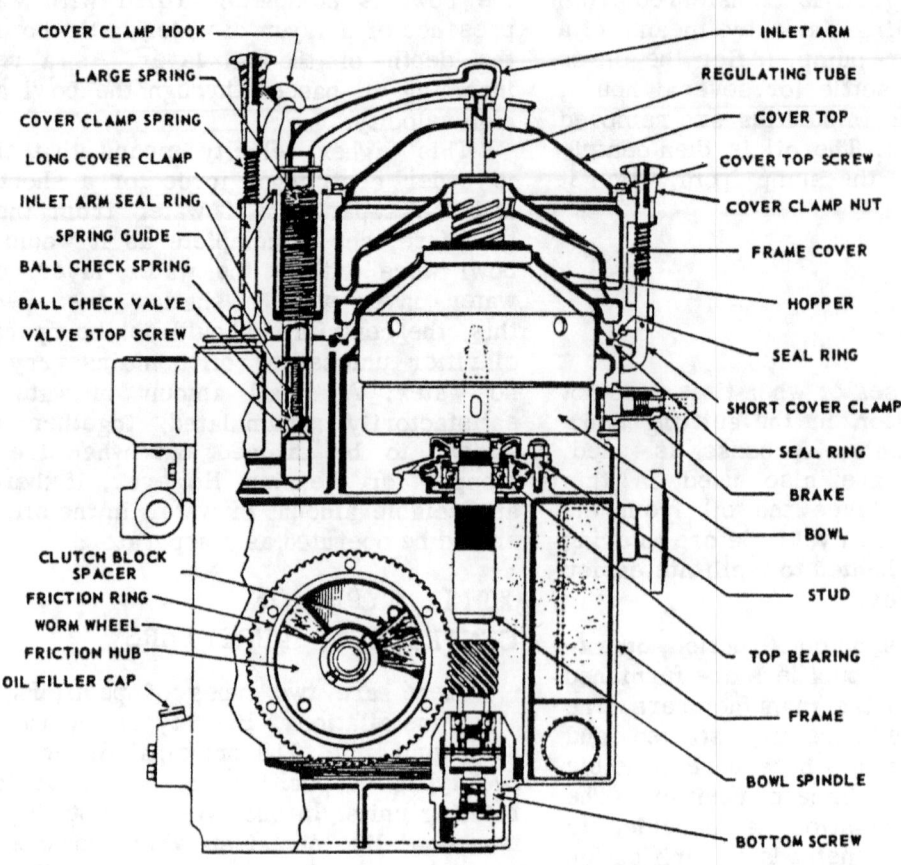

Figure 6.—Disk-type centrifugal purifier.

spaces. The liquid confined within each passage is restricted so that it can only flow along that passage. This arrangement prevents excess agitation of the liquid as it passes through the bowl and creates shallow settling distances between the disks.

Most of the dirt and sludge remains in the bowl and collects in a more or less uniform layer on the inside vertical surface of the bowl shell. Any water, along with some dirt and sludge, separated from the oil, is discharged through the discharge ring at the top of the bowl. The purified oil flows inward and upward through the disks, discharging from the neck of the top disk (fig. 8.)

A cross section of a tubular-type centrifugal purifier is shown in figure 9. This type of purifier consists essentially of a hollow rotor or bowl which rotates at high speeds. The rotor has an opening in the bottom to allow the dirty lube oil to enter and two sets of openings at the top to allow the oil and water (separator) or the oil by itself (clarifier) to discharge (see insert, fig. 9). The bowl, or hollow rotor, of the purifier is connected by a coupling unit to a spindle which is suspended from a ball bearing assembly. The bowl is belt-driven by an electric motor mounted on the frame of the purifier.

The lower end of the bowl extends into a flexibly mounted guide bushing. The assembly, of which the bushing is a part, restrains movement of the bottom of the bowl, but allows sufficient movement so that the bowl can center itself about its center of rotation when the purifier is in operation. Inside the bowl is a device consisting essentially of three flat plates equally spaced radially. This device is commonly referred to as the three-wing device, or just the three-wing. The three-wing rotates

# LUBRICATION AND ASSOCIATED EQUIPMENT

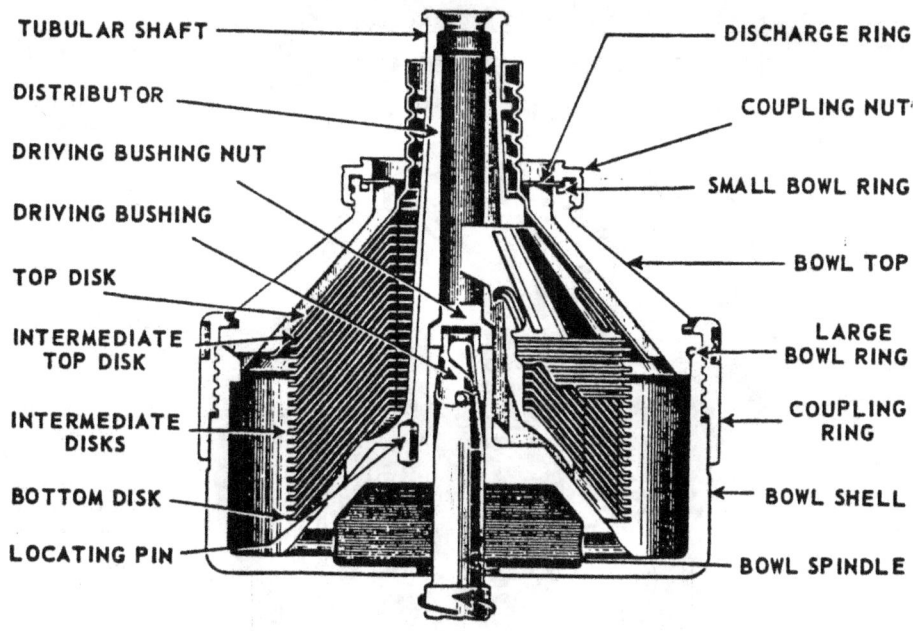

Figure 7.—Parts of a disk-type purifier bowl.

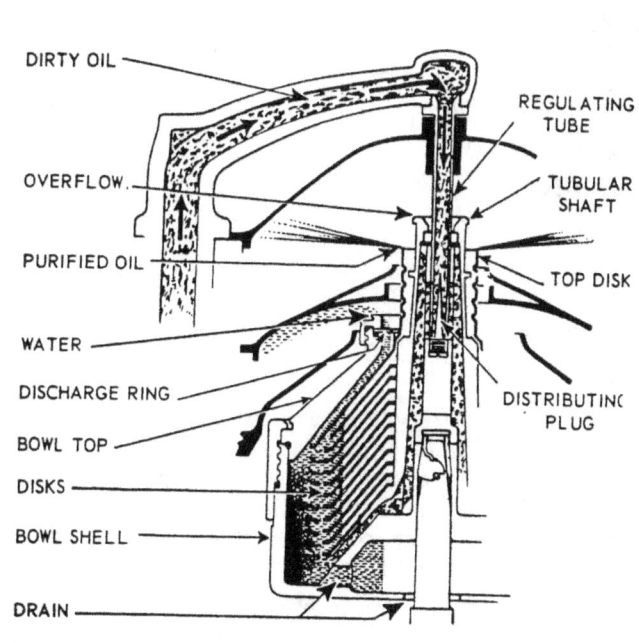

Figure 8.—Path of contaminated oil through disk-type purifier bowl

with the bowl and forces the liquid in the bowl to rotate at the same speed as the bowl. The liquid to be centrifuged is fed into the bottom of the bowl through the feed nozzle, under pressure, so that the liquid jets into the bowl in a stream.

When the purifier is used as a lube oil clarifier, the three-wing has a cone on the bottom, against which the feed jet strikes in order to bring the liquid up to bowl speed smoothly without making an emulsion. Both types of three-wing devices are shown in figure 10.

The process of separation is basically the same in the tubular-type purifier as in the disk-type purifier. In both types, the separated oil assumes the innermost position and the separated water moves outward. Both liquids are discharged separately from the bowls, and the solids separated from the liquid are retained in the bowl (fig. 11).

## XIV. GENERAL NOTES ON PURIFIER OPERATIONS

The specific details for operating a given purifier should be obtained from the appropriate

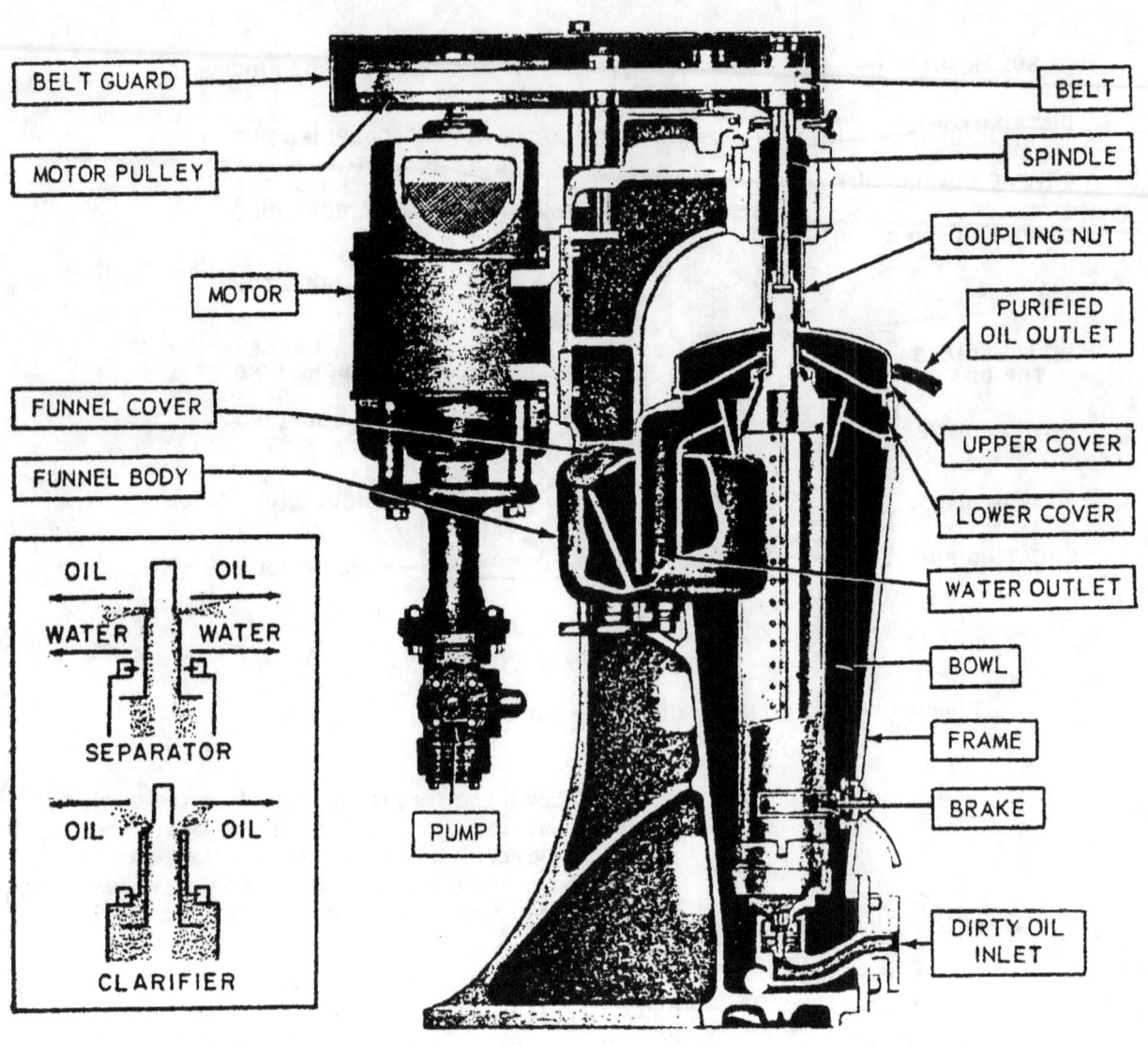

Figure 9.—Tubular-type centrifugal purifier.

instructions provided with the unit. Information provided here is, in general, applicable to both types of purifiers.

For maximum efficiency, purifiers should be operated at maximum designed speed and rated capacity. Since turbine oils are always contaminated with water of condensation, the purifier bowls should be operated as separators and not as clarifiers. An exception to operating a purifier at designed rated capacity is when a unit is used as a separator of 9000 series (compounded or additive-type-heavy-duty lube oils) detergent oil. Some engine installations using oils of the 9000 series are exposed to large quantities of water. If the oil becomes contaminated with water, the oil has a tendency to emulsify. The tendency to emulsify is most pronounced when the oil is new, and gradually decreases during the first 50 to 75 hours of engine operation. When an emulsion appears, the purifier should be reduced to approximately 80 per cent of the rated capacity and operation

## LUBRICATION AND ASSOCIATED EQUIPMENT

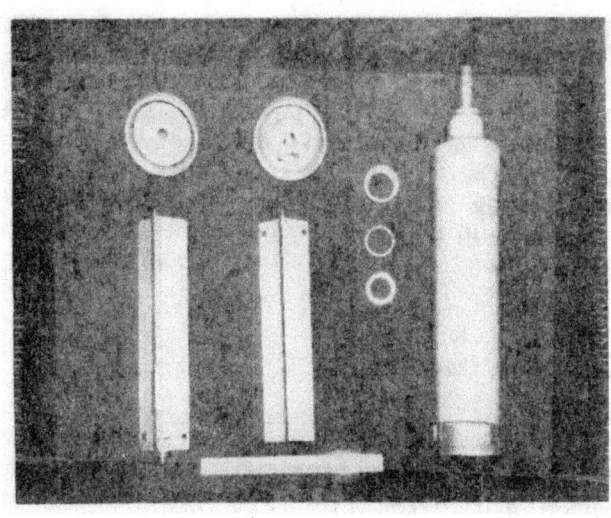

Figure 10.—Parts of a tubular-type purifier bowl.

continued as long as an appreciable amount of free water discharges along with the emulsion.

When a purifier is operated as a separator, PRIMING OF THE BOWL with fresh water is essential before any oil is admitted to the purifier. The water serves to seal the bowl and to create an initial equilibrium of liquid layers. If the bowl is not primed, the oil will be lost through the water discharge ports.

There are several FACTORS WHICH INFLUENCE PURIFIER OPERATION. The time required for purification and the output of a purifier depend upon such factors as the viscosity of the oil, the pressure applied to the oil, the size of the sediment particles, the difference in the specific gravity of the oil and the substances which contaminate the oil, and the tendency of the oil to emulsify.

The viscosity of the oil determines to a great extent the length of time required to purify lube oil. The more viscous the oil, the longer the time required to purify it to a given

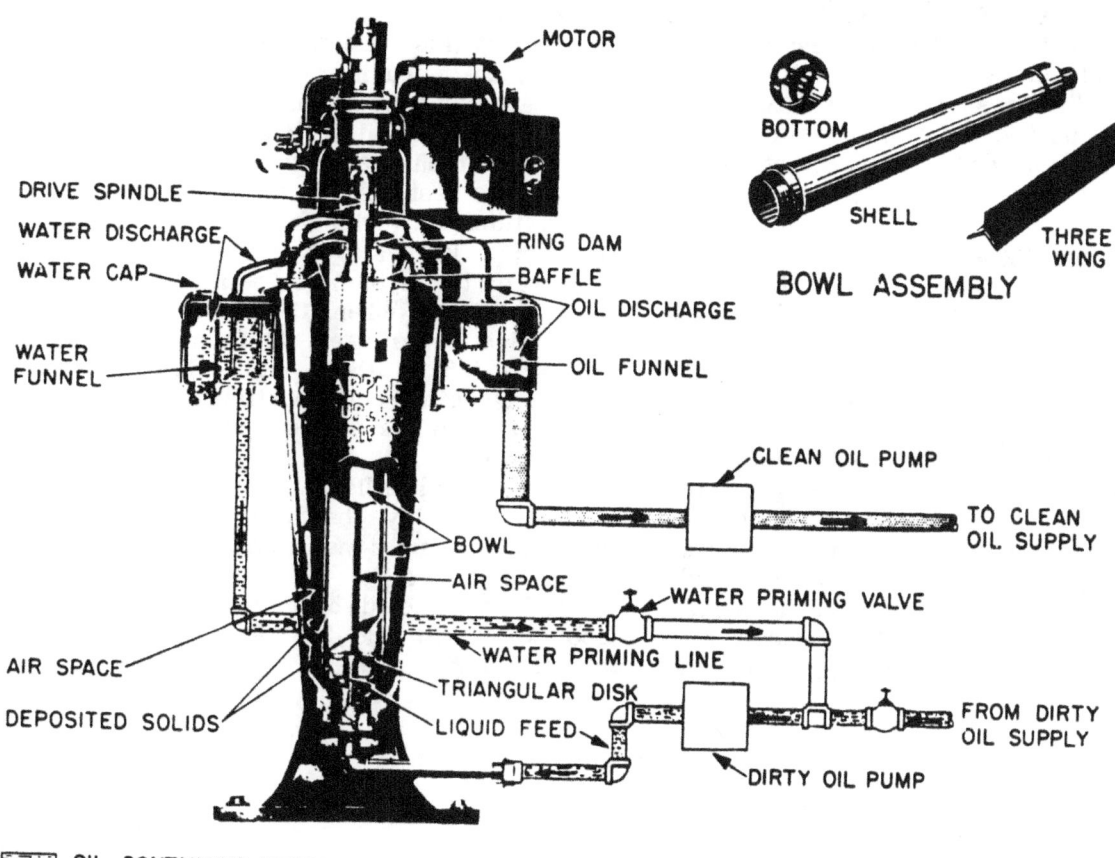

Figure 11.—Path of contaminated oil through a bowl type purifier (Sharples).

degree of purity. Decreasing the viscosity of the oil by heating is one of the most effective methods of facilitating purification.

Even though certain oils may be satisfactorily purified at operating temperatures, a greater degree of purification will generally result by heating the oil to a higher temperature. To accomplish this, the oil is passed through a heater where the proper temperature is obtained before the oil enters the purifier bowl.

Oils used in installations may be heated to specified temperatures without adverse effects, but prolonged heating at higher temperatures is not recommended because of the tendency of such oils to oxidize. Oxidation results in rapid deterioration. In general, oil should be heated sufficiently to produce a viscosity of approximately 90 seconds, Saybolt Universal (90 SSU).

Pressure should not be increased above normal in order to force a high-viscosity oil through the purifier. Instead, viscosity should be decreased by heating the oil. The use of pressure in excess of that normally used to force oil through the purifier will result merely in less efficient purification. On the other hand, a reduction in the pressure at which the oil is forced into the purifier will increase the length of time the oil is under the influence of centrifugal force, and therefore will tend to improve results.

If the oil discharged from a purifier is to be free of water, dirt, and sludge, and the water discharged from the bowl is not to be mixed with oil, the PROPER SIZE DISCHARGE RING (RING DAM) must be used. The size of the discharge ring to be used depends upon the specific gravity of the oil being purified. All discharge rings have the same outside diameter, but have inside diameters of different sizes. Ring sizes are indicated by even numbers and the smaller the number, the smaller the ring size. The size, in millimeters, of the inside diameter is stamped on each ring. Sizes vary by two-millimeter steps. Charts, provided in manufacturer's technical manuals, specify the proper ring size to be used with an oil of a given specific gravity. Generally, the size ring indicated on a chart will produce satisfactory results. However, if the recommended ring fails to produce satisfactory purification, it will be necessary to determine the correct size by trial and error. In general, the most satisfactory purification of the oil is obtained when the ring used is of the largest size possible without causing loss of oil with the discharged water.

MAINTENANCE
OF PURIFIERS

Proper care of an oil purifier requires that the bowl be cleaned frequently and all sediment carefully removed. The frequency of cleaning depends upon the amount of foreign matter in the oil to be purified. If the amount of foreign matter in an oil is not known, the machine should be shut down for examination and cleaning once during each watch, or more often if necessary. The amount of sediment found in the bowl at this time will give an indication as to how long the purifier may be operated between cleanings. The bowl should be thoroughly cleaned each time lube oil is run through for batch purification from the settling tank.

Periodic tests should be made to ensure that the purifier is working properly. Tests should be made at intervals of about 30 minutes when the oil in the system is being purified by the batch process. When the continuous process of purification is used, tests should be made once a watch. If these tests show oil free of water and sediment, the purifier may be operated at the rate of 12 hours per day and cleaned once a watch.

The general efficiency of the purifier may be determined by observing the clarity of the purified oil and the amount of oil in the separated water.

Purifiers should be tested and inspected in accordance with the 3-M Planned Maintenance System requirements.

# BASIC FUNDAMENTALS OF
# ENGINES, FUELS, LUBRICANTS, AND POLLUTION CONTROL

## CONTENTS

| | | Page |
|---|---|---|
| I. | Internal Combustion Engines | 1 |
| II. | Fuels and Lubricants | 7 |
| III. | Safety in Handling and Storage of Petroleum Products | 20 |
| IV. | Filters | 23 |
| V. | Environmental Pollution Control | 26 |

# BASIC FUNDAMENTALS OF ENGINES, FUELS, LUBRICANTS, AND POLLUTION CONTROL

As an equipment operator, you will be mainly concerned with operation of equipment. In order to perform these duties intelligently, it is important that you fully understand the principles of the internal combustion engine operation and the function of the various components that make up the internal combustion engine. This understanding will make your job easier when simple adjustments or repairs have to be made.

This chapter discusses basic principles of engine operation and explains some of the terminology related to engines. Various types of fuel and lubricants are described and information is given on the safe handling and storage of petroleum products. Information is provided on the types and purposes of filters used on automotive and construction equipment. Various methods are discussed on environmental pollution control so that you may effectively control pollution resulting from the combustion and spillage of fuels.

## I. INTERNAL COMBUSTION ENGINES

An internal combustion engine is one in which the fuel burns within the body of the engine. The burning that takes place inside the cylinders produces the energy that turns the crankshaft of the engine. Both gasoline and diesel engines operate on this principle.

Combustion is the act or process of burning. An internal or external combustion engine is defined simply as a machine that converts this heat energy to mechanical energy. To fulfill this purpose, the engine may take one of several forms.

With the internal combustion engine, combustion takes place inside the cylinder and is directly responsible for forcing the piston to move down.

In external combustion engines, such as steam engines, combustion takes place outside the engine. Figure 1 shows, in simplified form, an external and an internal combustion engine.

The external combustion engine requires a boiler to which heat is applied. This combustion causes water to boil to produce steam. The steam passes into the engine cylinder under pressure and forces the piston to move downward.

The transformation of HEAT ENERGY to MECHANICAL ENERGY by the engine is based on a fundamental law of physics which states that gas will expand upon application of heat. If the gas is confined with no outlet for expansion, then the pressure of the gas will be increased when heat is applied. In the internal combustion engine the burning of a fuel within a closed cylinder results in an expansion of gases, thus creating a pressure on top of a piston and causing it to move downward.

In an internal combustion engine the piston moves up and down within a cylinder. This up-and-down motion is known as RECIPROCATING MOTION. This reciprocating motion (straight line motion) must be changed to ROTARY MOTION (turning motion) in order to turn the wheels of a vehicle. A crankshaft and a connecting rod change this reciprocating motion to rotary motion, figure 2.

All internal combustion engines, whether gasoline or diesel, are basically the same. We can best demonstrate this by saying they all rely on three things — AIR, FUEL, and IGNITION.

FUEL contains potential energy for operating the engine; AIR contains the oxygen necessary for combustion; and IGNITION starts combustion. All are fundamental, and the engine will not operate without any one of them. Any discussion of engines must be based on these three factors and the steps and mechanisms involved in delivering them to the combustion chamber at the proper time.

The power of an internal combustion engine comes from the burning of a mixture of fuel and air in a small, enclosed space. When this

## ENGINES, FUELS, LUBRICANTS, AND POLLUTION CONTROL

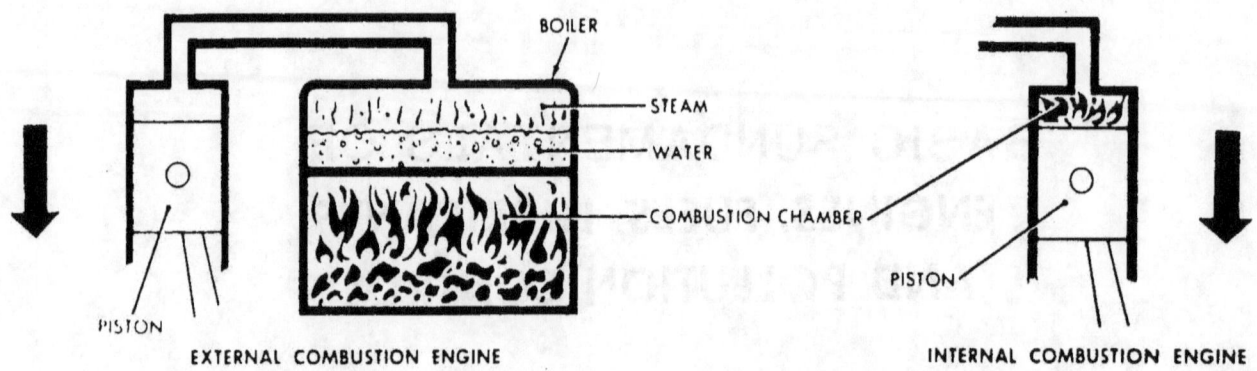

Figure 1.—Simple external and internal combustion engine.

mixture burns it expands greatly, and the push or pressure created is used to move the piston, thereby rotating the crankshaft. This movement is eventually sent back to the wheels to drive the vehicle.

Since similar action occurs in all cylinders of an engine, let's use one cylinder in our development of power. The one-cylinder engine consists of four basic parts as shown in figure 2.

First we must have a CYLINDER which is closed at one end; this cylinder is similar to a tall metal can which is stationary within the engine block. Inside this cylinder is the PISTON,

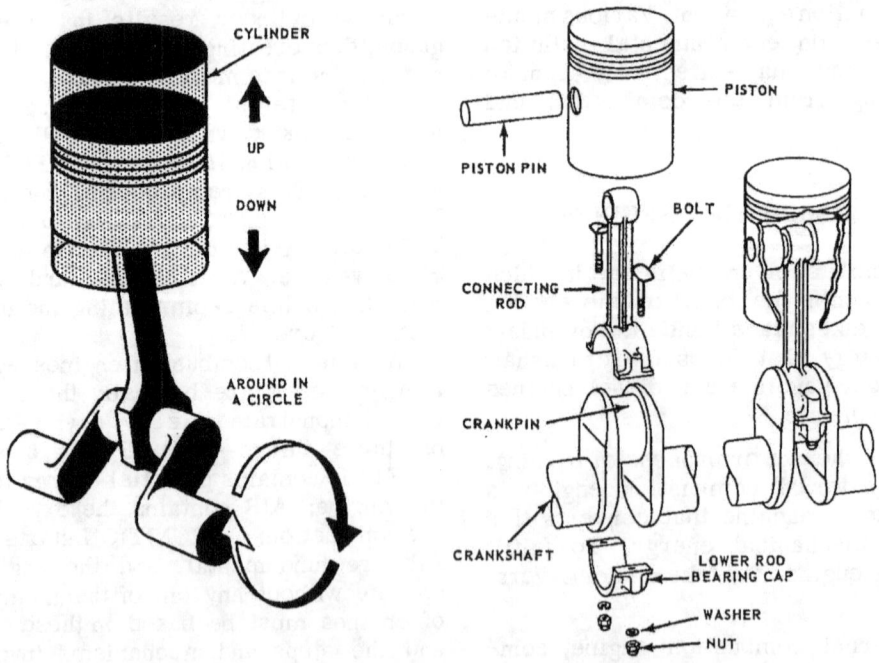

Figure 2.—Cylinder, piston, connecting rod, and crankshaft for one-cylinder engine.

a movable metal plug, which fits snugly into the cylinder, but can still slide up and down easily.

You have already learned that the up-and-down movement of the piston is called reciprocating motion. This motion must be changed to rotary motion so the wheels or tracks of vehicles can be made to rotate. This change is accomplished by a crank on the CRANKSHAFT and a CONNECTING ROD which connects the piston and the crank.

The crank is an offset section of the crankshaft, which scribes a circle as the shaft rotates. The top end of the connecting rod is connected to the piston and must, therefore, go up and down. The lower end of the connecting rod also moves up and down but, because it is attached to the crankshaft, it must also move in a circle with the crank.

When the piston of the engine slides downward because of the pressure of the expanding gases in the cylinder, the upper end of the connecting rod moves downward with the piston, in a straight line. The lower end of the connecting rod moves down and in a circular motion at the same time. This moves the crank which, in turn, rotates the shaft; this rotation is the desired result. So remember, the crankshaft and connecting rod combination is a mechanism for the purpose of changing straight line (or reciprocating) motion to circular (or rotary) motion.

FOUR-STROKE CYCLE
GASOLINE ENGINE

The operating principles of the gasoline and diesel engines are basically the same. Therefore, only the operating cycles of the four-stroke gasoline engine and the two-stroke cycle diesel engines will be discussed.

Each movement of the piston from top to bottom or from bottom to top is called a stroke. The piston takes two strokes (an upstroke and a downstroke) as the crankshaft makes one complete revolution. When the piston is at the top of a stroke (fig. 3), it is said to be at top dead center (TDC). When the piston is at the bottom of a stroke (fig. 4), it is said to be at bottom dead center (BDC).

The basic engine you have studied so far has no provisions for getting the fuel-air mixture into the cylinder or burned gases out of the cylinder. There are two openings in the closed end of a cylinder. One of the openings, permits an intake of air or an intake of a mixture of fuel and air into the combustion area of the cylinder. The other opening permits the burned

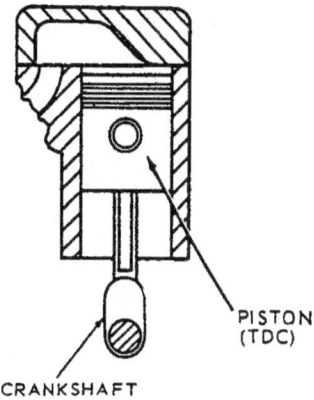

Figure 3.—Piston top dead center (TDC).

gases to escape from the cylinder. The two openings have valves in them. These valves, activated by the camshaft, close off either one or the other of the openings, or both of them during various stages of engine operation. The camshaft has a number of cams along its length that open the valves and hold them open for the correct length of time during the piston stroke. The camshaft is driven by the crankshaft through timing gears, or by means of a timing chain. On a 4-stroke cycle engine (fig. 5) the camshaft turns at one-half crankshaft speed. This permits each valve to open and close once for every two revolutions of the crankshaft. One of the valves, called the intake valve, opens to admit an intake of air or a mixture of fuel

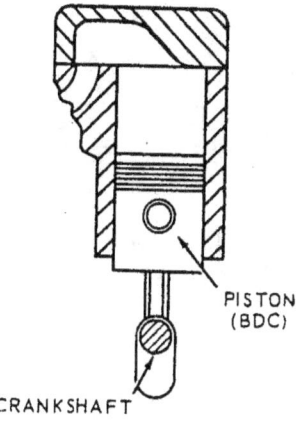

Figure 4.—Piston bottom dead center (BDC).

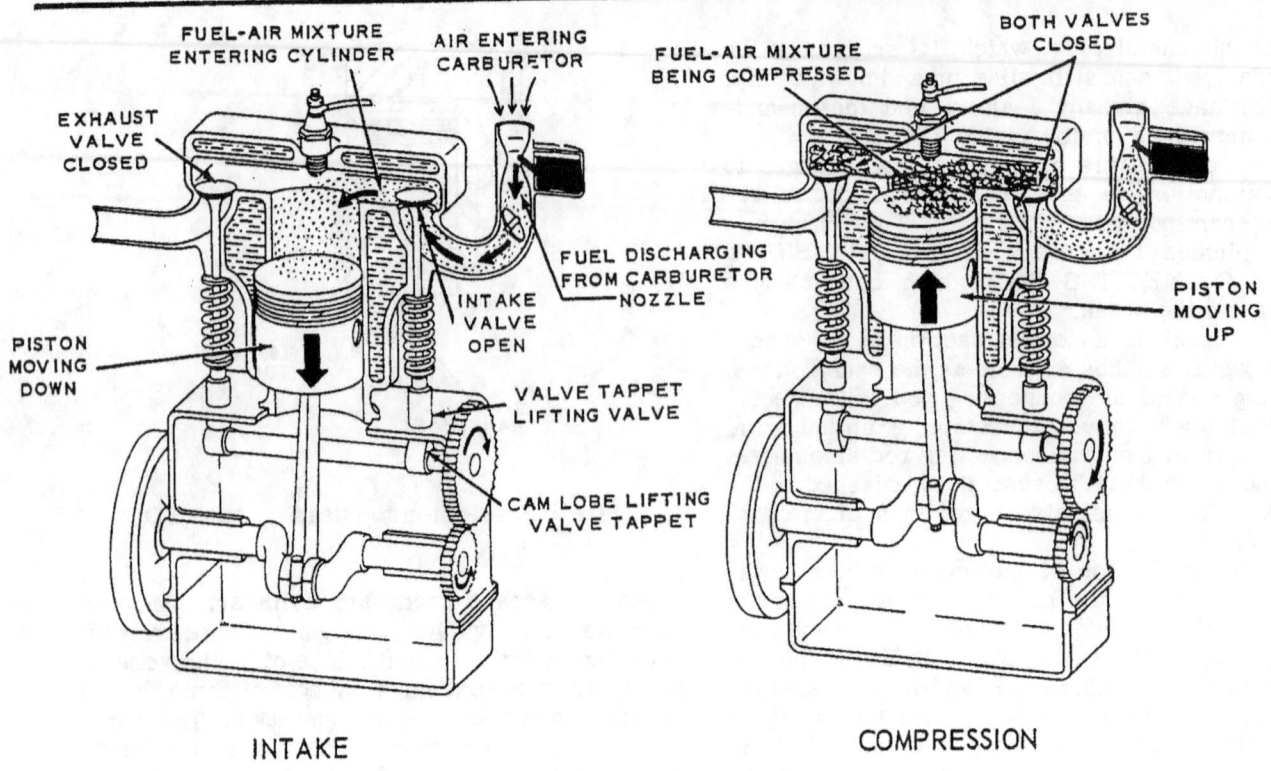
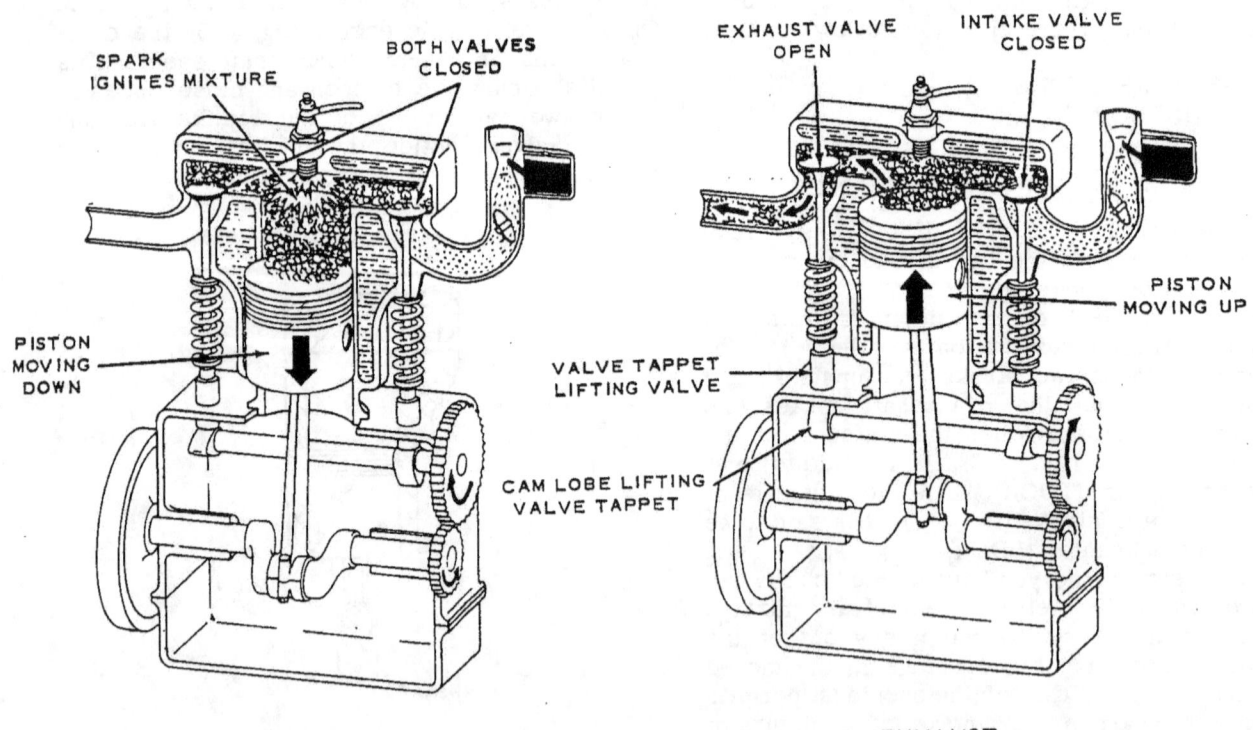

Figure 5. — Four-stroke cycle in a gasoline engine.

and air into the cylinder. The other valve, called the exhaust valve, opens to allow the escape of burned gases after the fuel-and-air mixture has burned.

The following paragraphs give a simplified explanation of the action that takes place within the engine cylinder.

Intake Stroke

The first stroke in the sequence is called the INTAKE stroke (fig. 5). During this stroke, as the crankshaft continues to rotate, the piston is moving downward and the intake valve is open. This downward movement of the piston produces a partial vacuum in the cylinder, and an air-fuel mixture rushes into the cylinder past the open intake valve. This is somewhat the same effect as when you drink through a straw. A partial vacuum is produced in the mouth and the liquid moves up through the straw to fill the vacuum.

Compression Stroke

When the piston reaches bottom dead center at the end of the intake stroke and is therefore at the bottom of the cylinder, the intake valve closes. This seals the upper end of the cylinder. As the crankshaft continues to rotate, it pushes up, through the connecting rod, on the piston. The piston is therefore pushed upward and compresses the combustible mixture in the cylinder; this is called the COMPRESSION stroke (fig. 5). In gasoline engines, the mixture is compressed to about one-eighth of its original volume, which is called an 8 to 1 compression ratio. This compression of the air-fuel mixture increases the pressure within the cylinder. Compressing the mixture in this way makes it still more combustible; not only does the pressure in the cylinder go up, but the temperature of the mixture also increases.

Power Stroke

As the piston reaches top dead center at the end of the compression stroke and therefore has moved to the top of the cylinder, the compressed fuel-air mixture is ignited. The ignition system causes an electric spark to occur suddenly in the cylinder, and the spark ignites the compressed fuel-air mixture. In burning, the mixture gets very hot and tries to expand in all directions. The pressure rises to about 600 to 700 pounds per square inch. Since the piston is the only thing that can move, the force produced by the expanding gases forces the piston down. This force, or thrust, is carried through the connecting rod to the crankpin on the crankshaft. The crankshaft is given a powerful turn. This is called the POWER stroke (fig. 5). This turning effort, rapidly repeated in the engine and carried through gears and shafts, will turn the wheels of a vehicle and cause it to move along the highway.

Exhaust Stroke

After the fuel-air mixture has burned, it must be cleared from the cylinder. This is done by opening the exhaust valve just as the power stroke is finished and the piston starts back up on the EXHAUST stroke (fig. 5). The piston forces the burned gases out of the cylinder past the open exhaust valve.

ENGINE CYCLES

The four strokes (intake, compression, power, and exhaust) are continuously repeated as the engine runs. Now, with the basic knowledge you have of the parts and the four strokes of the engine, let us see what happens during the actual running of the engine. To produce sustained power, an engine must accomplish the same series of events — intake, compression, power, and exhaust — over and over again.

This series of events is called a cycle. Remember that in a 4-stroke cycle engine it takes four complete strokes of the piston to complete one engine cycle, that is, two complete revolutions of the crankshaft. Most engines that you will deal with are of the 4-stroke cycle design.

2-Stroke Cycle Diesel Engine

In the 2-stroke cycle engine, the same four events (intake, compression, power, and exhaust) take place in only two strokes of the piston; one complete revolution of the crankshaft.

The 2-stroke cycle operation shown in figure 6 features the General Motors 71 series. This engine differs in two ways from the 4-stroke cycle engine previously discussed. Not only does it complete the four events in 2-strokes, but it depends upon the heat of compression rather than a spark for ignition. In the two-cycle engine, intake and exhaust take place during part of the compression and power strokes respectively.

# ENGINES, FUELS, LUBRICANTS, AND POLLUTION CONTROL

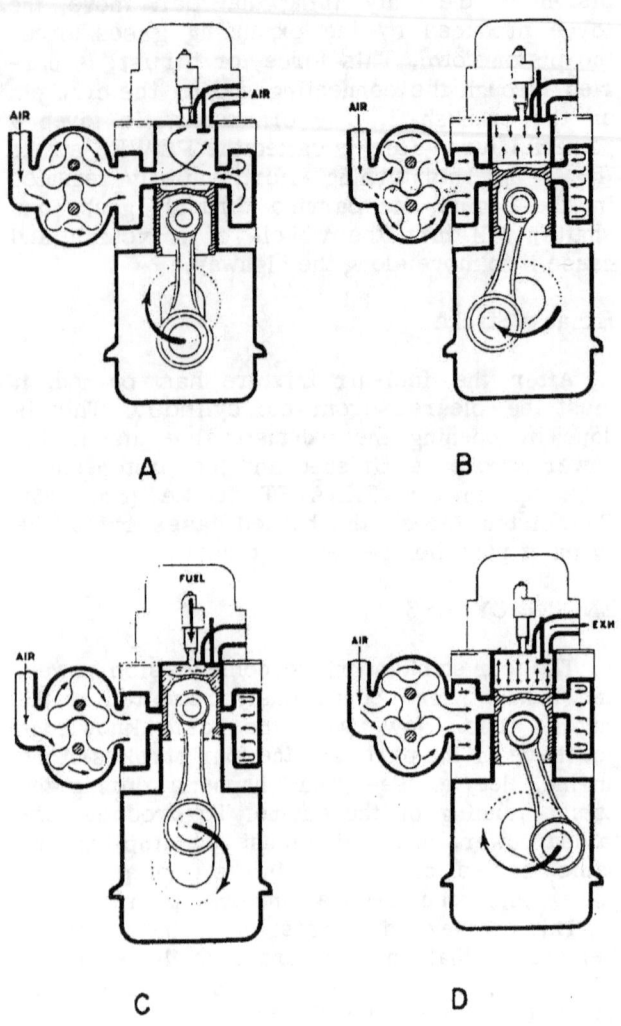

Figure 6.—Events in a 2-stroke cycle, internal combustion engine.

In contrast, a four-cycle engine requires four piston strokes to complete an operating cycle. A blower is provided to force air into the cylinders for expelling the exhaust gases and supply the cylinders with fresh air for combustion. The cylinder walls contain a row of ports which are above the piston when it is at the bottom of its stroke. These ports admit the air from the blower into the cylinder as soon as the top face of the piston uncovers the ports, as shown in view A, figure 6. The indirectional flow of air toward the exhaust valves produces a scavenging effect; this action leaves the cylinder full of clean air when the piston again covers the inlet ports.

As the piston continues on the upward stroke, the exhaust valves (2 per cylinder) close and the charge of fresh air is subject to compression, as shown in view B, figure 6. Shortly before the piston reaches its highest position, the required amount of fuel is sprayed into the combustion space by the cylinder's injector, view C, figure 6; the intense heat generated during the high compression of the air ignites the fine spray immediately and the combustion continues as long as the fuel spray lasts. The resulting pressure forces the piston downward on the power stroke. The exhaust valves are again opened when the piston is about halfway down, allowing the combustion gases to escape into the exhaust manifold, view D, figure 6. Shortly thereafter, the downward movement of the piston uncovers the inlet ports and the cylinder is again swept with clean air, as shown in view A, figure 6. This entire combustion cycle is completed in each cylinder for each revolution of the crankshaft and during two strokes of the piston thus; the term "two-stroke cycle."

## 4-Stroke Cycle Vs 2-Stroke Cycle

A power stroke is produced every crankshaft revolution within the 2-stroke cycle engine; whereas the 4-stroke cycle engine requires two crankshaft revolutions for one power stroke.

It might appear then that a 2-stroke cycle could produce twice as much power as a 4-stroke cycle of the same size, operating at the same speed. However, this is not true. With some 2-stroke cycle engines, some of the power is used to drive a blower that forces the air-fuel charge into the cylinder under pressure. Also, the burned gases are not completely cleared from the cylinder, reducing combustion efficiency. Additionally, because of the much shorter period the intake port is open (as compared to the period the intake valve in a 4-stroke-cycle is open), a relatively smaller amount of fuel-air mixture is admitted. Hence, with less fuel-air mixture, less power per power stroke is produced in a 2-stroke cycle engine of like size operating at the same speed and with other conditions being the same.

## MULTIFUEL ENGINE

The multifuel engine operates on a compression ignition, four-stroke cycle principle similar to conventional four-stroke cycle diesel and gasoline engines. Those pieces of military equipment which are equipped with the multifuel engine are designed to use several different types of fuel, such as gasoline, kerosene, diesel, and (JP) fuels. No modifications or adjustments are necessary when changing grades or types of fuel.

The multifuel engine operation cycle, is shown in figure 7.

## STARTING AND STOPPING PROCEDURES FOR GASOLINE AND DIESEL ENGINES

In the previous sections you learned about the operating cycle of the internal combustion engine, and how it is constructed.

In order to make the basic engine operational, it requires the addition of cooling, lubrication, fuel, and electrical systems. Before starting an internal combustion engine, certain pre-start checks must be made to determine if the engine will operate. Check for fuel, coolant, battery condition, loose wires, oil level, and the absence of leaks.

In this chapter, it is infeasible to state the correct procedures for starting and stopping every type of automotive or construction equipment, equipped with a gasoline or diesel engine that is used. Therefore, the procedures explained below apply to typical types of automotive equipment equipped with a gasoline engine. For information on a specific type of automotive vehicle consult the manufacturers operating manual. Procedures for starting and stopping a typical piece of construction equipment equipped with a diesel engine are covered in chapter 9.

Before starting the engine, be sure the hand or parking brake is set, and the gear selector lever is in NEUTRAL. On a vehicle with an automatic transmission, set the lever at N (NEUTRAL) or push in the N (NEUTRAL) button; otherwise the engine will not start. Some vehicles can be started also in P (PARK).

Next, turn on the ignition and depress the accelerator one-quarter of the way toward the floor. If the equipment has a clutch, disengage it before starting the engine to ensure that the vehicle will not move, and to keep the starter from turning the transmission.

If the engine does not have an automatic choke, pull the choke control out about half-way. Using the choke when the engine is warm will cause flooding and will hinder easy starting.

Now operate the starter until the engine begins to fire. The starter on some vehicles may be actuated by pushing in a starter button on the instrument panel; on others, by depressing the starter button on the floorboard. A few engines are started by depressing the accelerator pedal; on others, turning the ignition switch key to the extreme right starts the engine.

If the engine does not start within 10 seconds, stop to see whether you have properly performed all prestarting operations. If it does not start after several attempts, notify your chief.

Caution: Never operate the cranking motor for more than 30 seconds at a time. If the engine fails to start in 30 seconds, allow the cranking motor to cool for 2 to 3 minutes before resuming cranking operation. Prolonged use of the starter wears it out and discharges the battery.

As soon as the engine begins to fire, release the starter knob, or let the ignition switch key snap back to ON position. Release the clutch pedal slowly, if you have depressed it, and push the choke control back in. After the engine is operating smoothly, ease off the throttle, and allow the engine to idle till it warms to the proper operating temperature. The warm-up period allows the oil in the crankcase to circulate and lubricate the engine pistons, bearings, and the cylinder surfaces. Putting a vehicle into motion before the engine is at proper operating temperature will cause undue wear of the moving parts of the engine.

The following are typical procedures for stopping automotive gasoline engines: (1) Allow the engine to operate at low idle for 3 to 5 minutes, (2) check gage readings; for water coolant within normal range, lubricating oil pressure within range, ammeter showing a charge, fuel gage indicating sufficient fule, and air pressure gage (if so equipped) indicating normal air pressure, and (3) turn the electrical system ignition switch to the OFF position.

## II. FUELS AND LUBRICANTS

Fuels and lubricants for gasoline and diesel engines are byproducts of petroleum. Petroleum, often called crude oil, means "rock oil." Petroleum products include gasoline, kerosene, diesel fuel, lubricating oils, gear lubricants, and greases. Many different products are added to the raw byproducts to obtain a fuel or lubricant that will perform efficiently in modern equipment.

Crude oil would ruin an engine if the impurities were not removed. The impurities are removed by the refining process, which also

# ENGINES, FUELS, LUBRICANTS, AND POLLUTION CONTROL

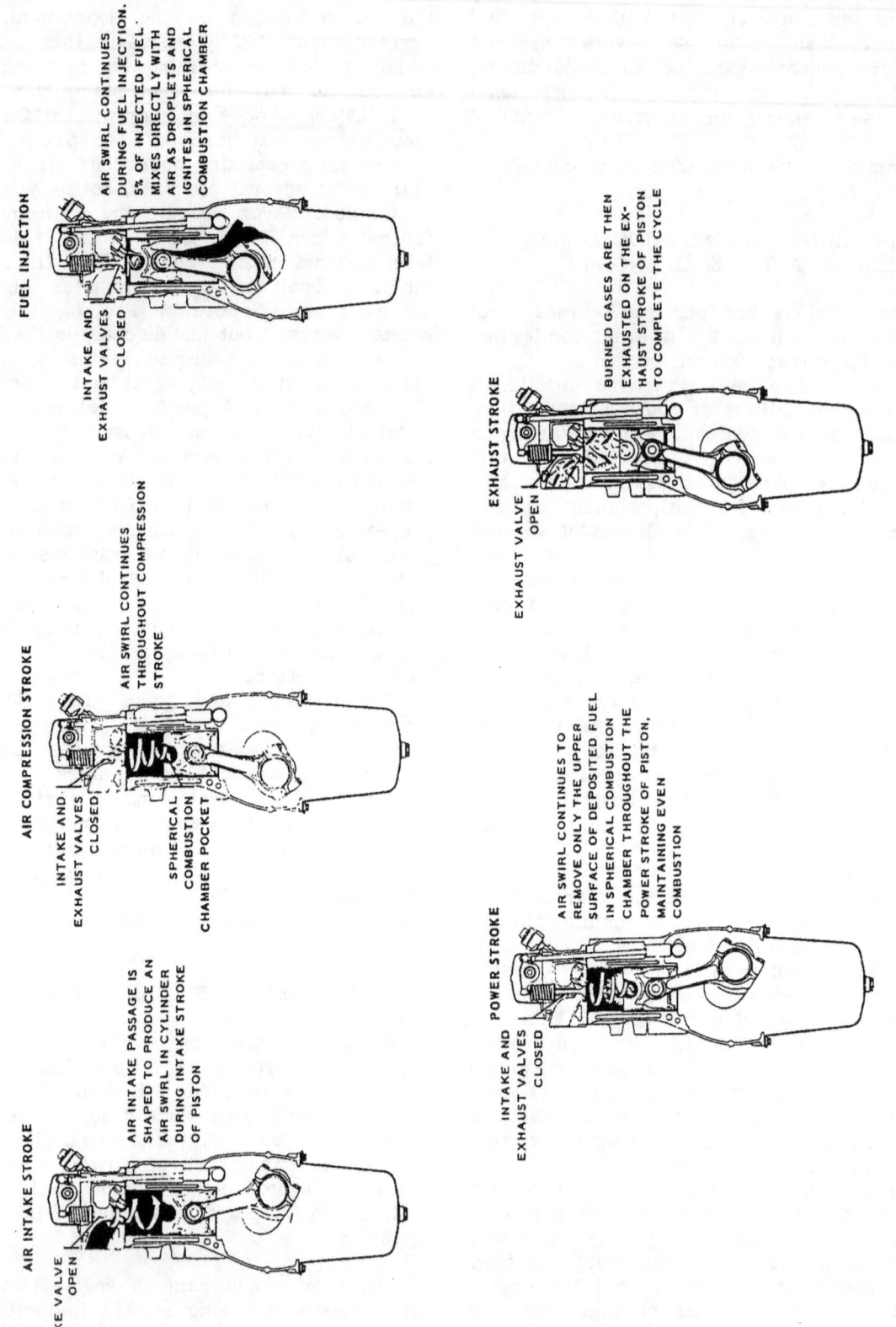

Figure 7. — Multifuel engine operation cycles.

separates the oil into various petroleum products. (See fig. 8.)

You have seen a teakettle boil. Heating the water in the kettle changes it to gas or vapor in the form of steam at a certain temperature. Many kinds of liquids change to gases, or are said to VAPORIZE, at different temperatures. Heating petroleum, which is a mixture of liquids, will change the liquids to gases one by one. Cooling changes each gas back to liquid form through condensation. This process of separating substances from one another is called DISTILLATION.

Distillation drives gasoline vapors from the crude oil first, because gasoline has a lower boiling point and vaporizes before other petroleum products. Substances with higher boiling points, like kerosene and the gas-oil from which we get most of our diesel fuel, are given off next. After the gas-oil has been collected, lubricating oils are distilled, the lightest first (lube distillates), and then the heavier ones (commonly called bottoms). (It is to be noted, bottoms are where we get asphaltic products.) (See fig. 8.)

You will hear also about propane and butane fuels, which are byproducts of natural gas. (Notice in figure 3-8 that gas is taken from a cavity in the earth that is between the oil and the rock formation just above the oil.) These liquids must be collected and stored under pressure because they change into gas when released to the atmosphere. Liquid propane becomes a gas at a temperature of -43°F; liquid butane, at -33°F. Although seldom used as a fuel for automotive equipment, small amounts of these liquid gases have been used to start engines in very cold climates. Some manufacturers believe that internal combustion engines can operate more economically with butane fuel than with gasoline. Gasoline and diesel oil, however, continue to be the most common fuels for internal combustion engines.

PROPERTIES OF GASOLINE

Gasoline contains carbon and hydrogen in such proportions that the gasoline burns freely and liberates HEAT ENERGY. If all the potential heat energy contained in a gallon of gasoline could be converted into work, a motor vehicle could run hundreds of miles on each gallon. However, only a small percentage of this heat energy is converted into power by the engine. Most authorities consider the power losses within the engine to be as follows:

| Engine | Percent of Power Loss |
|---|---|
| Cooling System | 35 |
| Exhaust Gases | 35 |
| Engine Friction | 5 to 10 |
| Total | 75 to 80 |

The question of what is ideal gasoline is more theoretical than practical. Every manufacturer recommends the octane rating of the gasoline he feels is best for the engines he produces. Besides engine design, factors like the weight of the vehicle, the terrain and highways over which it is to be driven, and the climate and altitude of the locality also determine what gasoline is best to use. All other factors being equal, these may be considered as some of the properties of the best gasoline: good antiknock quality, a minimum content of foreign matter, and a volatility which makes starting easy and allows smooth acceleration and economical operation.

Volatility

The blend of a gasoline determines its VOLATILITY — that is, its tendency to change from a liquid to a vapor at any given temperature. The rate of vaporization increases as the temperature of the gasoline rises.

No standard for gasoline volatility meets all engine operating requirements. The volatility must be high enough for easy starting and acceleration. Ordinarily the proper starting mixture is about 15 parts of air to 1 part of fuel, but in very cold weather more fuel must be admitted to the cylinders through the use of the choke in the carburetor for quicker starting. In polar regions, a gasoline of higher volatility makes starting easier; it also helps keep the crankcase from becoming diluted by gasoline seeping past the piston and the piston rings while the engine is being choked.

On the other hand, a gasoline of low volatility brings about better fuel economy and combats VAPOR LOCK (the formation of vapor in the fuel lines in a quantity sufficient to block the flow of gasoline through the system). In the summer and in hot climates, especially, fuels with low volatility lessen the tendency toward vapor lock.

# ENGINES, FUELS, LUBRICANTS, AND POLLUTION CONTROL

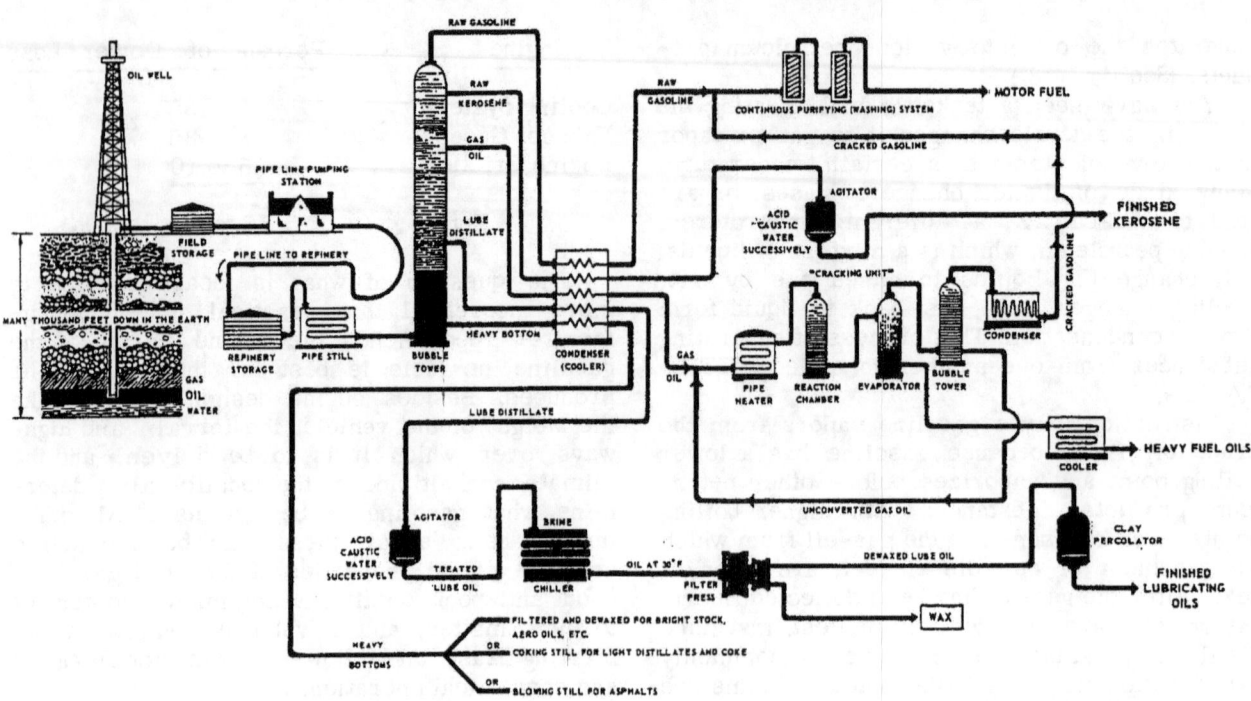

Figure 8. — Typical chart tracing crude oil from well to finished product.

## Purity

Engine efficiency depends to some extent on the PURITY of gasoline. Gums and sulfur are removed from crude oil in the refining process. Gums in gasoline cause sticking valves and form hard baked surfaces within the cylinders. Residue unites with moisture to form sulfuric acid, which corrodes engine parts. Modern refining processes have reduced the sulfur and other foreign matter content of gasoline, thus minimizing the damage to engine parts as well as cutting down engine maintenance.

## Antiknock Quality and Detonation

Reviewing the process of combustion will help you understand the ANTIKNOCK quality of gasoline. When any substance burns, its molecules and those of the oxygen in the air around it are set into motion, producing heat that unites the two groups of molecules in a rapid chemical reaction. In the combustion chamber of an engine cylinder, the gasoline vapor and oxygen in the air are ignited and burn. They combine, and the molecules begin to move about very rapidly, as the high temperatures of combustion are reached. This rapid movement of molecules provides the push on the piston to force it downward on the power stroke.

In the modern high compression gasoline engines the air-fuel mixture tends to ignite spontaneously or to explode instead of burning. The result is a knock, a ping, or a DETONATION. In detonation the spark from the spark plug starts the fuel mixture burning, and the flame spreads through the layers of the mixture, very quickly compressing and heating them. The last layers become so compressed and heated that they explode violently. The explosive pressure strikes the piston head and the walls of the cylinder, and causes the knock you hear in the engine. It is the fuel, not the engine, that knocks. Besides being an annoying sound, persistent knocking results in engine overheating, loss of power, and increased fuel consumption. It causes severe shock to the spark plugs, pistons, connecting rods, and the crankshaft. To slow down this burning rate of the fuel, a fuel of a higher octane rating must be used.

Octane Rating

The property of a fuel to resist detonation is called its antiknock or OCTANE rating. The octane rating is obtained by comparing the antiknock qualities of gasoline in a special test engine against reference fuels.

Octane numbers range from 50 in cheaper gasolines to over 100 for those required of modern high compression engines. The octane number has nothing to do with the starting qualities, potential energy, or volatility of the fuel.

The octane rating of gasoline can be raised in two ways: by mixing it with another fuel, or treating it with a chemical. In this country a chemical is added to gasoline to improve its octane rating. The most efficient additive used for this purpose is tetraethyl lead compound, which is added to the gasoline with ETHYL FLUID. In addition to the tetraethyl lead, ethyl fluid contains other chemicals that prevent lead deposits from forming within the engine. Lead oxide causes considerable corrosion.

The LEAD CONTENT of ethyl fluid is very poisonous. Ethyl gasoline should be used only for engine fuel and for no other purpose. It should never be used as a cleaning agent.

An engine which does not knock on a low octane fuel will not operate more efficiently by using a fuel of high octane rating. An engine which knocks on a given fuel should use one of a higher rating. If a higher octane fuel does not stop the knocking, some mechanical adjustments are probably necessary. Retarding the spark so that the engine will fire later may end knocking. However, an engine operating on retarded spark will use more fuel and will overheat. It may be less expensive to use a higher priced, high-octane gasoline with an advanced spark than to use a cheap, low-octane gasoline with a retarded spark.

Engine knocking is not always the result of using too low an octane rating; it can be caused by preignition. In preignition the fuel-air mixture begins to burn before the spark occurs. This condition may be caused by an overheated exhaust valve head, hot spark plugs, or glowing pieces of carbon within the combustion chamber. In figure ·9, you see the diagrammed course of the fuel-air mixture in the cylinder under circumstances of preignition and detonation, as well as in normal combustion.

DIESEL FUEL

Diesel fuel is heavier than gasoline because it is obtained from the residue of the crude oil after the more volatile fuels have been removed. As with gasoline, the efficiency of a diesel fuel varies with the type of engine in which it is used. By distillation, cracking, and blending of several oils, a suitable diesel fuel can be obtained for almost all engine operating conditions. Slow speed diesels use a wide variety of heavy fuels; high speed diesel engines require a lighter fuel. Using a poor or an improper grade of fuel can cause hard starting, incomplete combustion, a smoky exhaust, and engine knocks.

The properties to be considered in selecting a fuel for a diesel engine are VOLATILITY, CLEANLINESS, VISCOSITY, AND IGNITION QUALITY.

Volatility

The volatility of a diesel fuel is measured by the 90 percent distillation temperature. This is the temperature at which 90 percent of a sample of the fuel has been distilled off. The lower this temperature, the higher the volatility of the fuel. In small diesel engines, a fuel of high volatility is more necessary than in large engines if there is to be low fuel consumption, low exhaust temperature, and little exhaust smoke.

Cleanliness

Cleanliness of diesel fuel is very important. Fuel should not contain more than a trace of foreign substances; otherwise, fuel pump and injector difficulties will develop. Because it is heavier and more viscous, diesel fuel will hold dirt particles in suspension for longer periods than will gasoline. In the refining process, not all foreign matter can be removed, and harmful matter like dirt and water can get into the fuel while it is being handled. Water will cause hard starting and misfiring. Dirt will clog injectors and spray nozzles and may cause an engine to misfire or stop altogether.

Viscosity

The viscosity of fuel is the measure of its resistance to flow. Viscosity is expressed by the number of seconds required for a certain volume of fuel to flow through a hole of a certain diameter at a given temperature. The viscosity of diesel duel must be low enough to flow

# ENGINES, FUELS, LUBRICANTS, AND POLLUTION CONTROL

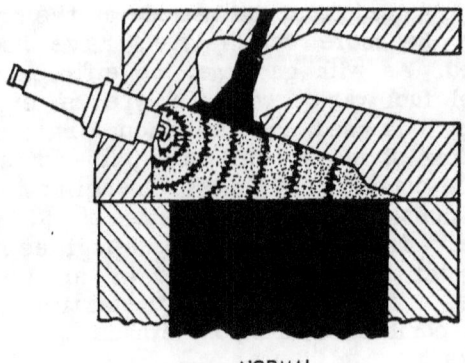

NORMAL

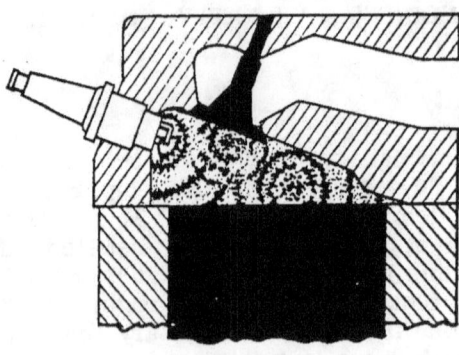

DETONATION

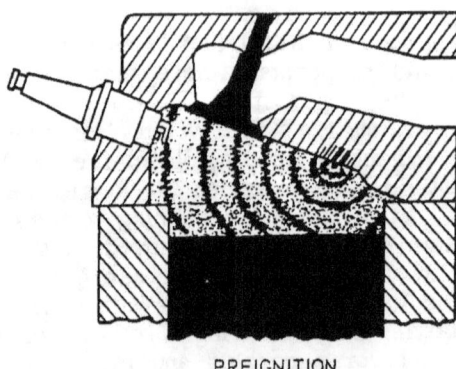

PREIGNITION

Figure 9. — Combustion process.

freely at low temperatures, yet high enough to lubricate the pump and injector plungers properly and lessen the possibility of leakage at the pump plungers and dribbling at the injectors. Viscosity is measured by an instrument (fig. 10) called the SAYBOLT VISCOSIMETER and is expressed in SAYBOLTSECONDS, UNIVERSAL (SSU).

A Saybolt viscosimeter consists of an oil tube, a constant-temperature oil bath which maintains the correct temperature of the sample in the tube, a 60-cc (cubic-centimeter), graduated receiving flask, thermometers for measuring the temperature of the oil sample and of the oil bath, and a timing device.

The oil to be tested is strained and poured into the oil tube. The tube is surrounded by the constant-temperature oil bath. When the oil sample is at the correct temperature, the cork is pulled from the lower end of the tube and the sample flows through the orifice and into the graduated receiving flask. The time (in seconds) required for the oil to fill the receiving flask to the 60-cc mark is noted.

The viscosity of the oil is expressed by indicating three things: first, the number of seconds required for 60 cubic centimeters of oil to flow into the receiving flask; second, the type of orifice used; and third, the temperature of the oil sample at the time the viscosity determination is made. For example, suppose that a sample of lubricating oil is heated to 125°F and that 170 seconds are required for 60-cc of the sample of flow through a Saybolt Universal orifice and into the receiving flask. The viscosity of this oil is said to be 170 seconds Saybolt Universal at 125°F. This is usually expressed in shorter form as 170 SSU at 125°F (or 20 weight oil.)

Other oils have other temperatures that are used for obtaining Saybolt Universal viscosities. Thus, it is important that the temperature be included in the statement of viscosity.

## Ignition Quality

The ignition quality of a diesel fuel is its ability to ignite when it is injected into the compressed air within the engine cylinders. Ignition quality is measured by the CETANE RATING of the fuel. A cetane number is obtained by comparing the ignition quality of a given diesel fuel with that of a reference fuel of known cetane number in a test engine. This reference fuel is a mixture of alphamethylnapthalene, which is difficult to ignite alone, and cetane, which

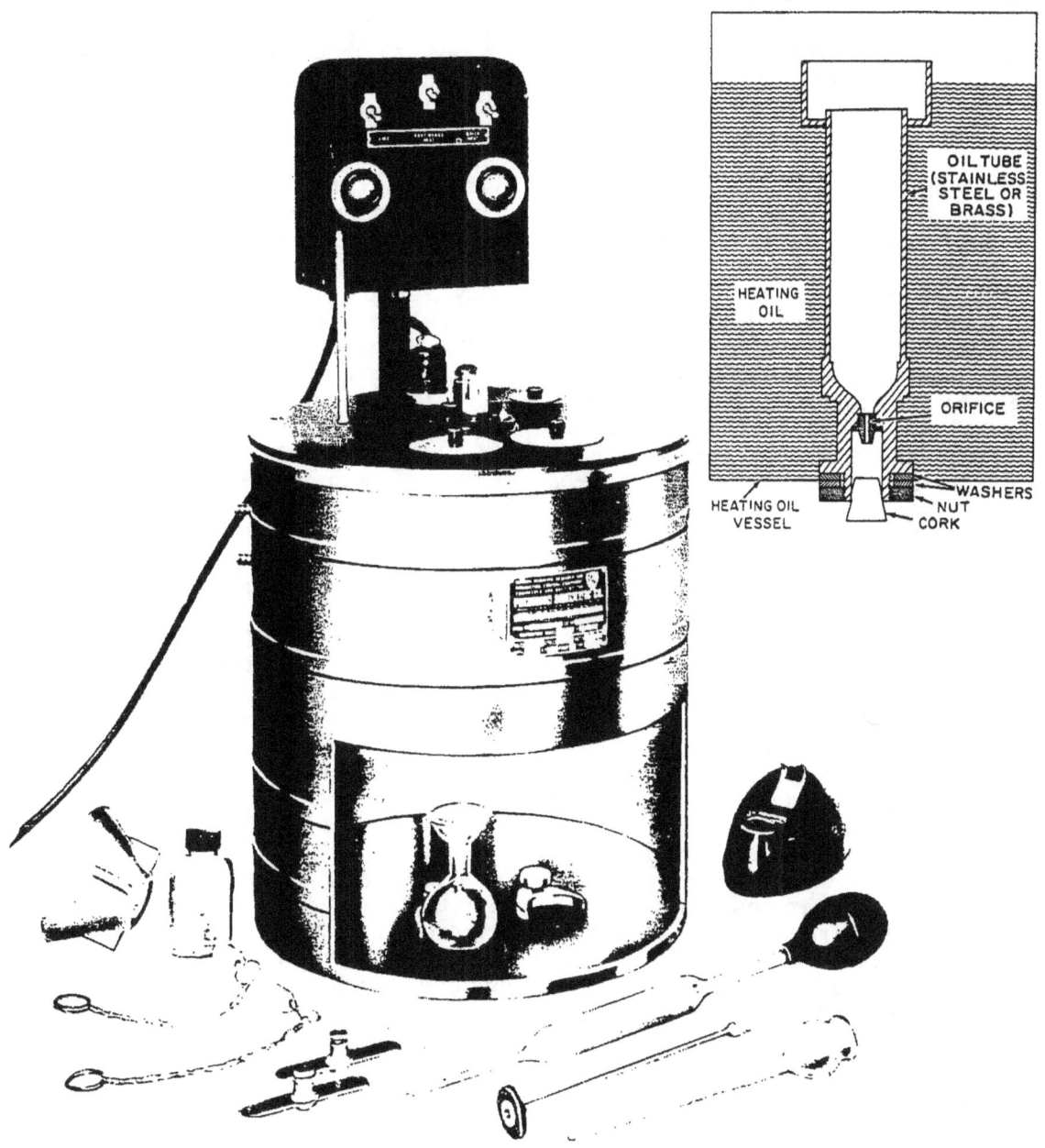

Figure 10.—Saybolt viscosimeter.

will ignite readily at temperatures and pressures comparable to those in the cylinders of a diesel engine. The cetane rating indicates the percentage of cetane in a reference fuel which will just match the ignition quality of the fuel being tested. The higher cetane numbers indicate more efficient fuels. The large slow diesels can use a 30 cetane fuel, but the high speed diesels must use at least a 40 cetane fuel, while some require as high as a 60 cetane fuel.

The ignition quality of a diesel-fuel depends also on its FLASH POINT and its FIRE POINT. The flast point is the temperature to which the fuel vapors must be heated to flash or ignite. The minimum flash point for diesel fuel is 150°

## ENGINES, FUELS, LUBRICANTS, AND POLLUTION CONTROL

F. A fuel having too low a flash point is dangerous both to handle and to store.

The fire point is that temperature at which the fuel vapors will continue to burn after being ignited. It is usually 10 to 70 degrees higher than the flash point.

You will sometimes hear knocks in diesel engines. They are believed to be caused by the rapid burning of the fuel that accumulates in the delay period between injection and ignition. This delay is known as IGNITION LAG or IGNITION DELAY. When the fuel is injected into the cylinders, it must vaporize and be heated to the flash point to start combustion. The lag between vaporization and flash point depends upon the ignition quality of the fuel and the speed of the engine and its compression ratio. In high speed engines the delay varies from 0.0012 to 0.0018 of a second. Ignition lag decreases with the increase in engine speed because of a swifter air movement in the cylinders that makes the injected fuel heat better.

## LUBRICANTS

A lubricant is a substance, usually a thin film of oil, used to reduce friction. There are three types of kinetic friction: sliding friction, rolling friction, and fluid friction. Sliding friction exists when the surface of one solid body is moved across the surface of another solid body. Rolling friction exists when a curved body such as a cylinder or a sphere rolls upon a flat or curved surface. Fluid friction is the resistance to motion exhibited by a fluid.

Fluid friction exists because of the cohesion between particles of the fluid and the adhesion of fluid particles to the object or medium which is tending to move the fluid. If a paddle is used to stir a fluid, for example, the cohesive forces between the molecules of the fluid tend to hold the molecules together and thus prevent motion of the fluid. At the same time, the adhesive forces of the molecules of the fluid cause the fluid to adhere to the paddle and thus create friction between the paddle and the fluid. Cohesion is the molecular attraction between particles that tends to hold a substance or a body together; adhesion is the molecular attraction between particles that tends to cause unlike surfaces to stick together. From the point of view of lubrication, adhesion is the property of a lubricant that causes it to stick (or adhere) to the parts being lubricated; cohesion is the property which holds the lubricant together and enables it to resist breakdown under pressure.

Besides reducing friction and wear, lubricants act as COOLING AGENTS, absorbing heat from the surfaces over which they are spread. This is true particularly of engine oil, which carries heat to the engine sump, where it is dissipated. The water circulating through an oil cooler also helps to reduce this heat (not all engines have oil coolers).

Lubricants are also used as SEALING agents. They fill the tiny openings between moving parts, cushioning them against damage and distortion from extreme heat.

Lubricants are also important as CLEANING AGENTS. Any grit and dirt finding their way into the engine parts often are removed by the lubricants before damage can result. Foreign matter found in old oils and greases in the bottom of the crankcase is evidence of the cleansing quality of lubricants. Some lubricants have chemicals added to make them better cleaners.

The high temperatures, speeds, and cylinder pressures of modern engines have made necessary better grades of lubricating oils. To increase efficiency, certain chemicals, called ADDITIVES, are put into oils. Additives are resistive agents which are used against oxidation and other kinds of metal deterioration. Oil which contains additives specifically designed to help clean the piston rings and other parts of the engine as it lubricates is known as DETERGENT OIL.

It is especially important for you to keep up with the latest developments in lubricants as presented in Navy and other technical publications. Your chief will tell you where you can get this information.

### Types of Lubricants and Their Uses

Oils and greases are the two general types of lubricants. The modern high-speed gasoline or diesel engine must be properly lubricated with the proper grades and types of lubricating oils and greases. Present-day refining methods have produced lubricating oils and greases with certain special qualities. In engines operating at high speeds and temperatures, these oils do a better job than ordinary oils can do. Engines operating at low speeds or in cold weather may require an oil with other special qualities.

Greases are used where it is difficult to keep oil in place and where the lubricant is subjected to varying pressures. In some cases, greases are used when centrifugal forces tend to throw the lubricant from moving parts. This is especially true in gear boxes and wheel bearings.

OILS.—Lubricating oils serve four purposes: (1) prevent metal-to-metal contact in moving parts of mechanisms, (2) help carry heat away from the engine, (3) clean the engine parts as they are lubricated, and (4) form a seal between moving parts. Moving parts that do not have enough oil will melt, fuse, or seize after a very short period of engine operation. All gears and accessory drives, as well as other moving parts of the engine subject to friction, must be bathed in oil at all times.

We have seen that viscosity is the resistance of a liquid against flow. It is the most important property of a lubricating oil. A lubricant of high viscosity spreads very slowly. You have heard of car owners using a HEAVY oil in summer and changing to LIGHT oil in winter. The heavy oil used in summer becomes too sluggish in cold weather, while the light oil used in winter flows too easily in hot weather. An oil used in any engine must flow freely and have enough body to resist friction between moving engine parts; it must pass readily through all oil lines and spread effectively over all surfaces that require lubrication.

The temperature of an oil affects its viscosity. The higher the temperature, the lower the viscosity. On a cold morning, the high viscosity or stiffness of the lubricating oil makes an engine hard to turn over.

The viscosity of an oil is figured by the number of seconds which pass while a certain volume flows through a small opening or hole of a definite diameter at a given temperature. The greater the number of seconds, the higher the viscosity. The Society of Automotive Engineers (S.A.E.) has standardized a code of numbers to indicate the viscosity of lubricating oils. You will be using military symbols for these lubricating oils, which are expressed in four digits, as indicated in Table 1. The last three digits indicate the viscosity in number of seconds required for 60 cubic centimeters of oil to flow through a standard opening at a given temperature. The first digit indicates the class and type of lubricating oil. You will use only the lubricant recommended for the particular engine which you service and lubricate. It is advisable to check with your chief from time to time for discontinued and new stocks and changed designations or specification numbers.

Oil is a mixture of many slightly different compounds, and therefore does not have a definite freezing point, but it does thicken as it cools. In order to determine the usefulness of an oil in cold weather, it is tested for its POUR POINT, which is the lowest temperature at which the oil will still flow. The pour point in which you will be interested is the lowest temperature at which the oil on the cylinder walls and bearings will permit the engine to be turned.

While the flash point and the fire point of an oil do not affect its lubricating qualities, they are useful in determining the amount of volatile fluids or compounds in the oil. As you learned concerning diesel oil, the flash point is the temperature at which vapors will ignite, but not sustain a flame. The flash point of a lubricating oil for your entire engine must range from 300°F to 500°F to keep the oil from vaporizing too readily in the crankcase and to make it withstand the heat of the engine. It is used also to determine the fire hazard in shipping and storing the lubricant.

Again, as you previously learned, the fire point is the temperature at which vapors given off continue to burn when ignited. Both the flash point and the fire point must be taken into consideration in the blending of an oil of proper viscosity for the type and condition of the engine in which it is to be used.

From the day that fresh oil is put into the engine crankcase, it gradually begins to lose its effectiveness because of dilution and contamination from engine operation. Gasoline or diesel fuel may dribble into the crankcase oil. Water and sludge also may accumulate. Carbon, gum acids, and dust in the air entering the engine (in the air-fuel mixture) all reduce the effectiveness of any lubricant. It is because of this accumulation of foreign matter that manufacturers recommend regular oil changes, and that regular lubrication is so important in preventive maintenance.

GREASES.—Greases are compounds of oil and soap. The soaps used are not ordinary laundry soaps but animal fats mixed with certain chemicals. The chief purpose of the soap is to provide a body or carrier for the oil that actually does the lubricating.

Grease is used where oil is impractical or unsatisfactory due to centrifugal forces, loads, temperatures or exposure. For instance, it maintains a film at high engine speed and temperature, or when the equipment is idle for long periods of time.

The chemicals in the grease classify it for a particular purpose or use. CHASSIS GREASES have a lime, sodium, or an aluminum soap base. Chassis greases are distinguished by their shiny, transparent appearance, and are used as a pressure gum lubricant for chassis, U-joints, track rollers, and low temperature ball bearings.

CUP GREASE, or WATER-PUMP GREASE, is a lime-base grease to which water or moisture is added to keep the soap from separating from the oil. The moisture gives the grease a somewhat cloudy appearance, and it will evaporate at a temperature equal to that of boiling water. Lime base greases are not recommended for parts subjected to high temperature. These greases are recommended when moisture resistance is required, and are satisfactory for water pumps and marine stuffing boxes.

WHEEL BEARING or FIBROUS GREASES have a sodium or mixed soap base. These greases only appear fibrous, for there are no actual fibers in them. They are recommended for wheel bearings because they stick or cling to parts. Since they are not water resistant, they can be used only on protected parts.

CABLE GREASE (wire rope and exposed gear grease) is a sticky black oil used to lubricate chains and wire ropes.

The black, tar-like sticky mass called CRATER COMPOUND is used to grease sliding surfaces and exposed gears on heavy duty construction equipment. It is applied by hand or with a brush and cannot be squeezed from between the gear teeth or the sliding surfaces. You will find a can of this grease on nearly every shovel or crane used.

Some form of dry lubricant such as GRAPHITE POWDER is available in the shop, to lubricate small parts and door locks, where a liquid would run off or otherwise be undesirable.

Petroleum refiners have developed greases to meet special lubrication requirements of modern machinery and equipment. Table 2 lists and describes the kinds of greases and their uses for proper maintenance.

## CONTAMINATION OF PRODUCTS

A contaminated product is one to which has been added some material not normally present such as dirt, rust, water, or another petroleum product. Such admixture may modify the usual qualities of the product permanently or add new and undesirable characteristics. In either case, the contaminated product may be unsuitable for its intended use. Contamination may result from accident, inability or neglect or follow prescribed procedures, gross carelessness, or sabotage. In most instances contamination of a product can be detected by its unusual appearance, color, gravity, or odor.

Dirt

The causes for the presence of sand, clay, or loam in appreciable quantity in petroleum products should be investigated at once and remedial action taken. It may be the result of carelessness or of sabotage. Most commonly it is the result of inadequate cleaning and inspection of tanks or containers, or the use of muddy water to flush pipelines.

In light fuels such as gasoline, in cans or drums, dirt settles in a few hours. The clear fuel may then be drawn off and the bottom (4 to 10 inches) recovered by filtration through a dry chamois. An alternative is to decant the fuel into larger containers for further settling by pouring off the fuel without disturbing the sediment in the bottom of the container. In bulk tanks the settling may require 12 to 24 hours. The clear fuel may then be run off to clean storage and the bottom layer passed through gasoline filters, if available, or downgraded. Tanks and other containers should be thoroughly cleaned before reusing. In heavier fuels such as diesel oils or JP-5 jet fuel, settling is much less satisfactory. Filtration is recommended if practicable. Otherwise it is usually necessary to downgrade the product. In the case of lube oils and greases, no remedial action can be taken. The product must be downgraded.

Rust

Rust is the common name for the product of corrosion which is formed when unprotected iron or some steel surfaces are subjected to prolonged contact with water or moist air. It is brittle and powders readily. It is insoluble in water and in petroleum products but may form troublesome suspensions because of turbulent flow in pipelines, the churning action produced while pumping into storage tanks, or the rough

Table 1.—Military and Commerical Designation for Gear and Lubricating Oils Used in Equipment Maintenance

| General Description | Military Designation and Specification Number | Typical Commercial Designation | Uses |
|---|---|---|---|
| Gear oil. Containing extreme pressure (EP) additives to maintain lubrication under extreme pressure conditions. | Lubricant, Gear, Universal, MIL-L-10324. FSN 9150-259-5443. | E.P. Hypoid Gear Lubricant. Universal Gear Lubricant for very cold climates. | For all gear lubrication including transmission, differentials, hypoid gears, tractor final drives, and steering gear mechanisms in cold climates when the prevailing temperature is below 0° F. |
| Gear oil. Containing extreme pressure (EP) additives to maintain lubrication under extreme pressure conditions. | Lubricant, Gear, Universal, MIL-L-2105. FSN 9150-577-5842. | SAE 80 EP Hypoid or Universal Gear Lubricant. MA 1327 | As above except that it is an SAE 80 gear lubricant for use where the prevailing temperature is between 0° and 32° F. |
|  | FSN 9150-577-5845. | SAE 90 EP Hypoid or Universal Gear Lubricant. MA 1328 | As above except that it is an SAE 90 gear lubricant for use where the prevailing temperature is above 0° F. |
| Mineral Gear Oil, SAE 140. NO ADDITIVES. | Military Symbol 5190. MIL-L-2105. FSN 9150-577-5848. | SAE 140 Mineral Gear Oil. Steam Cylinder Oil. MA 1329 | For use in tractor transmissions and final drives only in tropical areas. There are no extreme pressure chemical additives in this oil. DO NOT mix with extreme pressure lubricants. DO NOT use in hypoid gear drives such as truck or passenger vehicle differentials. |
| SAE-10 Heavy Duty Lubricating Oil. | Military Symbol 9110. FSN 9150-231-9039. | Gasoline and Diesel Engine Oil, SAE-10 and SAE-10W Grades. | For crankcase lubrication in both gasoline and diesel engines requiring an SAE-10 or SAE-10W oil and for general purpose lubrication. |
| SAE-20 Heavy Duty Lubricating Oil. | Military Symbol 9170. FSN 9150-231-6651. | Gasoline and Diesel Engine Oil, SAE-20 Grade. | For crankcase lubrication in both gasoline and diesel engines requiring an SAE-20 oil and for general purpose lubrication. |
| SAE-30 Heavy Duty Lubricating Oil. | Military Symbol 9250. FSN 9150-231-6655. | Gasoline and Diesel Engine Oil, SAE-30 Grade. MB 1702 | For crankcase lubrication in both gasoline and diesel engines requiring an SAE-30 oil and for general purpose lubrication. |
| SAE-40 Heavy Duty Lubricating Oil. | Military Symbol 9370. FSN 9150-912-9552. | Gasoline and Diesel Engine Oil, SAE-40 Grade. | For crankcase lubrication in both gasoline and diesel engines requiring an SAE-40 oil and for general purpose lubrication. |

ENGINES, FUELS, LUBRICANTS, AND POLLUTION CONTROL

Table 1.—Military and Commerical Designation for Gear and Lubricating Oils Used in Equipment Maintenance—Continued

| General Description | Military Designation and Specification Number | Typical Commercial Designation | Uses |
|---|---|---|---|
| SAE-50 Heavy Duty Lubricating Oil. | Military Symbol 9500. FSN 1950-231-9043. | Gasoline and Diesel Engine Oil, SAE-50 Grade. MB 1722 | For crankcase lubrication in both gasoline and diesel engines requiring an SAE-50 oil and for general purpose lubrication. |
| Medium VI Mineral Oil SAE-50. No additives. | Military Symbol 3100. FSN 9150-223-8893. | Mineral Oil SAE-50 | For lubrication of certain 2-stroke cycle gasoline engines where prescribed. Mixed with fuel in specified proportions such as outboard motorboat engines. For general purpose lubrication. |
| Hydraulic Transmission Fluid, Type C-1 | EO—Series 3 or MIL-L-45199A. Grade 10. FSN 9150-680-1103. | Lubricating Oil High Output. | For hydraulic systems and certain transmission and converter units as prescribed by the manufacturer. |

handling of small containers. Rust is a commonly occurring source of contamination when disused pipelines or containers are employed without proper cleaning. Its prevention in small containers—where it is most likely to occur—is best accomplished by thorough cleaning and subsequent rinsing of the container with a prescribed rust-preventive type oil or solution which will cling to the metal surface in a thin layer and provide temporary protection until the container can be filled with the product to be stored. While empty, the containers should be stored upside down. Active pipelines and large storage facilities do not normally permit the accumulation of rust in appreciable quantity. Rust may be removed from gasoline and heavier fuels by the same methods employed in removing dirt from these products.

Mill-Scale

Mill-scale is a magnetic product formed on iron and some steel surfaces during the manufacturing process. It is largely responsible for the blue-black appearance of such surfaces. It has been observed as a very serious contaminant in bulk products pumped through new pipes during the first few days or weeks of use. The scale is brittle and cracks readily. Corrosion begins at these cracks and proceeds to spread under the scale causing it to flake off. The scale is then carried along by the oil flow and is broken up still further before it reaches terminal storage. Here it may remain suspended for days. Settling is not, therefore, a satisfactory method of elimination. The scale is not removed completely by segregators and consequently, screens are quickly choked. Filtering of such stocks is recommended.

Water

In bulk storage, water can very often be a reason for fuel contamination. Water is sometimes employed as a bottom, to a depth of a few inches, to underlie light products such as gasolines and jet fuels. However, the use of water bottoms should be avoided if at all possible, and only employed when authorized by proper technical authority. It is sometimes used to separate and prevent mixing of products when two products, such as motor gasoline and

Table 2.—Military and Commerical Designations for Greases Used in Equipment Maintenance

| General Description | Military Designation and Specification Number | Typical Commercial Designation | Uses |
|---|---|---|---|
| Grease, Chasis—Lime, soda or aluminum soap base grease. | Lubricant, General Mil-G-10924 Mil Sym GAA FSN 9150-530-7369 | Chassis Grease, Cup Grease, Pressure Gun Grease, No. 1—Soft. | For general use as a pressure gun lubricant, particularly chassis, universal joints, track rollers, ball bearings operating below 150° F. Lime and aluminum soap base grease types are water resistant. |
| Grease, Wheel Bearing Soda or mixed soap base grease. | Lubricant, General Purpose, No. 2 (Wheel-Bearing-Chassis Lubricant—WB). VV-G-632 Type B, Grade 2. FSN 9150-531-6971. | Wheel Bearing Grease, No. 2—Medium. | For wheel bearings, ball bearings, and as a pressure gun lubricant when operating temperatures are expected to be above 150° F. DO NOT USE TO GREASE UNIVERSAL JOINTS OR OTHER PARTS HAVING NEEDLE BEARINGS. Not water resistant. |
| Grease, Ball and Roller Bearing Soda or mixed soap base grease. | Lubricant, Ball and Roller Bearing. Mil-G-18709. FSN 9150-249-0908. | Ball and Roller Bearing Grease, BRB. | BRB and G-18709 suitable for ball and roller bearing lubrication, especially in electric motors and generators and clutch pilot bearings. Not water resistant. |
| Grease—Water Pump Lime soap base grease. | Lubricant, Water-Pump, No. 4. VV-G-632 Type A, Grade 4. FSN 9150-235-5504. | Water-Pump Grease, No. 4—Hard. | For gland type water-pumps of some engines not equipped with factory lubricated and sealed water pumps. Very water resistant. |
| Lubricant, Exposed Gear, Chain, and Wire Rope Sticky, viscous, black, residual oil. | Lubricant, Chain and Wire Rope. Mil-G-18458. FSN 9150-530-6814. | Exposed Gear Chain and Wire Rope Lubricant. Gear Grease. Wire Rope Grease No. 2. | For greasing cable, open gears or any open mechanism requiring rough lubrication. Usually heated before applying. Grade B is intended for use in temperate or warm weather and is suitable for open-air or under-water conditions. Not for cables in contact with earth. |
| | | As above, except that it is No. 3 or heavy duty type. | As above except that Grade C is for use in hot weather or for hard service and is suitable for open-air or under-water conditions. |

aviation gasoline, are to be pumped through a pipeline, one after the other. Again, this should be avoided if possible as there are better means for segregation of products. The legitimate and necessary uses of water provide ample opportunities for the contamination of light products unless they are controlled by strict adherence to standard operating procedures. Fortunately, water suspended in light products such as gasoline separates rapidly on standing; less rapidly in diesel oil and JP-5 jet fuel. In cold weather this settling may be delayed by the formation of ice crystals, which are lighter than water droplets. In suspension, these crystals may clog filters, fuel lines, or jets in equipment. The most effective precaution against water contamination is to ensure delivery of a well-settled product through a dry line into a dry container. In cold weather, even a small amount of water can cause the freezing of bottom outlet valves in rail tank cars and tank trucks. In the case of packaged products, water may become a contaminant through the use of open or damaged containers, through improper storage and handling methods, and by the breathing which normally occurs in drums and cans. (Breathing is the reverse of vaporization and is caused by a drop in temperature. In breathing, cooled vapors condense to liquids, the interior pressure of the storage tank or container decreases, and air is sucked into the tank or container.)

Water contamination of fuels supplied to consumers in drums or cans can be avoided, when the turnover is rapid, by the application of prescribed methods of inspection, storage, and handling. However, long-term storage in drums, (strategic reserve stocks) cannot fail to result in some contamination. The condensation of some water from the moist air sucked in during the night is inevitable since this water settles and, therefore, is not expelled with product vapors during the heat of the day. During several weeks of storage, this water accumulates in surprisingly large amounts. Not only does it constitute direct contamination, which may have very undesirable consequences if transferred to equipment, but it is the cause of serious additional contamination by rust, and increases container maintenance. For this reason, periodic technical inspection is required and provision must be made for the regular replacement of such stocks at relatively frequent intervals. The length of intervals is determined by climatic and other conditions. Accumulated water can best be removed by decantation, settling, and refilling. Lacking time or facilities for this, a small pump may be employed to remove the lower layers from individual containers.

The most effective and proper protection for lubricants is to keep them well covered, preferably in inside storage. Should damaged containers permit water to contaminate engine or gear oils, the water may remove some of the essential additives. Even more undesirable is the fact that water tends to emulsify in the oil and does not settle out, thus decreasing effective lubricating action. Water can be poured off from greases. When this is done, about an inch of surface grease should also be removed. After removal, the surface grease should be burned or buried.

Commingling of Products

Commingling of products may result from inadequate cleansing of lines or containers; from the use of unmarked or improperly marked containers; and from the mishandling of manifolds. In such cases it can be minimized by supervision sufficient to ensure strict application of the prescribed petroleum handling procedures. Commingling may also result from leaks in tanks or valves aboard tankers, and from leaky valves or insufficient protective facilities in shore installations. These sources can be minimized by proper inspection and maintenance procedures. Nevertheless, serious contamination of one product by another can and does occur occasionally in field operations. This is one of the most compelling reasons for the continuous inspection procedures and the routine testing programs prescribed by the military departments.

Commingling can be negligible or serious depending upon the product contaminated, the contaminating agent, and the amount of contamination. Some of the more important serious effects are:

1. Loss of power in fuels.
2. Increase in volatility (producing a fire or explosion hazard in kerosene or diesel fuels).
3. Increase in gum content.
4. Formation of heavy sludge.

III. SAFETY IN HANDLING AND STORAGE OF PETROLEUM PRODUCTS

Although the handling of petroleum products presents many hazards, both bulk and packaged products can be handled safely and with remarkable freedom from accident if proper precautionary measures are taken. All personnel involved with the receipt, storage, issue, and use of flammable and combustible petroleum products must be familiar with and observe applicable safety precautions.

Precautionary measures must be taken to prevent fire and explosion when handling any petroleum product. The degree of hazard involved depends on the properties of a given product. Therefore, for safe handling purposes, petroleum products are divided into groups or classes according to the temperature at which the product will give off flammable vapors.

Any material which can be ignited easily and which will burn with unusual rapidity is said to be flammable. (The terms flammable and inflammable are identical in meaning, but the former is preferred since the prefix in suggests non flammable.)

All petroleum products, being composed of carbon and hydrogen, will burn and are therefore combustible materials. However, classification for safe handling purposes distinguishes products according to their tendency to burn.

Combustible liquids, according to the National Fire Protection Association (NFPA) Standards, are those liquids having flash points at or above 140°F and below 200°F.

Flammable liquids, according to the NFPA Standards, include all liquid petroleum fuels which give off flammable vapors below temperatures of 140°F.

Volatile products are products which tend to vaporize; that is, give off flammable vapors at comparatively low temperatures are said to be volatile. Because volatile products such as gasoline and JP-4 jet fuels will give off sufficient vapors to be flammable at relatively low temperatures, they are the most hazardous of all petroleum products to handle. For example, gasoline has a flash point of about -45° and JP-4 jet fuel has a flash point slightly higher, while crude oil has a flash point of about 60°F. This varies, however, according to the source of the crude oil. Volatile products such as gasoline and JP-4 jet fuel are normally handled at atmospheric temperatures above -45°F and, therefore, give off sufficient vapors to flash or burn at all times. Products which give off flammable vapors only above 100°F and are relatively nonvolatile are relatively safe to handle at ordinary temperatures and pressures. Such petroleum products as kerosene, JP-5 jet fuel, diesel and light and heavy fuel oils are included in this category.

It is noted, however, that if products such as kerosene, JP-5 jet fuel, diesels and fuel oils are handled at elevated temperatures they are just as hazardous as the volatile products. For example, kerosene, which has a flash point of about 110°F will not ignite at ordinary atmospheric temperatures, but if it is heated above 100°F will give off sufficient flammable vapors to burn or explode. All products which have a flash point above 100°F when heated to temperatures equal to or higher than their flash point, should be treated as volatile products with respect to fire and explosion hazards.

Some precautionary measures to be strictly observed when handling petroleum products are listed below. Most of these precautions apply to the handling of any flammable or volatile product at ordinary temperature, and higher flash or less volatile products at high temperature.

1. Reducing Or Controlling The Discharge Of Vapors
a. Take care that no spills occur.
b. Avoid spills from overflow when loading storage tanks by gaging tanks prior to loading.
c. Never neglect leaks. Make frequent inspections for leaks in tank seams, tank shells, and pipe joints.
d. If spills or leaks occur, clean them up immediately. Soaked ground should be washed with water or covered with sand or dry earth. The area should be policed until flammable vapor has been eliminated.
e. When temperatures are excessively high, cool storage tanks by sprinkling, or by playing water over them.
f. Keep containers for volatile products, whether empty or full, closed tightly.
g. Beware of empty fuel containers.
h. Ensure proper ventilation of all enclosed spaces in which vapors may accumulate.

2. Eliminating Sources Of Accidental Ignition
a. Do not smoke.
b. Do not carry "strike anywhere" matches or automatic lighters that open and light with a single motion.

## ENGINES, FUELS, LUBRICANTS, AND POLLUTION CONTROL

c. Do not perform any mechanical work or repair involving hot work such as burning, cutting, or welding, unless a permit is issued by proper authority.

d. Inspect electrical apparatus frequently and correct any condition likely to cause sparking.

e. Open switches and pull fuses before work is done on electrical equipment.

f. Shut off gasoline tank truck engines during the entire period of filling or discharging unless the truck is designed for engine operation, to drive transfer pumps through a power take-off.

g. Ground flammable fuel hose nozzle to the tank before starting the flow of fuel. Maintain this bond throughout the filling operation.

h. Never load or unload volatile or flammable products during electrical storms.

i. Use only self-closing metal receptacles for discarding oily waste or rags and dispose of such collections daily.

j. Never use volatile petroleum products such as gasoline for any cleaning purpose.

k. Keep gage tape in contact with gage hatch during gaging operations.

l. Immediately remove any clothing which has become soaked with fuels.

3. Safety Precautions For Handling JP-4 Fuel:

In addition to the safety precautions required for handling all volatile fuels, Grade JP-4 fuel, because of its tendency to accumulate and discharge static electricity and its low vapor pressure, requires additional handling precautions. Like other volatile fuels, JP-4 still requires a source of ignition. Unlike the other volatile fuels, the static electricity generated in pumping, transferring and loading JP-4 is an inherrent source of ignition which requires careful handling to control. JP-4 fuel is unique in that its rate of vaporization under most handling conditions will create an atmosphere (vapor/air) well within the explosive range, within the tank above the liquid surface. The atmosphere within a fixed roof tank storing gasoline will normally be too rich to be ignited or to burn within the tank, but in the case of JP-4, any ignition at gaging hatches, or vents will travel into the tank and cause a violent combustion (explosion). This hazard is not normally present in the case of Grade JP-5 fuel because of its relatively high flash point (140°F). To minimize the generation and accumulation of static electric charge in JP-4 fuel, the following procedures and/or precautions are recommended:

a. Do not use overhead fill lines which permit a free fall of product through the air.

b. The entrance of air into fill lines should be minimized or eliminated if practicable.

c. Where feasible the storage of JP-4 in concrete tanks or other poor electrical conducting materials should be avoided.

When handling petroleum products, care must be taken to ensure they do not become contaminated with foreign matter. Since all petroleum products will burn, fire is an ever present hazard. The degree of fire hazard increases as the volatility of the product increases.

Inhaling gasoline vapors may cause headaches, dizziness, nausea, or even unconsciousness. If any of these symptoms are noticed among men handling gasoline or working in an area where gasoline has been spilled, the men should leave the area at once. If anyone has been overcome, he should receive immediate medical attention.

Gasoline may cause severe burns if allowed to remain in contact with the skin, particularly under soaked clothing or gloves. Clothing or shoes through which gasoline has soaked should be removed at once. Gasoline should be washed from the skin with soap and water. Repeated contact with gasoline removes the protective oils from the skin and causes drying, roughening, chapping, and cracking and, in some cases, infections of the skin. Rubber gloves should be worn as protection by persons handling petroleum products.

If gasoline gets into a person's eyes, first aid should be given immediately. Fresh water may be applied, and medical attention should be secured.

If a person swallows gasoline by accident, first aid should be given immediately. Giving the victim warm salty water to induce vomiting is an effective aid. Medical attention should be secured promptly.

Slipping and falling are common accidents which occur when handling petroleum products. This danger is particularly grave while climbing to and from loading racks, storage tanks, or stacks of drums or cans. Tools, pieces of lumber, and other objects should not be left lying where they may cause accidents.

On a hot day, gasoline vapors mixed with air may be flammable for a distance of 20 feet from an open container. By using underground tanks there will be less chance of a fire or an explosion, and less gas will be lost by evaporation. Areas near gasoline storage tanks should ALWAYS BE WELL POSTED WITH WARNING SIGNS.

Gasoline storage tanks should be placed underground and covered with at least 3 or 4 feet of earth. The tanks must be equipped with vent pipes which extend well above the ground (6 to 8 feet) so that the vapors may spread and disappear. (See fig. 11.)

Diesel fuel is not as volatile, flammable, nor as dangerous to handle as gasoline. But it will burn, and in closed unventilated places, diesel vapors can be explosive.

Diesel fuel is generally not stored in the same way as gasoline. Figure 12 shows a typical diesel fuel storage tank. The tank is generally placed above ground on a raised platform. The platform should be high enough to permit the fueling of equipment from the tank by gravity flow. The tank must be provided with an air vent at the top and a drain cock at the lowest point. The outlet for the fuel should be at least 6 inches from the bottom of the tank, so that any water and dirt which have accumulated and settled in the bottom will not be drained into the fuel tanks of the equipment being serviced. The water and sediment that collect in the bottom of the tanks should be drained off daily. When you fill a diesel fuel storage tank, remember to leave enough room for expansion of the fuel. Lubricating oil and greases are furnished in various sizes of containers. More lubricant is wasted because it has become contaminated than for any other cause. All containers should be clearly marked as to their contents and dates received. The lubricants that have been in stock the longest should be used first. Make sure that all openings of lubricant containers are properly secured. This will decrease the chances of lubricants becoming contaminated.

## IV. FILTERS

In discussing diesel fuel, it was emphasized that it must be clean for proper diesel engine operation. So important is clean fuel, that besides the precautions observed in handling and storing diesel fuel, manufacturers have built fuel strainers and filters into the fuel systems or diesel engines.

## FUEL OIL FILTERS

In addition to a metal strainer, most diesel-fuel systems also contain a filter to remove any remaining small particles of dirt that might clog the injectors. Fuel-oil filters are manufactured in various models by a number of manufacturers. All fuel entering the injectors first passes through the filter elements. The filter elements are made of cotton fiber or mineral wool and glass cloth. After continued use, these filters will become packed with dirt filtered from the fuel, and the flow of fuel to the engine will be reduced to a point where the engine ceases to function properly or stops. Most types of heavy equipment have fuel pressure gages which will indicate when filters are dirty. Filter elements are easily removed and should be replaced with new elements when they start to restrict the flow of fuel to the engine.

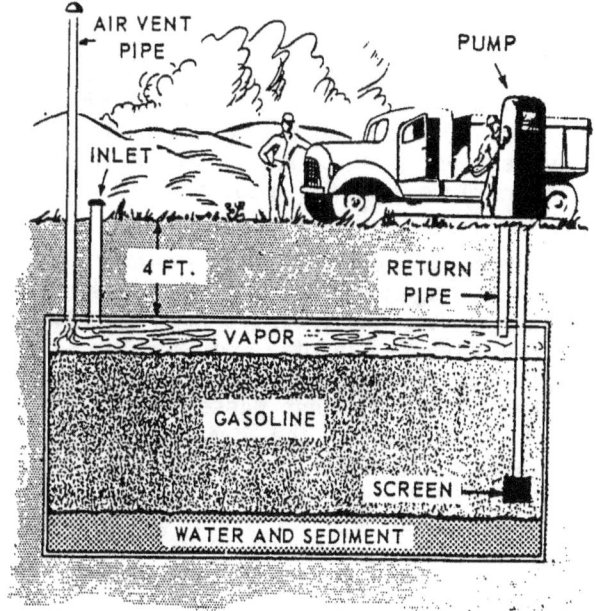

Figure 11. — Underground gasoline storage tank.

ENGINES, FUELS, LUBRICANTS, AND POLLUTION CONTROL

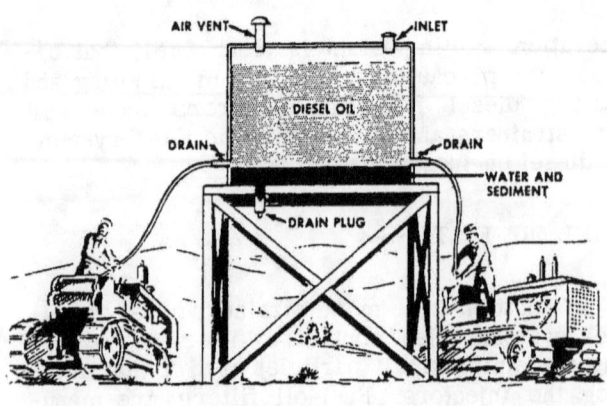

Figure 12.—Storage tank for diesel fuel.

## LUBRICATING OIL FILTERS

Most internal combustion engines are equipped with an oil filter. This device filters out the dust, dirt, and grit that enter the oil during operation of the engine.

Construction equipment lubricating oil filters (fig. 13) contain a filtering element for their filtering action. When this filtering element is saturated with solid particles, it ceases to function. It is good practice to replace the element with a new one every time the crankcase is drained and new oil is added. By such replacement you are assured of clean oil and a minimum of wear on engine parts.

The three types of oil filter systems used on automotive engines are the bypass, full-flow, and shunt types. The bypass type of oil filter is bracket mounted to the cylinder head or manifolds with connecting oil lines to the engine. The oil from the oil pump passes through the oil filter and then to the crankcase in the bypass system. The full-flow type of oil filter is integral with the engine. The oil is directed under pressure through the filter and then to the engine bearings. When the oil is too cold to circulate through the filter in the full-flow system, a bypass valve directs the oil around the filter element. The shunt type filters only a portion of the oil at a time, as does the bypass system, but the oil which is filtered is passed directly to the engine bearings.

Bypass systems use three types of filters. They are the throw-away type (fig. 14), the screw-on type of throw-away filter (fig. 15), and the replaceable element type of filter (fig. 16). The full-flow and shunt systems use the replaceable element type of the screw-on type of throw-away filter. A replaceable element for a full-flow type filter is shown in figure 17.

The throw-away type of oil filter is replaced as a complete unit. You have to disconnect the oil line fittings at the filter. Detach the filter from its bracket and remove the brass fitting from its filter housing. Throw away the filter. Place a bolt or plug into the brass fitting when you are removing or installing it. Brass is malleable (easily bent) and may be crushed by excessive wrench pressure.

The screw-on, throw-away type filter is also replaced as a complete unit. You unscrew

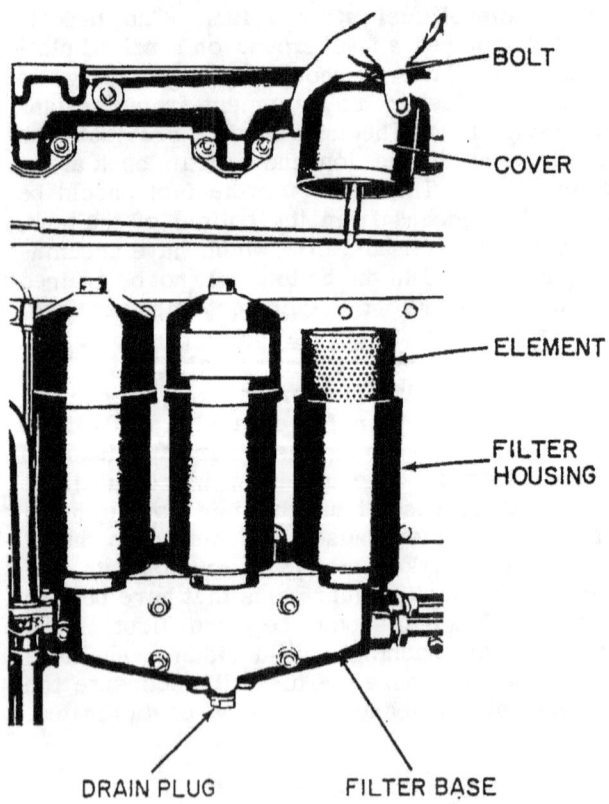

Figure 13.—Lubricating oil filter for construction equipment.

the filter from the base by hand and throw the filter away. Wipe the base clean with a cloth and screw a new filter onto the base by hand, tightening at least half a turn after the gasket contacts the base. Fill the crankcase to the full mark on the dipstick with the proper grade and weight of oil. Start the engine and observe the oil pressure and check for leaks around the oil filter. Stop the engine and add oil to the full level if needed.

To service replaceable element oil filters, you remove the fastening bolt, lift off the cover or remove the filter shell. Remove the gasket and throw it away. When removing the oil filter of the full-flow or shunt type, place a pan under the filter to catch the oil. Take out the old element and throw it away. Throw away the gasket from the top and bottom of the center tube if they are present. Place a pan under the filter and remove the drain plug if the filter is used in the bypass system. Clean the inside of the filter shell and cover. Install metal supports

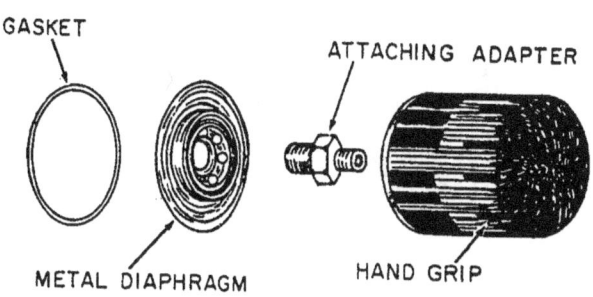

Figure 15.—Screw-on type of throw-away oil filter.

and a new bottom tube gasket. Insert a new element and a new top tube gasket. Insert a new cover or housing gasket (make sure that the gasket is completely seated in the recess). Replace the cover or housing and fasten the center bolt securely. Fill the crankcase to the full mark on the dip stick with the proper grade

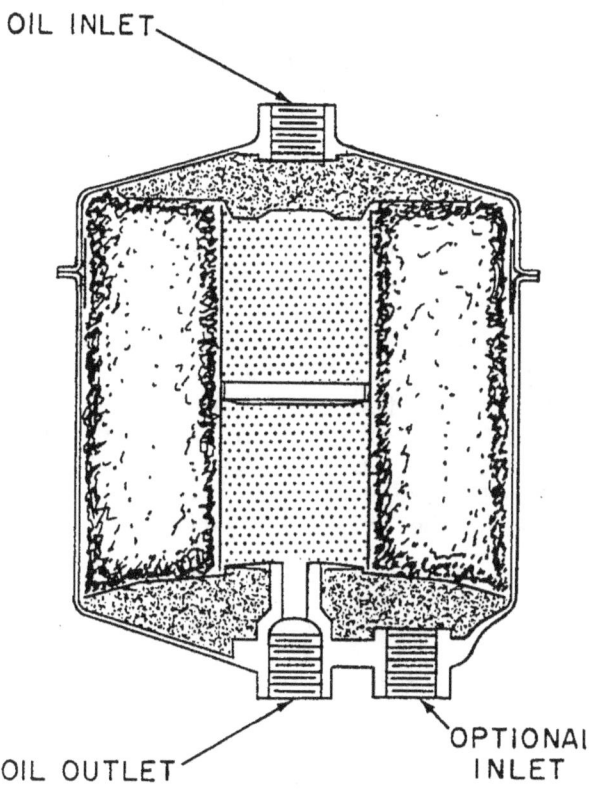

Figure 14.—Sealed type of throw-away oil filter.

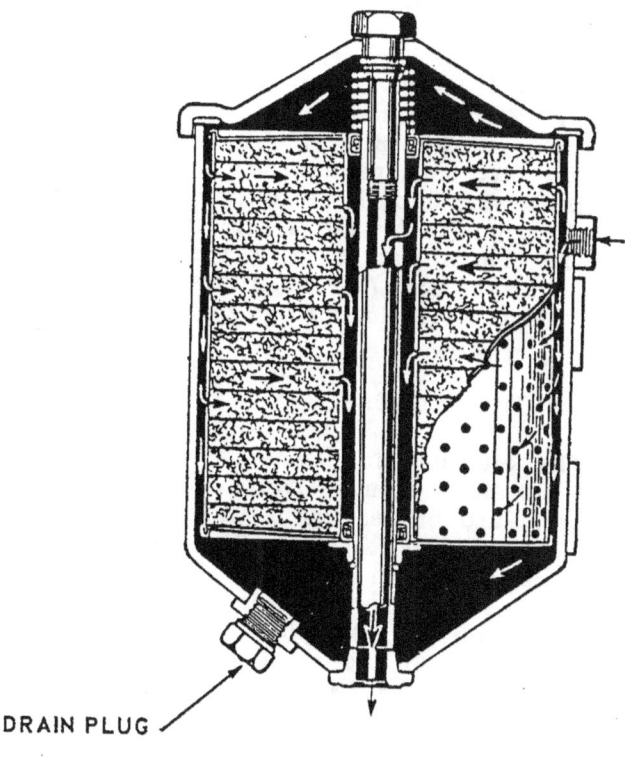

Figure 16.—Replaceable element type oil filter.

## ENGINES, FUELS, LUBRICANTS, AND POLLUTION CONTROL

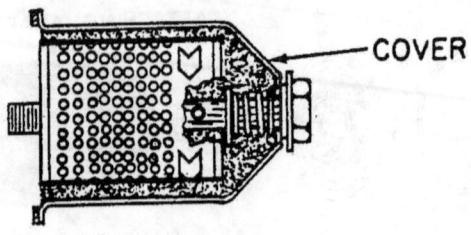

Figure 17.—Replaceable element, full-flow type oil filter.

and weight of oil. Start and idle the engine. Check the oil pressure immediately and inspect the filter for oil leaks. Then stop the engine and check the crankcase oil level and add oil to the full mark. The final step in the procedure is to mark the mileage on the sticker so that the element of the oil filter will be replaced at the proper interval.

### DRY-TYPE AIR CLEANERS

The heavy duty dry-type air cleaner illustrated in figure 18 uses a replaceable element. Air enters the cleaner through the air intake cap and screen (1) which prevents chaff and coarse dirt from getting into the air cleaner. After passing through the adapter (3) and rotonamic panel (4), the air is filtered as it passes through the replaceable dry-type element (5) and filter housing (6). The filtered air is then drawn into the engine through the intake manifold.

### OIL-BATH AIR CLEANER

The oil-bath air cleaner shown in figure 19 consists of main body, air intake cap, screens, and oil reservoir. Air enters the intake cap and inlet screen (1) which prevent large particles such as dirt, chaff, leaves, and so forth, from entering the air cleaner. After passing down the inlet pipe (2) to the center oil reservoir (3), the air is deflected upward through the screen (4), carrying drops of oil. The oil absorbs dirt from the air as it passes through the screen. The screen is sloped so the air sweeps the dirt laden oil toward the outside of the cleaner where it falls and re-enters the oil reservoir. The clean filtered air is then drawn into the engine through the intake manifold pipe (5).

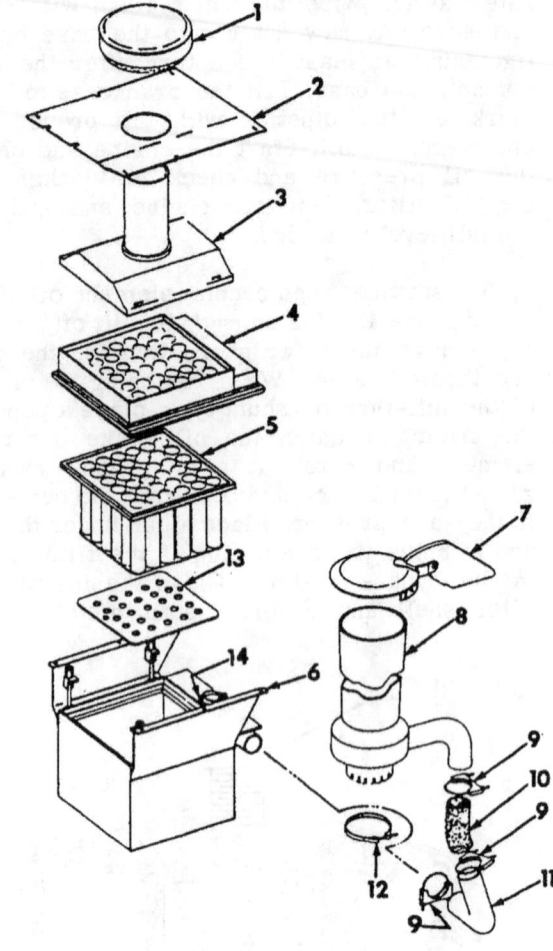

1. CAP, air intake.
2. PANEL, removeable.
3. ADAPTER, intake.
4. PANEL, rotonamic.
5. ELEMENT, filter.
6. HOUSING, air cleaner.
7. CAP, weather.
8. ASPIRATOR.
9. CLAMP.
10. HOSE.
11. ELBOW, exhaust.
12. CLAMP, aspirator.
13. PLATE, support.
14. GASKET.

Figure 18.—Heavy duty dry-type air cleaner.

### V. ENVIRONMENTAL POLLUTION CONTROL

Environmental pollution is that condition which results from the presence of chemical, physical or biological agents in the air, water or soil

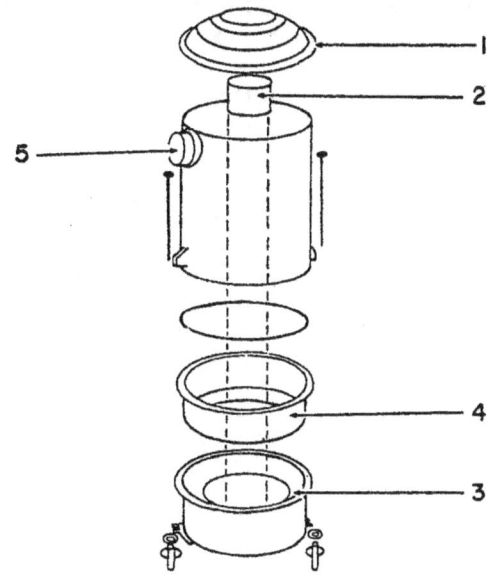

1. Intake cup and inlet screen.
2. Inlet pipe.
3. Center oil reservoir.
4. Screen.
5. Intake manifold pipe.

Figure 19.—Oil bath air cleaner.

which alter the natural environment. This causes an adverse effect on human health or comfort, fish and wildlife, other aquatic resources and plant life, and structures and equipment to the extent that economic loss is produced and recreational opportunity is impaired. Pollution causes nylon hose to disintegrate, masonry to crumble, steel to corrode, and skies to darken. It also damages vegetation, causes illness, and results in the loss of countless work days.

AIR POLLUTION

As an EO, you should be aware of the conditions which cause air pollution when operating equipment, and the efforts being made to minimize or correct these conditions.

When incomplete combustion occurs, unburned hydrocarbons and various other constituents in the basic fuel combine chemically to form some visible, noxious, and harmful byproducts which are emitted into the environment. Some of the fuel components and combustion products which have an adverse effect on the air are carbon monoxide, particulate matter, sulfur, oxides, unburned hydrocarbons, nitrogen oxides, and lead.

CONTROLLING AIR POLLUTION

The most effective means of controlling air pollution caused by fuel combustion is to maintain a well-tuned engine that provides an optimium fuel and oxygen mixture and proper timing; this results in most efficient combustion. Another alternative, not always under control of an operator, is to use only the best grade of fuel available which contains low particulate matter, low water and sulfur content, and other contaminates. Automotive manufacturers now provide systems on engine to return "blowby" (unburned fuel) to the carburetor for combustion, i.e., a pollution control system. Long range research and development is underway in developing systems to remove harmful constituents from engine exhausts, e.g., catalytic filter scrubber systems to remove oxides of sulfur and nitrogen, and others to remove lead.

WATER AND GROUND POLLUTION

In addition to creating a fire hazard, oil and other fuel products pose many possible pollution threats when spilled on the water or ground. Oil products on the ground can infiltrate and contaminate ground water supplies or can be carried into surface water supplies with ground runoff due to rain. Oil products carried into storm or sanitary sewers pose potential explosion hazards. Gasoline seeping into a sewer from a service station created an explosion which demolished several city blocks in a Chicago suburb

Oil on the water surface blocks the oxygen flow from the atmosphere into the water which results in less oxygen in the water for the fish and other aquatic organisms. Fish can be harmed by eating oil or smaller organisms that have eaten the oil. If the fish do not die from the oil coating their gills or from eating the oil, their flesh is tainted and they are no longer suitable for consumption by man. In addition to harming aquatic organisms and contaminating water supplies, oil products foul boats, water front structures, beaches, and in general create an unsightly mess along the waterfront.

Of all the oil introduced in the world's waters, spent oils from highway vehicles accounted for 37 percent, or 2 million tons in 1969. This is the largest single source of oil pollution, ever greater than tankers (11 percent), other ships (10 percent), offshore oil production (2 percent), refineries and petrochemical plants (6 percent), industrial and all other vehicles (31 percent), and accidental spills (4 percent).

## PREVENTIVE MEASURES FOR WATER AND GROUND POLLUTION

During automotive repair, drip pans and an absorbent material should be used to catch all unavoidable spills. Spilled oil or fuels should never be washed down a drain or sewer, unless an immediate fire hazard exists and an oil-water separator is present in the discharge line. Where spills are expected to occur (gasoline fill stands, etc.), absorbent material should be on hand. This material can be sprinkled on spilled oil or fuel, placed in a container, and disposed in a sanitary landfill or other non-polluting manner.

Spent crankcase oil, filters, contaminated fuel should be collected and disposed of in a non-polluting manner. Most naval activities collect and dispose of waste oil periodically through a contractor, by burning in a boiler plant, or reprocessing in an oil reclamation plant. Naval supply fuel farms usually have means to properly dispose of waste oils.

Open vehicle repair or maintenance areas located near water-courses or bodies of water should be landscaped and diked so spilled oil products cannot easily or directly flow into the nearby water.

www.ingramcontent.com/pod-product-compliance
Lightning Source LLC
Chambersburg PA
CBHW082044300426
44117CB00015B/2607